GOSPEL AND CHURCH

GUSTAF WINGREN

GOSPEL AND CHURCH

Translated by
ROSS MACKENZIE

Associate Professor of Church History
Union Theological Seminary
Richmond, Virginia

OLIVER AND BOYD
EDINBURGH AND LONDON
1964

OLIVER AND BOYD LTD
Tweeddale Court
Edinburgh 1

39A Welbeck Street
London W1

A translation of *Evangeliet och Kyrkan* by Gustav Wingren
Copyright C. W. K. Gleerup, Lund, Sweden

ENGLISH EDITION
First published 1964

TRANSLATION © OLIVER AND BOYD LTD 1964

PRINTED IN GREAT BRITAIN BY
OLIVER AND BOYD LTD., EDINBURGH

FOREWORD

THE present work has its origin in the foreword to my earlier book, *Creation and Law*, published in English in 1961. It will be to the reader's advantage if he can also study this earlier work. I have attempted, however, to make this new study complete in itself, and intelligible even to those who have not studied the previous book, although, of course, it is incomplete apart from its predecessor.

The same holds true in relation to my earlier work on preaching which was published in English as *The Living Word* in 1960. A complete study of the Gospel and the Church would quite properly give a much fuller place to preaching than will be found here. I have not, however, considered it necessary to repeat in detail what I have said earlier. The reader who seeks a fuller discussion is therefore referred to my two earlier books already mentioned.

I am again most grateful to Dr Ross Mackenzie for translating this work and preparing it for the English edition.

GUSTAF WINGREN

Lund, Sweden

CONTENTS

PART I
THE GOSPEL

CHAPTER I

PREACHING AND THE SACRAMENTS

Baptism and the Eucharist

CHRIST is not limited to Palestine, nor does He belong merely to the first few decades of the present era. The sphere in which He has chosen to work is the world—the whole world. The period in which He has chosen to work is our own time and every age. If we propose to speak about Christ and His work we must begin with the events and institutions in which He is at work now or will be in the future. It is for this reason that we take our starting-point not in an historical episode that lies in the past but in His present activity in preaching and the sacraments. By adopting this point of departure we are beginning with Christ as He is. It is His nature that He cannot do other than call His Church into being. This is how it has always been, and how it will be in time to come.[1]

Preaching and the sacraments are events. They cannot be what they are unless they are received by men. There are many other events which can take place without our being involved in them, but not preaching, baptism, or the Eucharist. These are gifts which have been given to men, and they can be bestowed only as they are received in faith. Where they are so received the Church comes into being. Those who are in the Church are recipients. Moreover these gifts can be bestowed only as they are given through human hands or spoken by human lips. As soon as we speak of preaching and the sacraments we are speaking of the ministers and the ministered unto, of those who administer the gifts and preach the Word and of those who receive. In this sense the ministry is grounded in the Gospel and in Christ Himself, for Christ

[1] Cf. Anders Nygren, *Christ and His Church*, 1957, pp. 90-91.

3

commanded His apostles to administer the sacraments and to preach, and with these offered His salvation to men.[2] The whole of this ministry is grounded in the Gospel, which in turn rests on the once and for all event of Christ's own mission and ministry.

Those who receive His gifts in word and sacraments and who thereby constitute the Church are both created by God and fallen. But when Christ comes to them in grace He gives them the true life which they have lost. If we cannot conceive of Christ apart from the Church it is because man cannot regain apart from Christ the life which he has lost by disobeying his Creator. The salvation which He offers is the restoration of our corrupt humanity. When the first article of the Creed is accepted as it stands and the prehistory of which we read in Genesis I-XI is interpreted as the story of Everyman, the idea of Christ restoring or redeeming can be maintained in an absolute sense whenever He is referred to as "Saviour." But when the first article is misplaced and the second consciously or unconsciously adopted as the point of departure in theological thinking, this same word "Saviour" comes to have a Marcionite meaning. This is our situation today, and we find an indication of it in the modern discussion of the Church. When men can look on love, birth, labour, disease, suffering, and death as events which occur in isolation from the will of God, or when it is argued that God's dealings with a man begin only when he hears the word of scripture or comes into the Church, their picture of God has become a Marcionite one, and He is conceived of as the higher or "good" God and as Saviour but not as Creator. The Church then ceases to be concerned with humanity and the work of restoring fallen human life to health and freedom. Rather, it becomes an institution and a community of a higher quality than the ordinary daily life from which it has now turned away. At the same time it is characterised not primarily by freedom but by a higher system of rules and regulations than is known in the world outside it.[3] This Marcionite view of the Church has penetrated deeply into modern Protestantism in which the point of contact

---

[2] Cf. Joachim Heubach, *Die Ordination zum Amt der Kirche*, 1956, pp. 84-87.

[3] Cf. Gustaf Wingren, *Creation and Law*, 1961, pp. 92-93, 147-148, 158-159, 169-170, 196-197.

between eighteenth century revivalism and nineteenth century ritualist movements has not infrequently been this particular interpretation of the Church.

In our discussion of the Gospel and the Church in the following chapters we have attempted to replace this view with an understanding of the Church as the gathering together of those whose lives have been restored, redeemed, and delivered under their Lord in whom all things have been created from the beginning. It is only on this level that we can see the connexion between the Gospel and the Church. The Gospel gave birth to the Church, and in everything that it does the Church is governed by the Gospel. In our discussion, therefore, we shall deal first with the Gospel and afterwards with the Church. This sequence is important. But in order to have a clear picture of the Gospel and the Church we must at least for the present keep well in view the background against which we are to examine our subject. The background is *creation and the law*, first creation and then the law, and again the sequence is important.[4]

The work of the law is to restrain men from evil-doing, and even to instil fear into them, while they await the freedom which is in Christ. Since the power of sin is active even in the believer, the tight grip of the law will not be relaxed until the last judgment. Man's full freedom, well-being and true nature belong to the future as the objects of his hope. In spite of baptism the believer has not yet wholly died. But the last times with their resurrection, freedom, and offering of praise have already begun with the first Easter. So there comes into being a Church which is the first fruits of a restored humanity. Day by day it turns to the Gospel for its life and to nowhere else. It lives out its life in this world of God's creation, making use each day of the things God has made and having joyful dominion

___

[4] See *ibid.*, Foreword p. vi and also pp. 119-120. Eternal life in the world of the resurrection will mean full restoration and total freedom. Prior to this the final death and the final judgment will have taken place, but until then the law remains in force. The Church is eternal life in the midst of death and judgment, i.e. in the midst of the transition to incorruption. Just as death and judgment are at work throughout the world, so also is the law of God. But Christ's purpose in founding the Church is not to establish a rule of law. What the Church gives is life in the world of death and the Gospel in the world of law, and from this new reality flow new works, exhortations and commandments, always, however, in freedom.

over them. The man whom we see in Christ's Church is the man whom we know in the created world, now freed to make proper use of the good things that God has created. But these are the same good things which were still wholly good even in man's sin. They are the same now as they were then, though formerly they were put to an evil use of man's own devising. Evil exists in man, and it is man who is brought into the Church. Preaching and the sacraments come to men, not to trees or to animals.[5] What God does in the Church He does wholly for man, and in the strictest sense of the term this work of God is man's "conversion" by which the flaw in his nature is put right. But those who have been so "converted" through baptism continue to live in the same world as before. What happens is simply that they begin to treat this external world in the right way, which means that they now serve those with whom they come in touch rather than exploit them. It is the work of the Gospel to bring this new relationship into being.

We see the character of Christ's work of converting, transforming, and restoring men most clearly in baptism. In one sense all that follows in the subsequent discussion is an extended explanation of the meaning of baptism. In the present introductory section our particular emphasis is on the connexion between baptism and the death and resurrection of Christ on the one hand, i.e. on the Christological significance of baptism, and on the connexion between baptism and creation and the fall on the other, i.e. on the significance of baptism in recapitulation. We shall finally stress the connexion between baptism and the whole subsequent life of the believer up to his death and the consummation, i.e. the eschatological significance of baptism. Baptism as an act and event embraces all three aspects which can be divided into three parts for analytical purposes. For this reason the act itself is richer in meaning than any explanation of its parts can ever be.[6] The same is true perhaps to a greater degree of the Eucharist.[7]

We shall begin, however, with baptism and its connexion

---

[5] Cf. Oscar Cullmann, *Königsherrschaft Christi und Kirche im Neuen Testament,* 2nd ed., 1946, pp. 38-39.

[6] Cf. on the sacraments in particular George S. Hendry, *The Gospel of the Incarnation,* 1958, p. 167.

[7] Cf. C. H. Dodd, *The Bible Today,* repr. 1948, pp. 161-163.

with the death and resurrection of Christ. More than any other, Oscar Cullmann has emphasised the connexion between baptism and the redemptive acts on man's behalf which were achieved in and through Jesus Christ, and notably His death at Golgotha—referred to by Cullmann as "the general baptism." What Cullmann is saying is that in the death and resurrection of Christ the true and proper baptism for all mankind has taken place. Each successive baptism thereafter represents the incorporation of new limbs into the baptised body of Christ. The origin of this terminology—for example, the reference to what took place at Golgotha as a "baptism"— is, of course, the synoptic Gospels where Jesus just before His death looks forward to the conclusion of His work among men as an agonising baptism which He had to undergo (Lk. xii.50, Mk. x.38).[8] In a similar way He speaks of His sufferings as the "cup" which He must drink, almost certainly a reference to the Eucharist (Mk. xiv.36, Mt. xxvi.39, 42, Mk. x.37-40, I Cor. xi.25, Lk. xxii.10, and Jn. xviii.11).[9] Whatever else the association of the death of Jesus with baptism may mean, Cullmann has succeeded in showing the inner unity between the two remarkably well, for he can also introduce into his discussion at this point the ritual baptism which Christ underwent at the beginning of His ministry when He was baptised by John in the Jordan. The voice which was heard speaking of the Beloved Son, the Spirit which overshadowed Him just after He was baptised, and the Baptist's words about the lamb that took away sin, represent both in the synoptic Gospels as well as in John a series of allusions to the Ebed Jahveh, the Suffering Servant of Isaiah (Mk. i.11, Mt. iii.17, Lk. iii.22, Jn. i.29-34, Isa. xlii.1, liii.7). But it is important to note that the narrative of the baptism in the Jordan alludes to the coming sacrificial death and is to be taken along with Christ's own words about His coming end as a baptism by which He is constrained until it is accomplished.[10] It is most significant of all,

[8] For what follows see Oscar Cullmann, *Baptism in the New Testament*, repr. 1958, pp. 19-20, and also 9-14, 22, 32-33.

[9] Cf. G. W. H. Lampe, *The Seal of the Spirit*, 1951, p. 39, and Regin Prenter, *Skabelse og genløsning*, 2nd ed., 1955, p. 498.

[10] Neville Clark, *An Approach to the Theology of the Sacraments*, 1956, pp. 30-31, is critical of Cullmann at this point.

however, to note that Paul's statements that we are put to death in baptism, buried in baptism, and raised in baptism, are no longer to be regarded as Pauline innovations but rather as concepts which are rooted and grounded in the four Evangelists themselves (Rom. VI.2-11, Col. II.12), and which are linked in many other ways with several important parts of the New Testament.[11]

We see this most notably in connexion with the use in the New Testament of terms and expressions which refer to "image" or "likeness." On the one hand Christ Himself is said to be the "image of God" (Col. 1.15, II Cor. IV.4, Heb. 1.3, Phil. II.6), but on the other hand it is man who is said to be changed into the same likeness in the Church (Col. III.10, II Cor. III.18). The effect of baptism, which brings the baptised into fellowship with Christ in such a way that he dies and rises with Christ, is thus to bring "the image of God" to fuller expression. Behind all these New Testament passages there lies without any doubt the declaration of the creation narrative: "Let us make man in our image, after our likeness" (Gen. 1.26). Cullmann maintains that those passages in the New Testament in which the terms image and likeness are used—terms which are central both for Christology and anthropology—are based wholly on the creation narrative and have been strangely neglected by systematic theology. Irenaeus, he argues, is unique in his grasp of this connexion, while only minor insights have been contributed by other theologians from his day to the present.[12] The Christological hymn (Phil. II.5-11) to Christ who emptied Himself and was highly exalted is comprehensible only if it is set beside the opposite account of Adam who exalted himself and fell (Gen. III.1-19). Christ achieved the intention of the Creator and through His sufferings produced the image and likeness which Adam had destroyed.[13] When a man is changed into the likeness of Christ

[11] Cf. Lampe, *Seal*, pp. 58-61.

[12] Oscar Cullmann, *The Christology of the New Testament*, pp. 189-192, and the important exegetical passages earlier on pp. 174-181. Cullmann is critical of Irenaeus on pp. 189-190.

[13] *Ibid.*, pp. 169-171. The temptation of Adam and the temptation of Jesus are thus contrasted, as in Irenaeus. Cf. Gustaf Wingren, *Man and the Incarnation*, 1959, pp. 127-128.

in the Church, the word spoken in the beginning—"Let us make man in our image"—is fulfilled (cf. Eph. IV.24, Rom. VIII.29). This likeness will be fully realised only in the eternal kingdom, and is thus in the meantime the object of hope (I Jn. III.2, Phil. III.10 f., 21).[14] Baptism unites us to Christ, and is thus not a finished work but will be completed only at the resurrection of the dead. In the Church we still have to die daily to the old nature until we finally pass from death to life. The baptised, who have put off the old nature (Col. III.9) and put on the new (Col. III.10) are exhorted to do what is clearly still to be done, viz. to put to death what is earthly in them (Col. III.5). Baptism has reference to the whole of the life of the Christian up to the final consummation. It is in no way incomplete, and the life of sanctification is simply the unfolding or manifestation of the inner meaning of baptism.[15]

We began by discussing the connexion between baptism and the acts of God in Christ, in particular His death and resurrection into which the baptised are incorporated. In looking at the Christological connexion we have passed spontaneously by our use of the Christological terminology of image and likeness to a discussion of creation. The terms referred to are derived from the creation narrative in which they are applied directly to the creation of man. They are thus anthropological terms and define the goal for man which God has appointed. When the New Testament takes these expressions and applies them to the believer and to what happens to him in the Church, i.e. to baptism and the life of sanctification, in both of which death and resurrection are central, it is clearly dealing with the aspect of recapitulation and therefore of restoration. The original purpose for man is fulfilled in the Church, and to be incorporated into the Church is to become man and to be

[14] Cullmann, *Christology*, pp. 176-177. Cf. too I Cor. xv.49, though here the emphasis is on the different results brought about by Adam and by Christ: the former brings death, the latter life. See also N. A. Dahl, "Christ, Creation and the Church," in *The Background of the New Testament*, 1956, pp. 422-443.

[15] Luther particularly stresses this in nearly all his baptismal teaching. Cf. Svend Lerfeldt, *Den kristnes kamp*, 1949, pp. 175-179, and also Prenter, *Skabelse*, pp. 508-509. See also Werner Jetter, *Die Taufe beim jungen Luther*, 1954, p. 317. In regard to the New Testament and especially Paul see Jacob Jervell, *Imago Dei*, 1960, pp. 197-256.

B

delivered from what is less than human.[16] But in discussing this connexion between baptism and recapitulation we have passed spontaneously—again by using the same terminology from Genesis—to a discussion of eschatology. In this event that still lies in the future man will be changed, but then finally and decisively, into the likeness of Christ "who will change our lowly body to be like His glorious body" (Phil. III.21). Even in those who have been baptised there is some sin that has to be put to death, and only when there is none left will the work of baptism be complete. It is the baptised whom Paul exhorts to "put to death what is earthly" (Col. III.5), while they await in hope that future state in which sin will no longer exist.[17] And when there is no more sin to put to death, death itself will no longer have power over men, but even this last enemy will have been destroyed (1 Cor. xv.26). Baptism comes to its fulfilment in the final resurrection from the dead, and then and only then will man attain to the likeness of God and sin disappear. Then and only then will man attain to the likeness of Christ and the freedom from death won by Christ extend to redeemed mankind.

Thus the purpose of the Creator to make man in His image is fulfilled in baptism, which in turn is fulfilled in the resurrection of the dead and the life eternal. Baptism has this double point of reference—backwards to creation and forwards to eternal life—because it is baptism into Christ and His death and resurrection. In Christ and in His resurrection on the third day one man stands before God in whom there is fulfilled the purpose which God intended for man when He created him at the beginning. This purpose is achieved in Christ but not at present in any other man. This is why the Church exists. This is the significance of its mission—that others too may come to fulfil God's purposes for them.[18] The Church exists for the sake

---

[16] In regard to the Church fathers see Lampe, *Seal*, pp. 247-248.

[17] In *Theologie der lutherischen Bekenntnisschriften*, 3rd ed., 1948, pp. 402-403. Edmund Schlink points out one difference between the New Testament and the Reformation: according to the former, he says, death has taken place in baptism, but according to the latter it takes place daily after the baptismal act. Schlink, however, does not cite Col. III.5 but only Rom. VI.1-11 in this connexion.

[18] Christ's own redemptive death is the death in our baptism, and this is definitively realised in our own physical death. Cf. Karl Rahner, *Zur Theologie des Todes*, 1958, pp. 61-63. The activity of Christ remains unique throughout, for by Him alone is death transformed.

of the unredeemed who are outside it. This is its *raison d'être*. If instead it exists only for the sake of its members it will be in continual conflict with its indwelling Lord. For Christ is the "light of the *world*." The Church is therefore to stand open to all mankind, her light is to be the light of the world, and the salt in her is to be the salt of the earth. The door which stands open to all mankind—to all unredeemed mankind—is baptism, the gateway through which those who are outside enter in and the act by which the Church "multiplies greatly" from Pentecost on and adds new stones to the building. The key question for any Church which tries to be obedient to the Lord's command to "go" and "baptise" can be rephrased in two separate but essentially related questions. The first is: How can baptism as a gateway into the Church be kept open in such a way that its administration witnesses to the truth that the Church is indeed open to all men? The second question is: How can baptism as a gateway into the Church remain just this, i.e. a way of entrance into a life which is different from that which is found outside? Baptism makes a man truly human and not just a member of a particular Church. If we keep this clearly in mind the gateway will always stand open. But we can never become truly human unless we die and rise again here and now on the level of daily life. If we keep this second aspect no less clearly in mind then death and resurrection really will take place inside the gate—within a congregation of ordinary men and women who have experienced God's dealings with them in the world, and who have the same humanity as the world outside and the same sorrow, sin, repentance, temptation, prayer, joy, and praise.[19]

What we have been speaking of as the open character of baptism is to be seen when we compare it with the more exclusive character of the Eucharist. Baptism is valid when it is administered "according to the institution of Christ." This view which is now general throughout the whole Church can be traced back to the period before the Middle Ages, and in essentials has been adopted by all the major denominations,

---

[19] On the operation in the Church, which is open to humanity, of Jesus's baptism in Jordan, His death, and His humanity, cf. also Hendry, *Incarnation*, p. 110.

though some, contrary to the practice of this early period, will not recognise heretical or schismatic baptism. Augustine argued that baptism is a single act and so cannot be repeated. A man who has been baptised in accordance with Christ's command is baptised once and for all. The charismatic gifts, it is true, will not be forthcoming as long as he remains in a schismatic group. But it is essential that baptism should not be repeated when the person who has received schismatic baptism is received into the true Church. His baptism is confirmed and rendered effective, but it is the original baptism which is so effected.[20] The "true Church" in the early period is, of course, the Church which is in communion with the Bishop of Rome. But gradually as this view of baptism was adopted by other Churches, some of which regard Rome itself as schismatic, the earlier idea of "recognition" came to mean that when a person transferred from one Church to another there was no question of rebaptism. Rather, the new member was regarded as having been truly baptised, wherever his baptism might have taken place. The distinguishing marks of baptism were derived from scripture—baptism is to be administered with water and in the name of the Father, the Son, and the Holy Spirit. There has generally been a reluctance to define which of the existing Churches is truly the Body of Christ. But when we come to the other sacrament the attitude of exclusiveness and grudging recognition which are found betrays in practice a sitting in judgment upon a Church whose baptism has equally in practice been acknowledged as Christ's own baptism.

There are no doubt traditional grounds for this different attitude as far as baptism and the Eucharist are concerned. The Eucharist was connected with ecclesiastical discipline, and the tendency was to make this sacrament the point of discrimination.[21] Early in the life of the Church baptism came to include the baptism of infants, and if an adult sinned after his baptism the point at which discipline was exercised had to be found elsewhere. Perhaps the most important factor was that

[20] See Lampe, *Seal*, p. 242-243. On the Synods of Arles, 314 A.D., and Nicea, 325 A.D., and their decisions on these questions, cf. Werner Elert, *Abendmahl und Kirchengemeinschaft in der alten Kirche*, 1954, p. 68.

[21] See Elert, *Abendmahl*, pp. 80-82 (and also 71-72), for a discussion of 1 Cor. v.11.

the whole problem of according recognition to the baptism of a sect developed in relation to those who were transferring *from* it, and that the problem was posed inside the body which took such converts into its membership. It was these converts who by their action passed a judgment against the Church which they had forsaken, while the Church that received them could refrain from passing any such judgment. But if there are traditional grounds for the quite different treatment of baptism and the Eucharist, it is no less clear that there is no scriptural basis for this treatment. True, we do find instances in the New Testament of disharmony in the Eucharistic fellowship, notably in the conflict between Paul and Peter in Antioch (Gal. II.11-16). But even in the heat of the disagreement both still remained members of the same undivided Church.[22] The apostles who heard the command to repeat the Eucharistic meal in remembrance of Jesus were the same in number, not fewer or narrower in outlook, as they were when told to go into the world and baptise. In fact, the number of those who took part in the Lord's Supper was twelve, including Judas Iscariot, while there were only eleven who were sent out to baptise and preach, Judas being missing (Mk. XVI.14-16, Mt. XXVIII.16-19). It is nowhere stated in scripture that Christ may have told others to baptise. It was the eleven whom He sent. Yet the responsibility of baptising belongs now to all Christians, ordained or unordained, men or women, and there is no question of finding biblical support for this way of doing things. On the other hand it is the traditional restriction in regard to the Eucharist which we attempt to justify on the basis of scripture; and since the arguments for these restrictions have from the first been quite arbitrarily chosen, the attempts to justify them threaten to bring all use of the Bible into disrepute. We have here a typical example of the universal phenomenon of a traditional practice gradually acquiring a scriptural basis in a manner which threatens to deprive the Bible of its authority.

[22] It is strange that in a book dealing with communion in the early Church Elert frequently discusses different passages in the New Testament without once referring to Gal. II.11-16, which in this connexion is the key passage in the New Testament. A positive treatment of the conflict at Antioch would undoubtedly have qualified Elert's confessional approach.

How then should the Church regard the Bible? What in fact has happened is that in this particular respect the historical and traditional openness of the Church in regard to baptism and an almost pathological narrowness in regard to the Eucharist have combined to draw the Church in modern times away from the Bible. Baptism has thus come to be thought of as a mere preliminary while the Eucharist has become the major sacrament.[23] The idea that baptism really unites men to the body of Christ has gradually disappeared, and the conception that the whole of the Christian life is simply a working out of the significance of baptism has come to be regarded as exaggerated and artificial. The proclivity of pietism to assign regeneration to an experience relatively independent of baptism and the denominational exclusiveness which makes the validity of the Eucharist depend on a specific form of ministry have both combined to rob baptism of its true significance and reduce it to an insignificant first stage in a process in which the matters of primary importance come later. In the New Testament, however, it is quite clear that baptism is the major sacrament and that it embraces everything else. There are solid Biblical grounds for making baptism central and using it as the point of reference for all other discussion.[24] At the present time this would mean a revolution in our thinking about theology and the Church. Among other things the remarkable extent to which the various Churches do recognise one another's baptism would have vast consequences in regard to proposals for intercommunion and there too bring about a correspondingly broad approach. But above all baptism would be closely connected with the Christian life at every point and be seen to be the sufficient basis for Christian morality.

[23] Cf. again Jetter, *Taufe*, p. 317, on the difference between Augustine and Luther: "Luther versteht die *Einmaligkeit* der Taufe neu: sie meint nicht den einmaligen Vorgang, sondern seine einmalige Qualität. War sie bis dahin letzten Endes rituell verstanden worden, so begreift Luther sie jetzt eschatologisch: der neue ordo, den uns die Taufe eröffnet, in dem die Strahlen der Gnade von Christus her das Leben im Glauben durchströmen, ist in Zeit und Ewigkeit unser eines, einziges Heil." Luther, as Jetter says, is here breaking with an interpretation of baptism a thousand years old but not with the New Testament. On the contrary, he returns to the early Christian view of baptism.

[24] Cf. T. F. Torrance, "The Atonement and the Oneness of the Church," in the *Scottish Journal of Theology*, 1954, p. 267-269.

Baptism, as we have said, is the means of entrance into the Church and of incorporation into it. The Eucharist is quite different in character. It is only by baptism that the Church is increased in size (Acts II.41). The Eucharist draws together those who have once and for all been incorporated or ingrafted into the body through the unrepeated act of baptism. It is at this point that we can see the more exclusive aspect of the Eucharist, for the Supper has no place in the mission of the Church, and unlike baptism was not commanded by Jesus when He sent His apostles into the world (Mk. XVI.15 f., Mt. XXVIII.19). Of the two sacraments baptism is prior and the Eucharist in the strict sense secondary.[25] The sequence cannot be altered. Baptism cannot be repeated any more than the crossing of the Red Sea could be repeated. But the Eucharist by its very nature is something that is done again and again, just as manna and water were given in the wilderness again and again to those who had been delivered from the sea (I Cor. x.1-4). Baptism and the Eucharist differ from each other, but in such a way that their very difference unites them and establishes a profound inner connexion between them. To say that baptism takes place once and for all and is never repeated means that Christ's death and resurrection embrace the *whole* life of the baptised. But this same Christ comes and gives Himself, the Crucified and Risen, in a Supper, i.e. in something which is continually repeated and which is not done once and for all.[26] Baptism is the greater and all-embracing sacrament. The Eucharist is included within this greater act and continues to renew what baptism has already bestowed. This strong connexion between baptism and the Eucharist is radically broken when it is assumed (as it is frequently today) that although baptism as practised in other Churches may be regarded as Christ's own baptism and therefore the means by which the baptised are manifestly ingrafted into His body, yet the Eucharistic acts of these same Churches cannot be allowed to exhibit His real presence. There is no question of a second baptism. But still the table is barred. Baptism is thus reduced

[25] Cf. Oscar Cullmann, *Early Christian Worship*, repr. 1954, pp. 31-32, 82-83.
[26] See J. G. Davies, *The Spirit, the Church, and the Sacraments*, 1954, pp. 123-124, and C. F. D. Moule, *The Sacrifice of Christ*, 1956, pp. 30, 42-43.

to a ritual formality and loses its connexion with all that follows in the life of the baptised, including physical death. It would be surprising if after this complete misinterpretation of baptism the Eucharist could retain its true character. Because of the intimate connexion between baptism and the Eucharist a false view of baptism will inevitably produce errors in the interpretation of the Eucharist.

One such error particularly worth noting in a work which deals with the Gospel and the Church is the lack of any clear theological connexion between the Eucharist and daily life. The Reformation was marked by its vigorous criticism of the idea of sacrifice as it was then applied to the celebration of the Lord's Supper.[27] This negative attitude in regard to sacrificial terminology is to be understood in the light of the attack on the medieval doctrine of the sacrifice of the Mass.[28] According to Luther the death and resurrection which are experienced in baptism bring about in faith a daily crucifixion of the old nature and a daily rising to life of the new. And the old nature is confronted by the Cross in the midst of human life and not apart from it. The life of baptism is to be lived in the worldly vocation of the Christian with all its drudgery and difficulty. It is here that our neighbour is to be served and here that praise and a readiness to make sacrifices are to be found. If baptism and the Eucharist are connected in this way, both will have consequences in the world outside the sanctuary and bring those who have participated in them into a fellowship of service in daily life. In the New Testament this aspect of the Christian life is quite boldly spoken of in terms of self-offering and sacrifice (Rom. XII.1-21).[29] We should see more clearly the connexion between baptism and the Eucharist and the connexion between both of these and the Gospel and the Church if we would fully grasp the profound theological

[27] See Carl F. Wisløff, *Nattverd og messe*, 1957, the summary on pp. 200-202. Cf. however, the different view in Gustaf Aulén, *Eucharist and Sacrifice*, 1958, pp. 81-87.

[28] Vilmos Vajta, *Die Theologie des Gottesdienstes bei Luther*, 1952, pp. 312-316, Alan Richardson, *An Introduction to the Theology of the New Testament*, 1958, pp. 381-382.

[29] Cf. Richardson, *Introduction*, pp. 297-300, 379, 385-387, and also Vajta, *Theologie des Gottesdienstes*, pp. 311-312. Cf. also Yngve Brilioth, *Eucharistic Faith and Practice, Evangelical and Catholic*, 1953, pp. 278-279.

unity which holds together the sacrifice involved in daily work and the offering of praise in divine worship. The cross of the Christian's daily work and the praise which he offers in the sanctuary are both aspects of the truth that death and resurrection are present realities to be experienced both in work and in worship. The Christian's whole life and not just the hour of worship on Sunday abounds in an eschatological expectation which extends from the altar to even the most rudimentary of human occupations.

It is an accepted fact that the Lutheran Reformation emphatically rejected any idea that the minister or worshipper has the active part to play in the celebration of the Eucharist and God, as it were, the passive. There is no suggestion, according to the Reformers, that anything is "offered" to a passive God in the sacrament. He is rather the God who Himself gives to men and acts on their behalf, and who comes in Christ and gives salvation to those who await Him. Every Eucharist must therefore culminate in *communion*. The Gospel is at work in the Eucharist, and in it Christ is continually giving Himself anew to His gathered people. But the more strongly we emphasise this real presence of Christ with all His benefits, the more clearly we shall perceive the connexion between the Eucharist and our service of our neighbour.[30] The social implications which follow from this do not weaken the eschatological expectation which is so prominent a part of the sacrament. On the contrary, this eschatological aspect becomes predominant. If eschatology is defined merely in terms of the contrast between a lower physical world and a higher spiritual one, or between an earthly dimension of existence "down here" and a heavenly realm "up there," then to underline the social significance of the sacrament will imply a corresponding diminution of its eschatological character by lessening the emphasis on "that which is to come" and concentrating on "that which is." But baptism brings us into the death of resurrection of Christ, the same Christ who comes to us in the Eucharist and there brings us again face to face with

[30] See Prenter, *Skabelse*, pp. 539-540. Peter Brunner in "Zur Lehre vom Gottesdienst der im Namen Jesu versammelten Gemeinde," in *Leitourgia*, Vol. I, 1954, e.g. pp. 245-247, strongly emphasises the eschatological aspect.

the events of death and resurrection. The soldiers who scourged Jesus Christ and the bystanders who saw Him take the vinegar were all but standing in the bright light of the resurrection. So near and yet so far! No living soul had every come so close as they, even through the most profound meditation.[31] But if eschatology is defined in terms of both the tension and the unity between death and resurrection, the communicant who takes part in the Eucharist does not reach out in faith to "that which is to come" when he shuts himself off from the affairs of the world but precisely when he leaves the table to become involved in them. The more basic and mundane a man's job in life, the more he is capable of abounding in hope, so long as he finds his true life in the sacraments.[32]

For this reason Luther's doctrine of the earthly government and human work are part of a total view which is essentially sacramental. Luther's writings from 1519 onwards point out quite clearly the connexion between baptism and vocation.[33] The points of contact between his doctrine of vocation and his teaching concerning the Eucharist are not so obvious, but there is no reason why we in our day should not try to trace out these relationships, taking baptism as our starting-point. There is abundant Biblical and patristic material at our disposal, and this new line of inquiry would not mean that we were departing from the stand-point and witness of the Reformation.

The Living Word

What we have called the living word comes to men in the sacraments and in preaching. It is not primarily a written but a spoken word. It is first the word of the Creator through which everything has been created. It has become flesh in Jesus Christ (Jn. 1.1-14), and is living and creating afresh in every word

---

[31] Cf. A. M. Ramsey, *The Gospel and the Catholic Church*, 1936, pp. 3-42. There is hardly any other theological work in our time which so vigorously treats the whole Church from the point of view of Christ's death and resurrection as this. Despite its errors the book is highly suggestive.

[32] Cf. H. Østergaard-Nielsen, *Scriptura sacra et viva vox*, 1957, pp. 163-165. Admittedly Luther is interpreted in the spirit of Grundtvig, but the interpretation of the sacrament and common life is of value. Cf. also Götz Harbsmeier, *Dass wir die Predigt und Gottes Wort nicht verachten*, 1938, p. 97.

[33] W.A. II.734, 14-33 (Sermon on the Sacrament of Baptism, 1519).

which He proclaims to men. It is by this word that the Church comes into being and is built up.[1] The phrase "word and sacraments" is liable to be misunderstood if it is interpreted to mean that the word exists independently of the sacraments and is wholly different from them. In fact the word underlies even the sacraments, and the Reformers recovered a fundamental insight of the early Christian Church by ascribing great importance to the words of the institution in the celebration of baptism and the Eucharist. By this recovery the Gospel again became central to both. The sacraments derive their validity from the word of God or of Jesus Christ, and this word commands a distribution, a giving of gifts to men. In the same way the real power of preaching consists in the fact that it is the word of God or of Jesus Christ which is addressing us, and this word commands—again—a distribution, a giving of gifts to men by the means of human speech. A subject that is to be debated, for instance, is first examined from every possible angle. Nothing more is involved. But the giving of a gift to someone is essentially an action that in some way or another affects the recipient. The gesture of giving is just this—a gesture or an action which alters some previously existing condition.[2] Much actual preaching is largely meditative or reflective in language or atmosphere, and as such stands in striking contrast with the strongly dramatic character of the scripture lessons on which it is based with their unmistakable insistence that their contents should be proclaimed. The proper expression is rather "preaching and the sacraments" or "sacraments and preaching." Underlying both and at work in both is the Word who is Jesus Christ. Christ has dealings with men in His appointed means, giving Himself to those who accept Him and thereby building up His Church.

In preaching human speech derives its power from the scriptural texts on which it is based, that is to say from a

---

[1] See Gustaf Wingren, "Die Sakramente und die Predigt als Träger des fleischgewordenen Wortes," in *Die Leibhaftigkeit des Wortes*, 1958, pp. 375-386.

[2] The part played by the Words of Institution in baptism and the Eucharist (clearly shown in the last two sections of Luther's Shorter Catechism) corresponds exactly to the part played by the text in preaching. In both cases the words introduce a dividing of the Word. Cf. Henrik Ivarsson, "Predikans funktion," in *Svensk teologisk kvartalskrift*, 1955, pp. 103-104, 108, 115-116.

written word, in the same way as the sacraments derive their validity from the written down words of institution. But if preaching and the sacraments issue with power from a written word, it is even more fundamental that both were in existence even before the Gospel was reduced to writing. It is nowhere stated that Christ ever wrote a single word.[3] On the contrary we are frequently told that He spoke to men and told His disciples to speak rather than to write. We know too that He was baptised and had the Supper with His friends and also that He promised them that they would share both in His baptism and His "cup," and commanded them to repeat these acts. All four Gospels unmistakably testify that the spoken word preceded the written word, and all four become truly "gospel" when they are preached. They are Gospels to be proclaimed by the spoken word, and are not merely written documents. This is of a piece with the characteristic Biblical belief in Christ as the Word. He is the Word of the Creator in Genesis and before His incarnation spoke through the prophets who in ancient Israel also addressed the living word to men.

We can best understand the Gospel which the apostles were commissioned to preach to "all nations" by looking at it as we looked at baptism in the previous section and from the same three aspects. In the first place we have to note the connexion between the Gospel and Christ's death and resurrection. The Gospel is primarily a message about something that has happened and is of importance to those who hear it. This is the significance of "Gospel" in the New Testament.[4] The term may accordingly also be used of the documents which are designated "Gospels" and which are kerygmatic rather than analytical or reflective in character. As soon as the Gospels recount the last events in the earthly life of Christ, the resurrection and the ascension, they come abruptly to a conclusion.[5] In the second place we have to note the obvious connexion

[3] For what follows cf. Regin Prenter, *Spiritus Creator*, 2nd ed., 1946, p. 127, Gustaf Wingren, *The Living Word*, 1960, pp. 65-67, Henrik Ivarsson, *Predikans uppgift*, 1956, pp. 21-23, Per Erik Persson, "Predikan och Kristi realpresens," in *S.t.k.*, 1958, pp. 314-324.

[4] Cf. C. H. Dodd, *The Apostolic Preaching*, new ed., 1944, pp. 7-40, Heinz-Dietrich Wendland, "Das Heilsgeschehen in Christus und die Predigt im Neuen Testament," in *Schriften des teologisches Konvents*, No. 7, 1955, pp. 16-18.

[5] See Dodd, *Apostolic Preaching*, pp. 45-56.

with the last times. The word which is preached in all the world is received in a variety of ways. It sifts men in secret. It is a judgment, a crisis. It comes to its climax in the "End," which is the last of all judgments when nothing is left to be judged and which is therefore called the last judgment with its final separation and the fulfilment of men's hopes or fears. In the third place we are also to note the connexion between the Gospel and creation, that is, its recapitulatory aspect. The Gospel is brought to all nations—all those nations of whom the prehistory in Genesis speaks, all of them created, fallen, and disobedient. Every human being on earth is "in Adam." But now men are born anew and find their true life in the Gospel which is the creative word and able to bring a "new creation" into being.[6]

In the present section, however, we have chosen to follow a slightly different order and begin with eschatology and conclude with Christology. In our discussion of the latter we shall be giving some attention to matters of some complexity but of vast importance to us. Each of the four Gospels speaks of a Christ who exercised His ministry in a restricted geographical area, mainly Galilee and Judea. In the Acts and the Epistles the scene is suddenly changed and now takes in the whole world. Between the two there occurs the ascension into heaven which is mentioned both at the end of the Gospel (Mk. xvi.19 f., Lk. xxiv.50-53) and at the beginning of Acts (Acts 1.4-11). It is included appropriately in each place, for it constitutes the conclusion of the ministry of Jesus and the beginning of the acts of the apostles. The ascension clearly does not mean that Jesus passed from one particular geographical area to another, but that He went to the place of divine power, to "the right hand of God," and that He now has power to be everywhere and in all things. For this reason the preaching of the early Church is the same as its mission. The goal is the world for both of them. For this reason too this world-wide preaching began at the very moment of the ascension: "And they went forth and preached everywhere" (Mk. xvi.20).[7] As the scene changes,

[6] Cf. Heinrich Vogel, "Viva vox evangelii," in *Evangelische Theologie*, 1947-48, pp. 351-352.
[7] Cf. J. G. Davies, *He Ascended into Heaven*, 1958, pp. 169-170.

the spotlight which had been focused for so long on a single
nation widens to include the whole of the world. Not since
Genesis XI, the story of the tower of Babel, the division of the
nations, and the call of Abraham, had Biblical history included
human history. And the object of this preaching was no absent
Saviour in a distant heaven or a remote age, but was Himself
in the word that was preached confirming the message (Mk.
XVI.20, Mt. XXVIII.20). The New Testament can even state
that Christ Himself is the subject of the preaching which began
with the open grave, and can speak of Him as the only true
preacher of the Gospel, who has suffered and died in order to
proclaim light to the Gentiles (Acts XVI.26). The Church,
which is raised to life through the preaching of the Gospel and
which in turn itself witnesses to the mighty act of God, exists
accordingly by an inner constraint for the sake of all
mankind.[8]

Thus the last times have already begun. Christ has already
passed through death and the resurrection and now declares
the Gospel from the right hand of the Father. Those who hear
Him have not reached their goal but are on the way and death
is still ahead of them. But when they hear the Gospel with its
word about the Son of man they come to see themselves as
they really are and even now have come to their appointed
end before the time. Now—in the word of the Gospel—is
their judgment and now the offer of life is being made.[9] It is
of no consequence whether or not they intellectually reject
the apocalyptic interpretation of the last times. They have still
to experience in their own lives events which they will not
escape even if they reject the Gospel and which are sufficient
indications of what is going to happen in the last times to all
men. Already they have a foretaste of the coming judgment.
The well-known passages in the New Testament which make
preaching one element in the events of the last times which have
begun with the ascension and Pentecost and will culminate
in the parousia (Acts I.4-11, X.39-43, Mk. XIII.10, Mt. XXIV.14)
are not of course to be interpreted in purely individual terms,
as if their only meaning were that the death of the individual

---

[8] Cf. Gerhard Koch. *Die Auferstehung Jesu Christi*, 1959, pp. 241-337.
[9] Cf. John VI.63, XII.48, III.18.

is identical with the last judgment, or that Christ's return from heaven is to be explained as the coming of the Gospel in preaching to those who accept it.[10] To demythologise the Gospel in such a way means to lose the possibility of speaking about the dealings which God and Jesus Christ have with all men, dealings which embrace the whole of life and in which the redemptive act on behalf of the individual has its proper though subsequent place. When the principal emphasis comes to be laid on what God does for the individual, those Biblical passages which plainly set forth what He has done or will do for all men at Calvary, Easter, the parousia, and the last judgment, are inevitably given a subordinate place through some kind of anthropological interpretation to the immediate response of the individual to the kerygma in face of the onset of his death. The fundamental error in this existential view is not that it does away with miracles, but that it gives quite mistaken prominence to the individual.[11] It is quite a different matter with the untheological and purely human events which we experience from day to day. While listening to the radio or perhaps while reading a page of the Bible a man may hear the Word of Christ speaking to him, and all of a sudden feel that he is both judged and at the same time entering into a new life. He has no idea of what Christ will do to the rest of mankind in the future. It is, he supposes, within the bounds of possibility that He may come and judge others as well. Be that as it may, for this man Christ is already present, dwelling in him, judging him, and regenerating him. For such a man the last times have already begun.

The New Testament speaks very clearly of the resurrection of Christ as a past event and of His return as a future hope. In the intervening period Christ comes again and again in the word of the Gospel which first began to be preached after the resurrection and will no longer be preached after His return.

[10] Rudolf Bultmann moves in this direction, e.g. in his reply to the theses of J. Schniewind in *Kerygma and Myth*, 1953, pp. 112-113.

[11] We see the same thing in Bultmann's tendency to include the work of the law in its "spiritual" use. In its spiritual use the law confronts the individual in his conscience. But in its civil use it has to do with all men, with questions of rule and order, and here I am only one among many, without any importance of my own. The isolation of the spiritual use of the law is always indicative of a fundamental individualism. Cf. Bultmann, *Kerygma and Myth*, pp. 191-211.

For this reason preaching itself is an eschatological event.[12] The demythologising theology which has made such advances in modern continental theology interprets the events of Easter and the parousia in such a way that both come to be identified with what is happening to me personally now and with the preaching to which I as an individual am listening. The significance of the personal experience of the individual is not derived from those objective events which concern all mankind corporately. It is my own personal experience which has become central.[13] We can understand the psychological attitude which so remarkably plays down the activity of God as a revolt against a doctrinal legalism or against the insistence of the Church on intellectual assent to certain redemptive facts which took place in the past and to a particular view of what will take place in the future. This revolt is a legitimate one. When Christ is openly "set forth" in preaching, which involves stating facts or portraying Him in some dramatic fashion, it in fact makes very little difference whether the hearer gives his intellectual assent to doctrinal propositions about past events or future expectations. The portrayal, i.e. the preaching of the Gospel, can destroy and refashion every intellectual difficulty. But more than this we may not say. We cannot say that the work of the Gospel is impeded when the hearer gives intellectual assent to dogmatic statements about past or future events. This insistence on an anthropological interpretation by existentialist theology has made it into a new dogmatic system, prohibitive in form and basically anti-human.[14] We are not to attach too great importance to the question of whether those who hear the Gospel accept it intellectually or reject it intellectually. The preaching of Christ is an eschatological event which brings its hearers into the last times now, however they may regard it intellectually.

But this "last" event is also from one point of view the restoration of the original pure creation. It is "recapitulation."

---

[12] See Oscar Cullmann, *Christ and Time*, 1951, pp. 157-164.

[13] Cf. too A. N. Wilder, "Kerygma, Eschatology, and Social Ethics," in *Background*, pp. 519-521, and also Gerhard Koch, *Auferstehung*, pp. 181-182.

[14] It might rather be maintained that theology should refrain from denying the fact of the resurrection if it does not want to destroy the Gospel it has to interpret. Cf. also Regin Prenter, *Ordet og Ånden*, 1952, pp. 61-83.

Preaching recapitulates the image of God in the same way as baptism. The Gospel declares that all that took place in the event of Christ's life is now becoming the experience of those who listen to its word. Now they can believe that they have died with Christ and are raised with Him (II Cor. v.14, Gal. II.16-21, Rom. vi.6 f.). But this transforming experience, so central to the message of the Gospel and realised in the event of baptism, is quite the opposite of what happened to Adam (Gen. III.1-19, Phil. II.5-11).[15] Adam is mankind, the man who hears the word of the Gospel and who is made in the image of God but is still far from the life for which he was created. The Christ who comes in the preaching of the Gospel *is* the image of God, who in our human flesh underwent the same temptation as Adam, but without being defeated. The purity which He attained in that struggle was not for Himself but for us, and having reached His appointed end and being now highly exalted above every living creature (Phil. II.9), He now comes in preaching and baptism to "all nations" (Mt. xxviii.19) and "the whole creation" (Mk. xvi.15). The New Testament closely connects the command to preach the Gospel with the prehistory of which we read in Genesis.[16] Since preaching is in essence the recapitulation of creation, it is also in essence missionary preaching. For mission implies being sent out to a lost mankind and seeking Adam who is still hiding from the presence of the Lord (Gen. III.8). The narratives of this prehistory deal with many other nations besides Israel, but from the time of the calling of Abraham these nations disappear into the background. In the world mission of the New Testament, however, they come back into prominence.[17] God's work within the limits of a single nation, Israel, has now come to fulfilment as a result of what He has done for men in Jesus Christ, and Adam's fall has been reversed through the temptation, passion,

[15] See Cullmann, *Christology*, pp. 180-181, and cf. Jervell, *Imago Dei*, pp. 173-175.

[16] When the New Testament refers to God's creation of the whole of mankind, it does so characteristically in its missionary preaching. Cf. Gösta Lindeskog, *Studien zum neutestamentlichen Schöpfungsgedanken*, vol. i, 1952, pp. 180-187, Bertil Gärtner, *The Areopagus Speech and Natural Revelation*, 1955, p. 169, 229-241.

[17] Cf. Gen. xii.3 with Gal. iii.8. See Wingren, *Living Word*, pp. 37-49, 96-103. To say that preaching sets forth the image of Christ (i.e. the image of God) is the same as to say that it is addressed to "all nations." Both things imply recapitulation.

C

and victory of a single new man. Once more the situation is what it was in the beginning. But now the movement is not as in Genesis from the pure creation to the fall and death. This time everything is reversed, and the movement is from sin and death to purity and life. This is why the Church stands open on one side to welcome fallen mankind, while on the other side it looks out to the resurrection of the dead. But this difference in outlook is only an apparent one, for in the light of the pre-history and the recapitulation the two are seen to be one. There is only one perspective, grounded in hope and directed towards all mankind.

In the New Testament the climax of this missionary preaching is generally a summons to *conversion* (Lk. xxiv.46-49, Acts ii.36-41, x.42 f., xiv.15, xvii.26-31).[18] The rebellion of the nations from their Creator is taken for granted, though at times it is explicitly affirmed (Acts xiv.15-17, xvii.24-30). There is a clear relationship between the kerygma with its emphasis on the death and resurrection of Christ, the conversion of the one who hears the Gospel, and his ensuing baptism (Acts ii.41, x.44-48). Central both to the kerygma and to baptism are the notes of death and resurrection. The significance of the summons to conversion must be understood in the light of this relationship. There is a tendency today to conceive of the kerygma of the early Church as an invitation addressed to those outside to come into the membership of the congregation. First, it is argued, comes the kerygma and then the didache or instruction given within the congregation and consisting largely of concrete rules and regulations.[19] It then becomes quite easy in trying to apply the New Testament to Church life today to ascribe the renewal of the Church to this didache rather than to the Gospel as it is proclaimed in the kerygma. Such an interpretation will ultimately give the question of what outward form and order the Church should have in the present time a greater significance than it actually

[18] Martin Dibelius, "Die Bekehrung des Cornelius," in *Coniectanea neotestamentica*, no. xi, 1947, p. 52, and also Harald Sahlin, "Die Früchte der Umkehr," in *Studia theologica*, vol. i, 1947, pp. 54, 66-67. See also Dodd, *Apostolic Preaching*, pp. 23-24.

[19] Cf. Harald Riesenfeld, "Evangelietraditionens ursprung," in *S.t.k.*, 1958, pp. 249-250. See also Dodd, *Apostolic Preaching*, pp. 7-9.

has. It would then be much more natural to speak of "the commandments of the Lord and the Church" than of "Gospel and Church." It seems as though this preference for such categories of thought is connected with the further tendency to relegate baptism (which, as we have seen, is the sacrament that is held open to the Gentile world) to some peripheral position and instead to put the more exclusive congregational act of the Eucharist into the centre. All these categories of thought and their consequences are closely connected. The significant fact is that neither baptism nor the preaching of the Gospel is given any place of consequence in the daily life of the Church or the Christian believer. They are made merely preliminary episodes, after which the Church turns elsewhere to find its real life.

This appeal for conversion in the missionary preaching of the Church is, however, only part of something deeper.[20] Those who hear the preaching of the Gospel are "in Adam." Underlying their own situation is the situation of Adam. But Christ's death and resurrection are the very opposite of what happened to Adam (Phil. II.5-11). Baptism brings the individual personally into this experience in which what happened to Adam is reversed and brings him through death to the resurrection. But this resurrection is fully attained only after physical death. The effect of baptism applies to the whole of daily life.[21] Since the rebellious element continues to exist in the old nature (cf. Gal. v.17, Col. III.5), the Gospel is not merely a beginning but a refuge to which we have to turn every day of life (cf. Rom. x.6-8, 17) and the resurrection is the object of our continual striving (cf. Phil. III.10 f., 21). All of this affects the convert. The actual point of turning, of course, is baptism and incorporation into the Church. But since the old movement from life to death is experienced in every temptation, it is now reversed in every temptation and every downward plunge which all men know, and to which Adam, but not Christ, succumbed.[22] The reversal of this movement means life for the "new man" and death for the "old." Conversion applies

---

[20] See also Bengt Hägglund, "Metanoia-Poenitentia," in *Studier tillägnade Hjalmar Lindroth*, 1958, pp. 81-82, 87-88.

[21] Prenter, *Skabelse*, pp. 265-267.

[22] Cf. Cullmann, *Christology*, pp. 94-97, 178-179.

to the whole of the Christian life, and is achieved in dying and rising day by day.

We can now see, as we noted earlier in regard to baptism, that the eschatological and recapitulatory aspects of preaching are inseparable from the Christological. We have discussed preaching as an event in the last times and as a restoration of creation, but each time we have been drawn inevitably to the heart of Christology, viz., the cross and resurrection. When Christ is set forth in preaching, two things happen to those who hear the Gospel: they have been brought into the situation in which the last times are even now upon them, and they see before them the pure and primal creation which is the image of God. The early Church went out to preach the Gospel and called the Gentiles in and brought them to baptism and this conversion of Adam's condition, a conversion which will finally be complete at the restoration of all things when "we shall be like Him" (1 Jn. III.2). For Luther this missionary preaching of the Church is the Gospel which we hear preached to the congregation Sunday by Sunday, while conversion is a continuing daily experience. When we regard conversion in this way, it means that baptism, which took place for the individual only once but which will exercise a powerful influence until the consummation, each day will disclose more of its real significance. Daily the old nature is put to death and the new raised to life.[23] This is what sanctification means, and sanctification is sustained by the Eucharist and preaching, both of which are given and addressed to the baptised believer over and over again. But even in those who have been baptised the "old Adam" still remains. The prehistory in Genesis has something to say about the lives of all who hear the Gospel. But the new creation too is found in the baptised, and in his preaching Luther speaks to exhort this new creature. It is not true that Luther has no place in his preaching for exhortation, admonition, and the example of Christ.[24] If it is historically

[23] Note the answer to the question, "What meaneth this baptism in water?" in the fourth section of Luther's Shorter Catechism, and the references to Rom. VI.3 f. Cf. Ruben Josefson, *Luthers lära om dopet*, 1944, pp. 162-167.

[24] We get the impression from Edwin Larsson, "Lag och frihet i Galaterbrevet," in *Svensk exegetisk årsbok*, 1959, pp. 111-112, 118-119, that it would be "Lutheran" to disregard these exhortatory aspects. If this is so, Martin Luther was not a Lutheran!

accurate to say that in the early Church moral instruction was given within the congregation after the Gospel had been preached to the world outside, our respect for Luther's intuitive grasp of the facts and his brilliant insight into the meaning of the biblical message cannot but increase. In his own preaching Luther has a place for moral exhortation and the example of Christ as a stimulus to good works. This all comes *after* the Gospel has been preached and after it has been accepted.

In the context of our discussion the most important fact to be noted is the parallel which Luther draws between conferring forgiveness of sins through preaching the Gospel and conferring the obligation to do good works through proclaiming Christ and through the exhortation to good works which follows from this. The preaching of the Gospel is essentially the same as absolution. It is the spoken, living word through which God Himself has dealings with those who hear it.[25] Preaching is not therefore concerned to analyse the situation of those to whom it is addressed, but rather to change that situation. It does not wait hopefully for faith to appear in a doubting soul, but brings faith about where it is lacking (cf. Rom. x.17). It does this by showing forth Christ as He is—and by showing the lost to whom Christ comes and gives Himself who they are. These helpless creatures are seen in the Gospel story in the company of Jesus so that in every age faith may come into being whenever the Gospel is preached.[26] Following this there comes the second subject of preaching, after the Gospel, viz. love, the good works which we are to do for the sake of our neighbour. This "ander stuck" of preaching, as Luther calls it, follows consistently and methodically from the first. Ivarsson, in his masterly work on the Reformer which may be unfamiliar outside Scandinavia, demonstrates quite conclusively that in the strict sense there are only two themes in Luther's preaching—faith and good works. Preaching has this double purpose: on the one hand it has a service to perform in relation to those who hear it, that is, its purpose is to elicit faith; on the other hand it directs us to the service which we have to perform

[25] Ivarsson, *Predikans uppgift*, pp. 19-69.
[26] See in particular *ibid.* pp. 48-49, and cf. Gerhard Ebeling, *Evangelische Evangelienauslegung*, 1942, p. 444.

for our neighbour, that is, its purpose is to elicit good works. Our works are "good" when they are to the benefit of someone other than ourselves. So when preaching reminds men of their obligation to do good works, it has in view the benefit of others than those who are listening to its message. Preaching then may not lose sight of this obligation to serve the needs of these others and is not concerned merely to state what a true Christian ought to be like. This would be to put those who hear it back into the centre, but they already have been made righteous through the Gospel and forgiveness of sins which have been declared to them. At this point preaching has to do with the goodness of their works. They themselves are no longer in the centre. It is their neighbour who has now come to the front.[27] Exhortations to do good for the sake of this neighbour are *identical with the preaching of Christ as the example of the believer,* for the work of Christ was to give Himself to the world in its need. To follow His example means therefore to give ourselves in service to our fellow-men. When preaching proclaims Christ as the example of what the believer should be, it is dealing *with the world.* Christ dwells actively in His word, and He is made flesh in the daily service rendered in the world by those who hear His word and obey in their actions. When the good works to which we are summoned by the Gospel are thus interpreted as a means of serving our neighbour and as being "good" in so far as they promote the well-being of our fellow-men, this is because (as Luther so well reminds us) the good works for which we are responsible are to be seen generally if not exclusively as tasks to be performed in the daily life of our fellow-beings. This is true even in the case of those outside the Church. Marriage, family, the rearing of children, the provision of food and care, home-making, farming, and trades—in every area of life the Creator is at work, sustaining the life He has created by means of activities such as these throughout the world. Only the Old Testament and the first article of the Creed can give us a true perspective of the inner meaning of all human activities.[28] But as soon as we isolate the New Testa-

[27] See Ivarsson, *Predikans uppgift,* pp. 115-132.
[28] Cf. Ivarsson, *ibid.,* p. 268, where the distinction between Luther and Swedish pietism is described.

ment from its historical setting and its unique interpretation of all human activity we make it into a denominational handbook and turn the Church into a sect which follows its own particular book of rules. What is more, we alter the character of the New Testament summons to good works in such a way that the good works which it enjoins become, instead, the marks of what the members of the Church ought to be, as opposed to other men.[29] Goodness is then something to be found by withdrawing from the world rather than something to be shared with the world. Christ exercises His Lordship in the Church by separating members of the congregation from the rest of the world and giving this separate group alone His words of counsel and command. The Gospel and baptism are regarded merely as preliminary events, related in the first instance to admission or entrance into the Church. Thereafter the congregation lives by rules which are unrelated to the Gospel and to this idea of sharing and indeed are incompatible with them. Luther's exposition of what the New Testament means in its exhortation to good works and his pointing to Christ as the example of what our own good works should be is much closer to the New Testament than this modern view of the Church as a society to be governed according to regulations.[30]

It is at any rate these New Testament passages in which Jesus is set before men as judge or example that Luther takes as his authority for preaching moral exhortation on the basis of the Gospel. In the first place the one particular aspect of the work of Jesus which they stress is His giving of gifts to men. The object of His giving, which we in turn are exhorted to imitate, is His people, His Church. We have *received* and must also give. The Gospel proclaims this self-offering of Jesus by which His Church is built up, and the basis of the constantly repeated exhortations to imitate His example is His dealings with men. Thus the Gospel is embedded in this moral instruction

[29] We can preach on one exhortatory passage after another and keep fitting what the New Testament says into this pietistic framework, which was constructed some time in the eighteenth century. See examples in Ivarsson, *Predikans uppgift*, pp. 259-268. On the preaching of Swedish pietism see Yngve Brilioth, *Predikans historia*, 1945, pp. 201-233.

[30] For what follows cf. Gustaf Wingren, "Was bedeutet die Forderung der Nachfolge der Christi in evangelischer Ethik?" in *Theologische Literaturzeitung*, 1950, pp. 390-392.

of which we have been speaking. It is heard afresh in these
ethical imperatives of which it is the ground and basis. But
when it comes to the service which we in our turn are to
perform, it is never to God or to Jesus that our works are said
to be directed,[31] but to our brethren, our neighbours, and to
"the least of these": "Whoever would be great among you
must be your servant, and whoever would be first among you
must be your slave" (Mt. xx.26 f.). This passage is characteristic
of many, and having given the command it at once provides
the reason: "The Son of man came not to be served but to
serve, and to give His life as a ransom for many" (Mt. xx.28).[32]
The narrative of the foot-washing culminates in a quite explicit
command: "I have given you an example, that you also should
do as I have done to you" (Jn. xiii.15). Christ is among his
disciples as One who serves, and they in turn are to follow His
example by being servants, not of God or of Himself, but of
their fellow-men: "You also ought to wash one another's feet"
(Jn. xiii.14). Even though we may interpret this phrase, "one
another," to refer to our fellow-members in the Church,
such a restricted interpretation of our obligation to render
service is impossible in other passages. The author of 1 Peter,
for example, defines the relationship which is to exist betwen
masters and servants, particularly masters who let their servants
suffer unjustly when they have done right. It is unlikely that
these masters were members of the Church, but it is quite
clear that even an evil master is still the neighbour of the
Christian servant and therefore the object of his care and
service, after the example of Christ. The motive for such
behaviour is explained: "Because Christ also suffered for you,
leaving you an example, that you should follow in His steps"
(1 Pet. ii.18-23). The Gospel lies behind and within exhortations such as these, and the service which is laid upon the
Christian is to be performed for the benefit of his neighbour
in daily life and even in objectionable ways.[33]

[31] This is not the case, e.g. even in ii Cor. viii.5 ff.
[32] See also the parallels in Mk. x.41-43, Lk. xxii.25-27. In all three Gospels
this comes after Jesus has spoken about "the cup."
[33] This is a key point in Luther's doctrine of works in our secular vocation, as
contrasted with the monastery. On Luther's sermons on this theme see Ivarsson,
Predikans uppgift, pp. 145-147.

Both in the Johannine narrative of the foot-washing and
the synoptic passages which speak of the follower of Jesus as
"slave of all" (Mk. x.41 ff. and parallels) reference is made
to the Lordship of Jesus (Jn. xiii.13 f.) and the "great men"
of the Gentiles (Mk. x.42, Mt. xx.25, Lk. xxii.25, 27). The
lowly position chosen by Jesus is set in contrast to the exalted
position sought by Adam. The questions which the disciples
asked concerning the places of honour and which gave rise to
Jesus's words about being the servants of all (Mk. x.37, cf.
Mt. xx.21, Lk. xxii.24) are, so to speak, Adam's questions.
They represent Adam's temptation (cf. Gen. iii.4 f.). And the
point made in all four Gospels is the same—the power of Jesus
Christ is greater than that of any other, yet He has chosen
to give Himself in service to man. His chosen way is the very
opposite of Adam's. Nowhere is this descent of Christ so simply
or so concisely expressed as in Phil. ii.5 ff., which speaks of
Him as the One who though He was in the form of God
emptied Himself and took the form of a servant.[34] It is easy,
however, to overlook the fact that this hymn of praise is actually
part of an exhortatory context in which the Apostle exhorts
his readers to imitate Christ. This imitation is expressed in
what they do to "others." "In humility count others better
than yourselves. Let each of you look not only to his own
interests, but also to the interests of others" (Phil. ii.3 f.).
The duty of serving one's neighbour in daily life is a simple and
direct consequence of the Gospel (cf. 1 Cor. x.31–xi.1, Rom.
xv.1-3, 7, Eph. v.25). When the Church at Corinth sent money
to Jerusalem it grounded its action on the example of Christ
who "though He was rich, yet for your sake He became poor"
(ii Cor. viii.9). The same pattern prevails throughout the New
Testament. The Gospel summons men to works of service
which are "good" in that they do good to others. In 1 Jn. iii.16
a parallel is drawn between the work of Christ and the duty of
the Christian: He gave His life for us and we must give our
lives for our brethren.[35] The Church comes into being through
the preaching of the Gospel which is continued in the exhortation to good works or the manner of life which is a consequence of the Gospel. Christ continues to give His gifts to

[34] See Cullmann, *Christology*, pp. 179-181.   [35] Cf. 1 John ii.6, Col. iii. 13.

men through these works which are thus demanded and encouraged in those who hear the Gospel. The Gospel is at work in the daily life of the Church and in the exhortation to good works which inspires service of different kinds in accordance with human need (e.g. money for Jerusalem, consideration of the weak, patient endurance in face of unjust government, etc.).[36]

Ivarsson's masterly treatment of Luther to which reference has already been made is notable not least for the fact that it avoids the rigid alternative of "law and Gospel" or "Gospel and law." Some may suppose that the exhortation addressed to the new man which we have discussed in some detail in the present section lends considerable support to Karl Barth's doctrine of "Gospel and law." The commandments, we have said, arise from the Gospel and presuppose faith and the new man. Much that Luther has to say would support such an interpretation. But this is only one side of the question. When, as in Luther, the main object of preaching is the offer of forgiveness, there is no less clearly presupposed the universal applicability of God's law and judgment in the whole world, and, correspondingly, the prevalence of guilt in every human relationship. In order to express this actual human condition it is quite common today to find the phrase "law and Gospel" being used to contradict the position of Barth. Ivarsson's work makes it clear, however, that neither of the two phrases can adequately express the unique character of Luther's preaching. We shall require to be much more discriminating in our use of language if we want to describe accurately the character of this preaching.[37]

This new interpretation of the Reformer's preaching admits both types of early Christian preaching, i.e. both a missionary

[36] Cf. here too N. A. Dahl, "Kerygma og kirke i de fire evangelier," in *Norsk teologisk tidskrift*, 1959, pp. 1-3, 19-20.

[37] In order to understand Luther we need to have access to *comparative material*, especially material from late Lutheranism, which, while preserving definitions from the period of the Lutheran Reformation, altered the whole interpretation of preaching and its effect on the listener. The best available material is pietistic preaching. In Ivarsson's *Predikans uppgift* the picture of Luther is given in very clear outline, through Ivarsson's constant comparison with later pietistic preaching (see pp. 167-276). Cf. also Erik Beijer, *Kristologi och etik in Jesu bergspredikan*, 1960, p. 329.

kerygma addressed to the Gentiles and a subsequent instruction given to the congregation of believers. To make any sharp distinction between these two will involve us in a double danger. In the first place the Gospel will be restricted to the missionary preaching of the Church and treated merely as a first stage rather than as the constantly new and repeated word by which the Church is permanently sustained. In the second place the exhortation and instruction addressed to the congregation will almost cease to have any connexion at all with the Gospel. Moral instruction then loses its flexibility and capacity to inspire different kinds of response in different situations. The "commandment of the Lord" becomes little more than a paragraph in a law of the Church. For the Gentiles Christ is Saviour, but for the Church a law-giver.[38] Luther's unwillingness to make this sharp distinction between the kerygma and the didache is a consequence of his anthropology and his view of the Bible. He does not conclude that the Gentiles are "in Adam" and the baptised "in Christ." The story of Adam in the Old Testament has something to say even to those who are baptised, and what it says to us it has to say for the whole of our lives.[39] When the Gospel speaks to "all nations" it continues to say something to me as long as the "old Adam" remains in me. In Adam we all die. In Christ we shall all be made alive (cf. 1 Cor. xv.22). And Christ, who will give us life in the last times, even now comes to us and gives Himself to us in the Gospel which gives birth to the new man and from which also commandments, summons to good works, and exhortation come into being.[40] When we take Christ's own giving as the pattern of what our response should be, our works will become like His. It is in the Church that we hear this summons to good works which is based on the Gospel. But when the Church responds in obedience to that summons, it is to mankind that it turns. The Church lives by receiving the Gospel anew each day, and the good works for which its members are responsible have the same goal and object as the Gospel itself—the restoration and healing of men.

[38] Cf George S. Hendry, *The Holy Spirit in Christian Theology*, 1957, pp. 57-58.
[39] Cf. Bengt Hägglund, *De homine*, 1959, p. 87.
[40] Cf. Ivarsson, *Predikans uppgift*, pp. 117-119.

The interpretation of preaching which we have been advocating is thoroughly biblical yet difficult to maintain in the present time. We are somehow to hold together both Gospel and exhortation. Both are creative. Both bring the new into being and impart it. It is remarkable that this biblical understanding of the word could be revived in so pure a form during the period of the Reformation. In the Augsburg Confession, for example, the doctrine of the word does not appear in the article which deals with the origin of the books of the Bible, indeed this subject is not even mentioned in the Confession, but is included in the discussion of the ministry (Art. 5).[41] The Spirit is given in the spoken word. We are not therefore to devote our attention so much to the relation between the authors of the books of the Bible and what they wrote as to the relation between the preacher of the word and those who listen. This is where the Spirit chooses to work. This is why the outpouring of the Spirit at Pentecost coincided not with the writing down of words in books but with the speaking of words to "every nation under heaven" (Acts II.1-11).[42] The Gospel goes out into the world and the Church is born.

Death and resurrection occupy a unique place in the Gospel. We shall therefore now take up for discussion first the death and then the resurrection of Christ.

---

[41] See Hendry, *Holy Spirit*, pp. 73-75, where other texts from the Reformation period are cited; cf. *ibid.*, p. 91. The ministry thus comes in one way to occupy a central place in the theology of the Reformation. But the ministry is not conceived as bestowing validity on word and sacraments, but as a distributive ministry which passes on what already has validity in itself through the real presence of Christ, viz., the word and sacraments. Cf. P. E. Persson, *Romerskt och evangeliskt*, 1959, pp. 33-39.

[42] Cf. Walther Zimmerli, 1 Mose 1-11, VOL. II, 1943, pp. 232-234.

CHAPTER II

CHRIST UNDER THE LAW

Adam, Man, and Christ

THE story of Adam in Genesis I-III is the story of Everyman. Every birth is an act of the God who creates Adam (Job XXXIII.4, 6, cf. XXXI.15, Ps. CXXXIX.13-16). Every man has been put on earth to have dominion over it and to rule over nature (Gen. I.26, 28, Ps. VIII.7 f.). But always man is brought sharply up against an unyielding earth and the fact of his own mortality (Gen. III.17-19), for always he is seeking to preserve his own life and setting his hopes on something in creation, however good it may be. That is to say, he bows down to the creature, instead of exercising dominion over it (cf. Rom. I.18-25).[1] But since God continues to be the God of all the world even in the face of man's sin, and since He continues His creation wherever life is brought into being or sustained (Ps. CIV.24-30), the gracious activity of God is brought to bear even on those who have rebelled against Him. They can go nowhere to escape His presence. In every human society force is used to prevent evil and encourage good, and in this "earthly government" God is active as the God of law and of wrath, constraining, compelling, and restricting (Gen. IX.1-7, Rom. XIII.1-7, I Pet. II.13-20).[2] It is true that those who exercise such government and bear such rule themselves misuse creation and worship it as an idol. But God can still get evil men to do what is good and use them to promote the life which He has created, just as He can create life through sinful parents who are still used despite their wickedness to continue

---

[1] See also Eph. V.5, Col. III.5. Cf. Isa. XL.19-24, XLI.6-7, XLIV.9-20, XLV.20, XLVI.6-11, and also Dietrich Bonhoeffer, *Creation and Fall*, 1959, p. 38.
[2] See Helmut Thielicke, *Theologische Ethik*, VOL. II, PT. II, 1958, pp. 288-290.

the process of conception and birth.[3] Here again the Creator is at work despite the sinfulness of particular individuals. Service of one's fellow-men is not a task that a selfish man would freely choose, but he still does what is required of him "in the sweat of his face." In whatever we do in order to keep alive we simultaneously benefit other lives than our own, and though we may never use the word "God" or take any interest in questions of right and wrong our whole life on earth is *under the law*, for it is a life *in Adam*.[4]

Christ has entered this life, "born of woman, born under the law" (Gal. iv.4). The climax of His coming into human life under the law was the cross and death. We shall deal with this in the following section. In the meantime we propose to discuss in more general terms the unity between Adam, man, and Christ.

It will be helpful to keep our eyes on the main problem from the first. Aulén has long maintained that the Christology of the early Fathers had the merit of holding together the incarnation and crucifixion—Christ "became" man in all that He did. The more He assumed of Adam's burden the more the purpose of the incarnation was fulfilled.[5] The death on the cross was the culmination of His becoming man. This early interpretation is based, of course, on the account of Adam in the prehistory of the Old Testament. To be made man is not simply to become a living creature in distinction from other living creatures, e.g. animals. Were this so, the process of "becoming a man" would end at birth, to be followed by some other activity not of itself natural to every man and so having nothing to do with "becoming man." The inadequate treatment of the doctrine of creation in modern theology has meant that at times we have uncritically accepted in our Christology a doctrine of man which has not been examined theologically.

[3] The begetting of children is still a work of God, even in sin and under a curse (Gen. iii.16, iv.1, 25, ix.1, 7). On good works done by evil men see Matt. vii.11, 14-15.

[4] Cf. Wingren, *Creation and Law*, pp. 35-44, 85-91, 95-120, 162-182, 187-197.

[5] Gustaf Aulén, *The Faith of the Christian Church*, 1954, p. 221: "Traces can also be found of the genuinely Christian idea that the incarnation itself is completed in the accomplishment of the work of redemption. The divine and loving will become fully 'incarnate' when the work is finished." Cf. Hendry, *Incarnation*, p. 141.

A further consequence has been that almost unconsciously we have looked for some sort of cultural portrayal of Christ, some particular achievement for which He was responsible and which He passed on. But as far as culture is concerned, Christ did nothing. He died, arms outstretched on the cross to embrace all mankind. And yet it was precisely in this act that the early Church saw the fulfilment of His baptism.[6] The completed work and baptism of Christ are both to be seen against the background of what *Adam* did. We can say what "man" is only epically, i.e. by reference to the account of Adam in Genesis. And when we speak of Adam we are speaking of all men and the ruin of all human life. The Gospel represents the same kind of epic or narrative, but now the whole movement has been reversed. Unlike Adam, Christ does not grasp for what He does not have but gives away what He has and seeks to check the downfall of Adam. In the end He comes to His death, put to death as a criminal, suffering as only an innocent and sinless man could. Our understanding of what a sinless man is, is gradually formed in the events of His life and comes to completion at His death. Since that event "man" cannot be defined in terms of certain distinctive attributes, but only by speaking about him in preaching and the sacraments. But in the whole of this redemptive activity from His birth at Bethlehem to the administration of the sacraments in our own time it is not just humanity that is active but *God*.[7] This is the heart of the problem. What is the relationship between divine and human when the human really is sinless?

Several different factors complicate the problem, of which two deserve mention. *In the first place there is the crucifixion.* On man's side sinlessness or incorruption is expressed in giving and not in keeping to oneself. In each of the three temptations of Christ, in the wilderness (Mt. iv.3, 6), at Caesarea Philippi with Peter (Mk. viii.32 f.), and on the cross, the temptation

---

[6] Hendry, *Incarnation*, p. 110.

[7] In the theology of the early Church *recapitulatio* or *anakephalaiosis* was interpreted as a single act which begins with the Virgin Birth and continues through death and the resurrection, through baptism, the Gospel, and the Eucharist in the Church, and will be completed on the last day. From first to last it is a single act, the restoration of man. Cf. Wingren, *Man and the Incarnation*, pp. 79-97, 122-128, 170-175, 191-202.

had reference to the position of Jesus as the "Son of God"
(cf. Mt. xvi.16). He was tempted to hold on to what He had
to safeguard His life and to escape death. His obedience wa
expressed in the fact that He suffered death (Phil. ii.8, cf. Heb
v.8). Since man's freedom from sin consists in this willingnes
to give, in one way humanity is seen at its best in its own
destruction. But in this very act of giving, it is *God* who is
revealed as outgiving love. The greater the need on man's part
the more we see God's being revealed![8] *The second factor to be
considered is the resurrection.* Sinlessness on man's part is expressed
in exercising his dominion over the whole of creation and in
standing over it (Gen. 1.26 ff., Ps. viii.7). The power of death
over man, however, limits his dominion (Gen. ii.17, iii.17 ff.,
Rom. v.12), i.e. the power which is seen in Christ's resurrection on the third day is not simply divine power but something profoundly human. Man's primal dominion over creation
suddenly emerges in one particular man, sinless man (note the
connexion between Ps. viii.7 and e.g. Phil. ii.9 or 1 Cor. xv.27).[9]
The greater our deliverance from the destruction which
overwhelmed us in Adam, the more we see humanity
revealed!

The complex problem which has concerned us in the present
section makes it very difficult for us to determine the significance
of Christ's death and resurrection. It is easy to lose sight of the
victory in the face of death, and consequently we define the
passion of Christ in other categories, locating the victory
(mistakenly) only in the resurrection. But then the resurrection
and the ascension become some higher position to be grasped by
Christ. He would then have done at the end what according to
Phil. ii.6 f. He refrained from doing at the beginning when "He
emptied Himself." In a word, we have got the wrong idea of
victory here. Ours is the view of the old Adam, and we are
forcing it upon Christ. And since this is our interpretation of
"victory" we can see no victory in death. In contrast to all such
misinterpretations John in his Gospel sets forth his understanding of "glory" and "ascension." Jesus is "lifted up" when His

[8] A constructive work which powerfully illustrates this point is Olov Hartman,
Oxens tecken, 1955, e.g. p. 55-58.
[9] Lindeskog, *Studien*, pp. 230-231.

enemies put Him on the cross (Jn. III.14, VIII.28). This is the beginning of His "glorification" (Jn. XII.27, 33).[10] His victory is victory over the power which brought Adam to his downfall. Adam fell by grasping for something. The victor wins the victory by setting Himself against the same threat and thereby vanquishing the Tempter in His suffering and death. His very destruction abounds in victory.

But the crucifixion is also the beginning of something. Something comes after it that is not crucifixion. The New Testament consistently refrains from representing the subsequent resurrection and ascension as a prize grasped by Jesus. Here, too, "victory" as understood by the old Adam is utterly excluded. For the resurrection and ascension into heaven culminate in the preaching of the Gospel to all nations and also, let us notice carefully, in preaching *the forgiveness of sins* to all nations, i.e. in Christ's new descent into the depths of Adam's lostness, but now "in all the world." The victory in Christ's resurrection is of the same nature as the victory in His death—it is the triumph of self-giving. It is therefore impossible for the Victor to abide by Himself alone. The Church must come into being. Gathered together by the Gospel, the Church witnesses to the fact that Adam's acquisitive attitude, demanding and selfish, has been broken. This fact is of great significance for our concept of the Church.[11] The Church is the community of those who receive from Christ. But if the Church fails to pass on what it has received, it brings back into its body the mind of Adam. This means that it is impossible to define the relationship between Christ and His Church unless at the same time we define the positive relationship between the Church and the

[10] On the meaning of this obscure and enigmatic passage in John about "lifting up" and "glory" see C. H. Dodd, *The Interpretation of the Fourth Gospel*, repr. 1954, pp. 373-379, 360, 367-368.

[11] It is also of great importance for eschatology. When Christ's resurrection has been interpreted as an exalted position maintained by Christ, each individual life after death is interpreted in the same way as something which a man has gained for himself as distinct from others. But eternal life means to enter into a fellowship in which there is no consciousness of having gained something for oneself, a fellowship the essence of which is praise. It is futile, therefore, to try to force men to believe by frightening them with hell after death. We cannot bring men to Christ by forcing them to ask Adam's questions. The "faith" which fear begets is the kind which grasps and holds. See Prenter, *Skabelse*, pp. 618-619.

D

world.[12] If we omit this latter element and are content merely
to state the points of connexion between Christ and His Church,
we are left, oddly enough, with an "Adamic" Church—a
Church which grasps and keeps to itself, fed by the streams which
flow into it, but failing to allow the streams to pass out from it.
This is the strange fact about Adam's power, that he can
misuse even the streams of life which flow from Christ, just as
from the beginning Adam perverted the streams of life which
flowed to him from the Creator.

But even if this specific anti-Adamic view of victory is allowed
to dominate the resurrection, and even if the resurrection has
thus the same outgiving character as the death of Christ,
it is still to be distinguished from His death. It is the opposite
of death. The contrast, however, is not evident to all. The
crucifixion and death were visible to all, but the Risen Christ
showed Himself only to those whom He had chosen as "witnesses" (Acts x.40 f.). His self-manifestation is identical with
His *sending* them into the world with the *Gospel*.[13] The Church
gathered together by the Gospel lives by faith and not by
sight (II Cor. v.7, I Pet. I.8). What the New Testament says
about what the apostles saw does not apply to the Church's
experience of Christ, for the Church comes into being through
the *preaching* which originated in what the apostles saw in
Christ. In every passage in the New Testament which
speaks of appearances of the Risen Christ the action and
the giving are always those of the One who is seen—it
is *He who gives* by means of what His witnesses see. He
gives, moreover, not only to those to whom He shows
Himself, but to "all nations" (Mt. xxviii.19, Lk. xxiv.47),
"the Gentiles and kings" (Acts ix.15), "the people (Acts
xxvi.17), "all men" (Acts xxii.15), "the whole creation"

---

[12] The chief defect of Nygren's *Christ and His Church* is his failure to treat the
question of the relationship of the Church to the world as an independent problem.
When he describes the relationship between Christ and the Church, the main
problem for Nygren is the relationship between different denominations (pp.
108-115), i.e. a problem within the Church.

[13] This is the point made in all three passages in Acts in which Paul's experience
on the road to Damascus is described. See Acts ix.15-20, xxii.10-15, xxvi.15-17.
In Jn. xx.29, too, according to Dodd, *Fourth Gospel*, pp. 185-186, 443, a similar
point is made.

(Mk. xvi.15), "to the end of the earth" (Acts 1.8).[14] But the garb in which the Risen Christ appears to all nations, the garb of preaching and the sacraments, makes it difficult to see where He breaks out of Adam's dominion. The last act of His life to be seen by men was Calvary, and His death was Adam's death, the death of every man. The final and open reversal of Adam's destiny is the continuing object of hope and expectation even in the Church. Only in the parousia when the last and decisive judgment of all takes place and death is finally destroyed will the dominion of Adam be wholly broken. In the present stage of change and transition faith prevails. To express the mode in which the resurrection of Christ is effective in the life of the individual in the present time we must speak of the faith of the individual. Faith is not blind. It experiences and partakes of the resurrection. It senses its reality and gains power from it.

But in this faith is not conscious of a divine object as distinct from other objects. The life of faith is a wholly human life and faith partakes of the life which all men know, Adam's life, with its birth, work, love, and death. In all God is at work. There is not a single living soul who does not have dealings with God every day and in every action.[15] The reality encountered by faith in Christ is not a new and hitherto unexperienced object, but a new power *to live and to hope* even in the midst of death. The man of faith still lives the life of Adam which the whole world lives and in which God is universally at work. There, however, He is at work without the Gospel. The new factor in the Gospel is the *resurrection* in the midst of this life of Adam. This is something which God has done only through the *Crucified*, but which He now continues to do for all who believe the Gospel. Labour, sorrow, and death remain, but are now only part of the story, and move steadily towards their destruction. The work of God in the cross and resurrection

---

[14] H. Eklund, *Tro, erfarenhet, verklighet*, 1956, pp. 140-148, misses the point in these New Testament passages, and consequently can find parallels to them in the documents of mystery religions.

[15] This is the meaning of the prehistory in the Old Testament: man's life has been appointed by God and God is at work in it. *The consequences of the biblical prehistory are of importance for Christology and for our view of faith and the Church.* In our present discussion we can mention only a few of these consequences.

of Christ encompasses us in faith on all sides, so that the old
life of Adam does indeed "die every day," but the new life in
Christ "is raised every day." This is the new reality which will
endure for ever, but it does not die only in the future beyond
death. It is a present fact and can be tasted and experienced
now. It is not experienced, however, as something other than
human life affords, but as a different and unexpected "feeling,"
the opposite of the attitude felt in unbelief: ". . . I am content
with weaknesses, insults, hardships, persecutions, and cal-
amities" (II Cor. XII.10), ". . . rejoice in that day, and leap
for joy" (Lk. VI.23).[16] Faith lives the life of Christ, which is the
same as Adam's life but moves in an opposite direction and
therefore also has a different feeling and a different attitude to
all it experiences.

Never, however, is there any suggestion of a new object for
faith or of God as some new reality encountered in a "religious
experience." Such a view would constitute a denial of the first
article and the belief in creation.[17] God completely surrounds
every man from birth to death. To be human means to encounter God unceasingly, but apart from the Gospel. The
Gospel is the new work which "converts" and transforms
everything. We are brought into this transformed new life
through baptism, which is the sacrament of death and the
resurrection, and which carries out its work of conversion in the
midst of our ordinary life each day and brings it to completion
in the death of the body and the resurrection of the dead.
God is never different from what He is in the death and
resurrection of Christ. The doctrine of the first use of the law
and of the earthly government is not an appendix to the doctrine
of Christ and the Church. The God who demands of us honest

[16] See also II Cor. VI.9-10. Paul's letters are full of these "opposite reactions."
Cf. Claus Westermann, *Das Loben Gottes in den Psalmen*, 1953, p. 5-6.

[17] When Eklund, *Tro*, pp. 146-148, speaks of "the character of reality," it is
clear that he has in mind a spiritual reality with which we have contact in certain
religious experiences, but not elsewhere. But this can easily pass into mysticism.
The passages which speak of the resurrection in the New Testament, however,
make no claim to convey any contact with reality of this kind. They speak of a
new work of God, whose works men have everywhere encountered before and
independently of Christ's resurrection. A scientific proof of the character of reality
is not possible. If we are going to prove anything at all, we must prove the whole
of the related context. But we cannot prove whether it really is the judgment
of God which we experience when we work in the sweat of our face.

toil is the same God who chastened Adam in order to redeem him, and He turns his discipline into redemption when the second Adam suffered at Golgotha and came from the grave to "proclaim light" to the people (Acts xxvi.23) and bring them into His own baptism. Baptism will perform its proper function only in those who remain involved in their daily contacts, for the discipline of God extends through all life. The Church does not seek to limit this activity of God in all life, but rather comes with the offer of life and hope to the daily life of men which apart from the Church would still have been lived in God's world, albeit without hope. This is the biblical view of God. Wherever a man may turn, God is there. This is why it is irrelevant to ask whether He "exists." The question implies a concept of the universe where a great many things "exist." Does God "exist" in the sense that these exist? The very question contradicts a biblical view both of God and of human life.[18] God then becomes a special kind of reality to be encountered in a "religious" experience. But in the Bible God has to do with *all* human experience. The two human situations in which we can fairly adequately speak about God are temptation and worship. Beyond these, words have no meaning in relation to the God who has all men in His hands.

The Bible says that redemption has been won for us in a single human life, but at the same time recognises that within this redeeming life God is active. In the period that stretches in the Gospel narrative from the birth at Bethlehem to the ascent into heaven we see a progression which runs counter to the movement which stretches in the prehistory of Genesis from Adam's creation to his expulsion from the "tree of life" (Gen. 1.26–III.24). Adam aspired to the heights and fell; Christ emptied Himself and was raised up again. At a very early period the ascension into heaven was quite clearly interpreted as corresponding directly to the "humiliation" (Phil. II.6-11). Neither the downward nor the upward movement of Christ are to be separated any more than the corresponding movements of Adam.[19] It is easy to interpret the

---

[18] Cf. K. E. Løgstrup, "Existenztheologie," in *Die Religion in Geschichte und Gegenwart*, VOL. II, 3rd ed., 1958, pp. 825-826.
[19] See Davies, *He Ascended*, pp. 178-179.

humiliation to mean that Christ descended from a pre-existent life in heaven to the manger at Bethlehem. His humiliation would then have been complete at His birth, while the ascension would be a movement to a localised heaven after His life on earth. It is quite clear, however, that His humiliation continued "unto death, even death on a cross" (Phil. II.8). We do not see the significance of Christ's self-emptying until we abandon every idea of two completely separate events and look instead at what is mentioned quite explicitly by the Evangelists, viz. the temptation. As long as Christ was being tempted, He was being humiliated, and His temptations were greatest in Gethsemane and on the cross. Having come triumphantly through every temptation, He was then raised up, for then He had passed the test which Adam failed, i.e. which we fail. His exaltation means freedom from temptation and power to "help those who are tempted" (Heb. II.18, cf. IV.14 ff., v.7 ff.).[20] When the humiliation becomes transformed into exaltation, the help which He renders to the tempted then comes into all the world and the Gospel is heard in the world of the law. This gives us the opportunity to define what we mean by the title of the present chapter, "Christ under the Law." *Christ is under the law as long as He is tempted.* It is clear from what we have said above that Christ had to be tempted in order to be able to save. Otherwise He could never have reversed what happened to Adam. *This means that the humanity of Jesus is to be regarded as of enormous consequence.* But the victory which He won in His temptations at exactly the point where Adam fell, i.e. where we ourselves fall, was attributable to the fact that in the heart of these temptations nothing less than the divine nature itself was at work. This is revealed most clearly in the crucifixion.[21] But it is also to be seen in all the other temptations of Christ from the beginning of His ministry and the baptism in the Jordan.

In all three synoptic Gospels the temptation in the wilderness follows immediately on the baptism in the Jordan (Mk. 1.12, Mt. IV.1, Lk. IV.1). Jesus's confrontation with the devil and his temptation is a work of the Spirit. In the doctrine of recapitulation in the early Church the Gospel accounts of the

---

[20] Cf. Cullmann, *Christology*, pp. 97-98.   [21] *Ibid.*, pp. 95-96.

temptation occupy a prominent place and are always regarded as corresponding to the account of Adam's temptation (Gen. III.1 ff.). There is a growing consensus of opinion among modern scholars that apparently would support this early interpretation of these passages.[22] In His temptation Jesus is addressed as the Son of God and tempted to make use of His Sonship in order to be spared hunger and pain and to gain power (Mt. IV.3-9). His victory lay in His refusal to cling to His prerogatives. This forced the devil to retreat and brought the angels to minister to Him (Mt. IV.11, cf. Lk. IV.13 where the devil merely departs "until an opportune time"). But of course His victory also involved a divine act. It was for the attainment of such victory that the Spirit drove Jesus out into the wilderness. But the victory was won decisively through the obedient submission of the Tempted to the law of the Old Testament, the commandments of which He cited against His tempter. Three times the phrase, "It is written," is heard from the lips of Jesus, and on each occasion His use of the phrase witnesses to the fact that He has set Himself *under the law* and stands before His accuser as a man among men *with no divine attributes*: "Man shall not live by bread alone" (Mt. IV.4, Lk. IV.4), "You shall not tempt the Lord your God" (Mt. IV.7, cf. Lk. IV.12), "You shall worship the Lord your God and Him only shall you serve" (Mt. IV.10, Lk. IV.8).[23] The man in the wilderness is emptied of divine power. One thing alone binds him to God—obedience. It is this obedience which is the central point in Phil. II.6-9, where the One who has emptied Himself is said to have been exalted because He was "obedient unto death." In the Epistle to the Hebrews also, which describes the humiliation of Jesus in starker colours than the synoptics dared to use even in their account of Gethsemane, obedience is the thread which holds together divine and human

[22] This is true even of a detail like the reference to the wild beasts and the angels in Mk. 1.13. Cf. W. A. Schulze, "Der Heilige und die wilden Tiere," in *Zeitschrift für die neutestamentliche Wissenschaft*, 1955, p. 282. See also Cullmann, *Christology*, p. 284.

[23] Deut. VIII.3, VI.16, VI.13. The passages are related to Jesus's cry from the cross, expressed in the words of Ps. XXII.2, a purely human cry, voiced in an extremity of need. In the depths of this temptation God achieved His act of redemption. Cf. here also Oscar Cullmann, *Immortality of the Soul or Resurrection of the Dead*, 1958, pp. 21-27.

nature: "Although He was a Son, He learned obedience through what He suffered" (Heb. v.8).[24]

The failure to accord to the humanity of Jesus the central place in soteriology which it undoubtedly has in the New Testament is due to the strongly anti-liberal attitude of almost all European theology since the First Word War. This is true even in Aulén's presentation of the classical theory of the atonement which he broadly bases on Irenaeus's doctrine of recapitulation.[25] In Aulén the major stress is on the downward movement of the divine and on the triumph of the divine over the forces of sin and death. This is right and proper, and we shall return to the point later in the section, "God, Christ, and Man," which will deal with the resurrection and the renewal of creation. But at the moment our concern is with Christ under the law and particularly with "Adam, Man, and Christ." We must therefore state that Aulén does not make clear what the humanity of Christ means, and to a large extent this is because he does not take creation as his starting-point, but begins with the New Testament and the second article. He has lost sight of the prehistory of the Old Testament and with its disappearance the significance of Christ's humanity has been weakened, i.e. His involvement in Adam's situation, the situation of man.[26] But underlying Aulén's position there is something even more ominous that affects our modern theological discussion more than we choose to admit. The approaches we adopt in many crucial issues are determined at least negatively by the earlier liberal theology. This liberal viewpoint had laid hold of Christ's humanity and in its criticism of the doctrine of Christ's divinity had used the passages in the New Testament which speak of His humanity to build up a purely "idealistic" picture of Christ. Jesus was regarded as an "ideal man," in the process of development and gradual growth as He faced His earthly mission.

[24] We really need a basic exposition of the meaning of "temptation" and "obedience" in the New Testament. This would be of help to systematic theology in its continuing discussion of Christology and anthropology. Cf. Dietrich Bonhoeffer, *Temptation*, 1955, pp. 14-30.

[25] See Gustaf Aulén, *Christus Victor*, 1931, pp. 32-51.

[26] Cf. the criticism of Aulén by Hendry, *Incarnation*, p. 123, and also Wingren, *Man and the Incarnation*, p. 113, especially footnote 13.

He was not a God, dealing with men in Christ, but on the contrary all men could be raised to His level by looking to Him as humanity's ideal. In the theological reaction that set in against such a liberal interpretation it was perhaps an obvious course to pit the work of God in Christ against this concept of the "ideal man." But this meant that the temptations and crises of Jesus, His humiliation and human destitution, were put out of the picture. The Bible can speak of God's act in Christ, and at the same time of His prayer to be allowed to avoid the cross (Mt. xxvi.39, cf. Heb. v.7), and His cry of dereliction in death (Mk. xv.34, 37).[27] It must be possible, then, to speak of the divine aspect of Christ's work without detracting from His humanity.

After Aulén had offered his interpretation of the classical theory of the atonement, many of his critics tried to defend Christ's *human* nature by attacking his theory. But this forced them into the position of defending the orthodox Lutheran doctrines of satisfaction, and to a greater or less degree they espoused what Aulén called the "Latin" type of redemption —Christ acts as man before God.[28] But if such an interpretation fails to begin with creation, the struggle undergone by Jesus will be regarded essentially as His appeasement of the wrath of God. It then gets harder to see that in His humiliation as a man Christ is dealing with *mankind* as the instrument of God's gracious love. But if on the other hand we take Adam's destruction of creation as our point of departure, Christ's obedience and humiliation "unto death" become the opposite of what Adam did and are therefore the restoration and deliverance of man. Here we can use all the terms of the "classical" theory to describe the divine triumph over the powers of destruction. Aulén can then be criticised from within his own theory, and there is no need to fall back on the so-called "Latin" type or later theories of satisfaction. The development of the classical concept will require a new and vigorous emphasis on the humanity of Christ as long as we employ the doctrine of

[27] See also Cullmann, *Christology*, pp. 97-98, Davies, *He Ascended*, p. 179.
[28] Osmo Tiililä, *Das Strafleiden Christi*, 1941, pp. 119-125, seeks support in Irenaeus for an interpretation of the atonement which harmonises with later theories of an offering of the punishment borne by man.

salvation as the recapitulation of creation to its fullest extent. In other words if we are going to treat the doctrine seriously we cannot start just with the second article and the New Testament. We must begin with the prehistory of the Old Testament and the first article. When we do, the simple references in the Gospels to the humanity of Jesus will fall into their proper place.[29]

When all this has been said, however, it is still true that in His humiliation and obedience Christ stands *under the law*. His whole life as man was lived under the law. At every point in life we are brought up sharply against the law, and none is free from it. Man has set himself defiantly against his Creator, against the very source of his life. Creature that he is, he is compelled to depend on something beyond himself for life, and since God remains Creator in all the world, wherever he turns for protection he is directly confronted by his Creator, even though he fails to live in conformity with the will of God, i.e. to realise the image of God in himself.[30] He clutches greedily at the gifts of God in creation, and cannot share them with his fellows. And it is down into this corrupt humanity that Christ has come. He cannot redeem man or turn him back from his erring course without being involved Himself in the same perversity, but resists it, halts it, and alters its direction. The term "temptation" expresses in a peculiarly vivid way this double aspect of Jesus's position. In the mind of Jesus the temptation to go a different way was a real possibility. So thoroughly involved is He in Adam's fall that at Gethsemane His will even comes into conflict with God's. But He has only shared in Adam's lot to check his ruin and to experience an even deeper humiliation (Mt. xxvi.39).[31] His victory was not won apart from his humiliation but in the midst of it. Thus the power which brought Adam down is destroyed. To be tempted

---

[29] A good example of the traditional criticism of Aulén is Paul Althaus, *Die christliche Wahrheit*, 3rd ed., 1952, p. 478. The key word is "Genugtuung," and the one to whom the work of Christ is primarily addressed is God. But in our interpretation these points of view cannot be decisive in any evaluation of Aulén's classical approach.

[30] Cf. C. A. Pierce, *Conscience in the New Testament*, 1955, pp. 66-74, 85-86.

[31] Cullmann in his analysis of the Gethsemane passages isolates Christ's fear in the presence of death, see *Immortality*, pp. 21-22. Cf., however, the same author's *Christology*, in which he discusses the temptation in a wider context, e.g. pp. 93-101, 174-181, 284-285.

as Jesus was is to be under the law, to have our will in conflict with God's. But to be obedient in temptation does not simply mean to fulfil the law but to put to an end once and for all every situation in which the will of God opposes man. Obedience means a return to the pure and undestroyed creation. The power of the law is not the normal condition which can continue because of Christ's obedience, but the abnormal situation which is removed as a result of His obedience. It is good only for dealing with disobedience. Where obedience supervenes, the law, wrath, and judgment give way and the law is fulfilled and put to silence.

When Jesus is tempted He finds His will in conflict with the will of God, which required of Him that He take the "cup" (Mt. xxvi.39, 42) and forced Him to submit to death. Within this death which loomed before Him at Gethsemane there lay the wrath of God.[32] It was not simply death in general to which He submitted, but a felon's death. This was the verdict passed against Him by the authorities, the servants of God's justice on earth. He could, of course, have protested that the verdict was unjust and that therefore He should refuse to submit to it, but only by holding Himself and His purity in God's eyes apart, i.e. by "grasping" at His likeness to God. But this was how Adam fell. He could just as easily have held Himself aloof in His purity at the river Jordan and refrained from undergoing "a baptism of repentance for the forgiveness of sins" (Mk. 1.4, 9). But He did submit to such a baptism, and now in Gethsemane and on the cross He has come to the end of it. He is not only Himself but He is all other men. He has been given for the world. In one sense He surrenders His life to the wrath of God. But in so yielding Himself in faith to God in the same act He gives Himself in love to all mankind and thereby is exalted above all creation.[33] In this He is what man ought to be and was created to be. He is the "image of God." But in

---

[32] When Paul speaks in Rom. xiii.4 of the authorities as "the servant of God to execute His wrath on the wrong-doer," not even Pilate is excepted (cf. John xix.11). The fact that Jesus is treated as a criminal subordinate to secular authority is the ultimate point in His self-giving and temptation. Cf. ii Cor. v.21, Rom. viii.3. On Rom. xiii.4 see Richardson, *Introduction*, pp. 78, 52-53.

[33] Cf. Wingren, *Creation and Law*, pp. 51-52, 130, on the unity of the relationships to God, to the neighbour, and to the world, or between faith, love, and "dominion."

what He does He also reflects, discloses and reveals God's nature. *God* is revealed precisely when Jesus comes in His anguish as a man to the furthest point of His humiliation. The most profound truth about God is His willingness to give, and it is this depth of His being that is revealed in the humanity of Christ.

What is true of the humanity of Christ has direct consequences for the humanity of the *Church*. The anti-liberal theology which vigorously affirmed the activity of God in the work of Christ but which also faced a number of difficulties when it had to give due place to His humanity, slowly become a theology of the Church.[34] What is distinctive for Christology is repeated at every point in the concept of the Church.[35] If Christ is regarded as an ideal man, the Church becomes the place where we find an idealistic concept of nurture that bears no relation to its own sacrament. If this idealism is changed into a theocentric emphasis on God's act in Christ the sacraments become central in the concept of the Church as God's acts in the present. But such an emphasis eliminates from Christology the humanity, temptation, humiliation, and forsakeness of Christ, and inevitably leads to the isolation of the divine nature of the Church. God acts in the Church, not men, and the life which is lived in the Church is not ordinary human life. The Church does not have those marks which Christology itself lacks. When the Church comes into contact with the world, however, both sides are well aware that the Church is itself acquisitive. To let this fundamental misunderstanding go uncriticised will bring us only too easily merely to a purely social or philanthropic alleviation of need through particular acts on behalf of needy groups. There is no question that such duties are inevitable, and will probably become greater after

[34] In the Continent this concentration on the Church developed quickly at the beginning of the 1930s, which were partly coloured by the political situation in Germany and the growth of the Confessional Church there. In Sweden a corresponding phenomenon was to be observed somewhat later, in the 1940s, when systematic theology in Lund entered into a close collaboration with New Testament exegesis in Uppsala. For a number of years the latter had directed its attention to the concept of the Church, the sacraments, etc. Typical products of this collaboration are, *En bok om kyrkan*, first published in 1942, and *En bok om bibeln*, 1947.

[35] Cf. also Claude Welch, *The Reality of the Church*, 1958, pp. 119-123, etc.

the basic misunderstanding has been put right. But the essential question at issue is the much more profound one of our interpretation of the *sacraments*.

The greater sacrament, embracing as it does the whole of the Christian life, is baptism.[36] Christ's baptism in the Jordan brought Him to Gethsemane and the cross. Baptism is the ground of the Church and brings us into a situation which continues throughout our life and restores us to the "image of God." This "image" is at one time man's true and natural being, that for which he was created at birth, and also Christ's turbulent earthly life in humiliation and servanthood. The "image" is the image of death and resurrection. It is the same image which is proclaimed in preaching Christ. Our baptism is realised in our earthly vocation, which is open to mankind and is the "philanthropic action" *par excellence*. But this very openness means that all who are baptised are more alone and more "tempted" than they would be if they sought for some particular holiness behind closed doors. But it is in this very loneliness and temptation that they are more firmly bound to Christ who gave Himself for all. Again and again Christ comes to His Church of tempted men, and when He comes He is the same as He was "on the night when He was betrayed." The Eucharist gives in a repeated form what baptism, the unrepeatable primary sacrament, gives us.[37] To live in the Church means to live by the sacraments, and therefore to be open to all mankind, to death, and to the resurrection of the dead. In such a fellowship everything is coloured by a "different feeling"—worship comes forth in the place where need dwells, for there the eschatological life is at hand. The fellowship of the Church flourishes in its purest form when it suffers and yet does not pay heed to its own distress but to the need of the world around. The body of the Church then breathes in Christ and the sacraments. But when its members make holiness a thing to be grasped in the sacraments with others who have similarly sought it, they are again "in Adam." Holiness is then conceived to be a quality which gains in purity in proportion as the Church shuts itself off from ordinary human relationships. Humanity then disappears

---

[36] On the relation between baptism and the Eucharist, see Davies, *Spirit*, p. 124.
[37] Cf. Moule, *Sacrifice*, pp. 30, 42-43.

from the Church. This is the profound significance of Genesis III. When man grasps at divinity he not only fails to attain divinity, but loses humanity as well.

We may raise the question of what theology is to do at this point. Can it keep men from falling? Theology can only give us a correct picture of the Church. This, then, is our answer— we cannot get a true picture of the relationship between Christ and the Church unless at the same time we define the positive relationship between the Church and the world, the Church and mankind.[38] A great deal of modern evangelical theology is deficient in this regard. Much of our modern malaise in the daily life of the Church is clearly attributable to theological misconstructions on the purely theoretical level.

The Cross

The subject which we now propose to take up is not entirely unrelated to the discussion of the previous section. What we had to say about Adam, man, and Christ had to do with the humiliation of Jesus which culminated in His death on the cross. We now propose, therefore, to investigate more thoroughly the meaning of "Christ under the law." The main problem is still the connexion between the divine and human nature of Christ, though the problem is now accentuated, for we have to deal with a victory, dominion and rule under the appearance of death and loss.

The authority to rule belongs to man in creation. He has been put in the world by God to "have dominion" over all creation and to "subdue" it (Gen. 1.28). The characteristic association of anthropology and Christology in the Bible means from a general point of view that humanity comes to fulfilment in Christ and not in Adam, i.e. in man. When we compare the two we see that pure humanity is to be found in Christ rather than in man. It is Christ who is the "image of God," not man. We tend instinctively to think of it the other way around:

[38] To put it briefly: a failure to express our doctrine of the work of the Christian in society is a failure to express our doctrine of baptism and the Eucharist. If we create a dichotomy between social ethics and the doctrine of the sacraments, both are misunderstood theologically.

we represent the human side, Christ represents something divine in contrast to what is human.[1] A corrupted form of humanity thus comes to represent normal and true humanity. A particular instance of this occurs when we take the kind of rule which we know on earth as the normal, undamaged form of rule, and then turn to Christ on the cross to see if this kind of dominion is to be found in His sufferings and death. The result is generally a failure to discern any such victory or lordship in His sufferings, and the consequent transference of His sovereignty to the resurrection alone.

But this is to do injury to the resurrection and to the Biblical idea of "rule." We have adopted this latter idea uncritically from its abnormal form which is based on fear and which in the prehistorical passages of the Old Testament is inserted with penetrating insight after the flood, when God began to deal with man in a new way since the sin in his heart was ineradicable.[2] Not until then did God permit the shedding of blood (Gen. IX.5 f.) and not until this point did fear on the part of those who were delivered into man's hand become the counterpart of man's power (Gen. IX.2). The whole of earthly government is marked by this kind of domination and is therefore passing and not eternal like the kingdom of Christ.[3] Christ's position as a man under the law means that in this world and under this kind of domination He is to bring about the pure and primal dominion over creation. This cannot be done through His assumption of earthly power. The law would not then be fulfilled by Christ but simply continue to be what it was before. It would still be unfulfilled and still have sin to deal with. But when the law has been fulfilled, it has no further evil to oppose. This is what Christ has done. He has risen and

---

[1] In recent years a great deal of Christology has been based on this false alternative, which makes it impossible to understand Christ as Saviour, i.e. the deliverer of man. We may employ the traditional formulations to assert that He is Saviour, but instinctively we think of Him as a divine being who appears in human dress and orders humanity according to His divine will, and therefore as a Lawgiver who is contrasted with man and nature. This is destructive of our concept of the Church. For a criticism of the antithesis of "God and man" cf. Ragnar Bring, *Till frågan om den systematiska teologiens uppgift*, VOL. I, 1933, pp. 35-37.

[2] Gerhard von Rad, *Genesis*, 1961, pp. 126-130, and also Zimmerli, *I Mose 1-11*, VOL. II, 1943, pp. 106-139.

[3] Cf. Thielicke, *Ethik*, VOL. II, PT. II, pp. 302-303, 284, 295.

ascended into heaven and is no longer tempted and no longer under the law. The cross was His victory over His final temptation, and therefore the cross is His dominion, though a dominion as it were, "in transition."

The fulfilment of the law in Christ is sometimes interpreted in such a way that the law actually comes to be regarded as the normal state, an "eternal law" which is binding both before the fall and after the final judgment. Sin is a falling short of this law and Christ's atonement the bringing of it to fulfilment. If then Christ is said to have fulfilled the law by depriving it of its power and putting it to silence by His judgment, this second type of fulfilment is almost invariably given an antinomian interpretation. Christ, it is argued, must therefore have abolished the law for the Christian. It hardly needs to be said that this interpretation becomes absurd when, as in the present work, the law is represented as having been fulfilled and superseded in the death of Jesus. The law has no dominion over the risen Christ, for all His temptations are now behind Him. Mankind is tempted and falls every day and is under the law. The Christian is tempted and also falls every day and is also under the law. The distinction between the Church and the rest of mankind is just that the Church knows the way out of this predicament, for the Gospel proclaims it and makes every part of divine law and judgment "old," something that will come to an end.[4] But the kingdom of Christ which He attained and established through His cross can never come to an end. It breaks in whenever the new man comes to birth. The old nature cannot be "old" or pass away without the new coming into being in some form or another. But it is not the law that breaks in, but Christ Himself, fulfilling the law. To summon men, therefore, to new works is not to proclaim the law but to proclaim Christ as our example to be imitated, that we should "follow in His steps" (1 Pet. II.21), through suffering and death

---

[4] If the law dominates our doctrine of the atonement, of necessity it also dominates the new creation and the activity of the new man, which means that the *Spirit* is subordinated to the law. The law in fact brings about the *death* of the old nature (in the second use of the law), but not the resurrection of the new (which is the work of the Gospel). This relation between old and new is anthropologically equivalent to the relation between Christ's cross and resurrection. For a discussion, see Ivarsson, *Predikans uppgift*, pp. 136, 153-154.

to life and resurrection.[5] It is Christ, the One who fulfils the law, who is eternal, not the law. After the last judgment it will not be the law that rules, but Christ, in whom all things were made.

For the present, however, our only concern is to see where Christ under the law fulfilled the law and achieved His dominion and "rule." It is at the cross. From what has already been said it will perhaps be clear that the crucifixion itself reveals the dominion which afterwards in the resurrection and ascension is expressed in Christ's *giving* to mankind, when He sends His apostles to "all nations" with baptism and the Gospel. His dominion is not exercised apart from the cross but is achieved precisely there. It was not something to be grasped, but was attained in an act of supreme self-humiliation, and is exercised in giving without limit to the whole of mankind.[6]

At this juncture we must go back to a point which was developed in our earlier volume, *Creation and Law*. We spoke then of the threefold aspect of sin. From the point of our relationship to God sin is unbelief—man grasps at power and tries to live apart from God. The same acquisitive streak is expressed in regard to his neighbour as the inability to give to those around him and therefore as a lack of love. There are not two sins, but a single sin, regarded from two different aspects. The same acquisitive characteristic is expressed in relation to creation as man's idolatry of nature. He is no longer capable of having dominion over it and subduing it. This idolising of prestige or wealth or health and man's bowing down and cleaving to them is not a third sin to be put beside unbelief in regard to God and selfishness in regard to his neighbour.[7] We have simply looked at the same one sin from a different aspect.[8]

At the cross, however, we see a single figure emerge unscathed from this whole involvement in sin. And he does so not at a level above sin but right down in it. Those to whom Christ came were caught in a predicament in which it was His

[5] See the entire context of 1 Pet. II.18-21, especially the part dealing with the imitation of Christ in daily work.

[6] Cf. Koch, *Auferstehung*, pp. 241-242.

[7] This bowing down and this loss of dominion contradict the decree of the Creator for man and creation (Gen. 1.26-29).

[8] Cf. Wingren, *Creation and Law*, pp. 51-52, 130.

E

responsibility to have no part. This makes the smallest detail of what took place at Calvary significant for the history of all mankind. Over and over again we hear references in the Gospels to Christ as "king" (Mk. xv.16-20 and parallels, Jn. xviii.37 and elsewhere). But the treatment He receives as king runs counter to the accepted idea of what a ruler should be—He is crowned with a crown of thorns and beaten and mocked. Before He dies the scoffing cry is heard again: "Let the Christ, the King of Israel, come down from the cross, that we may see and believe" (Mk. xv.32). Those who addressed Him thus had undoubtedly good grounds for their challenge in the Jewish conception of the Messiah. Like the devil in the wilderness they quote the Word of God against Him.[9] The words they use declare that the One on the cross is forsaken and humiliated in a threefold sense. He has none of the attributes of a ruler—he has no dominion over anything. He is, moreover, completely cut off from God, who affords Him no assistance (cf. Mt. xxvii.43, Lk. xxiii.39). And finally He is totally unable to give anything to anyone. He is unable to arouse faith in any of them, even in His disciples, who flee away. But those who taunt Him are themselves the prisoners of a mistaken view of what it means to rule, and to have faith in God, and to have love for men. They are all in error—only the Crucified knows the truth. And He is beyond the reach of temptation so long as He is free of those false ideas which would deflect Him from His chosen path.[10] He would not be fully human if He were not tempted in this sense, even to the extent of harbouring the thoughts of sinful men. The cry of dereliction, "My God, my God, why hast thou forsaken me?" (Mk. xv.34) accords with the view of God which all men share and therefore proves that Christ has really entered the condition of Adam, but without ceasing to give and move in a different direction from Adam.

In one sense it is true to say that God "is changed" by the death of Jesus from what He was before.[11] The God who gives

[9] On the role of the older concepts of Messiah in this connexion, cf. Nygren, *Christ and His Church*, pp. 50-88.

[10] Cf. Einar Billing, *Försoningen*, 2nd ed., 1921, pp. 96-97.

[11] See also Aulén, *Christus Victor*, p. 167, on the conflict between "blessing" and "cursing" in God.

up man to death becomes the God who is present with all His benefits in one man's death. But we must bear in mind that the new thing that was done at Calvary was the fulfilment of the purpose of God at the beginning, and it is the same God who acts in both. Until Calvary there had never been any pure human being in creation. Only in the humiliation and death of Christ do we see humanity in all its purity.

There is also, however, a sense in which it is true to say that it is man and not God who is changed by the atoning death of Jesus. In this case we are to keep in mind that the change is not brought about by a psychological influence wielded over men by Jesus. It is He, the Crucified, who is man. He endures the same temptation as Adam but alters everything by his obedience "unto death." To be man means something different to Jesus, and this change is brought about by the fact of the crucifixion. From Calvary onwards "man" is to be seen in Him, and therefore only in baptism does man become truly man. The Church is the new and uncorrupted humanity, brought about among "all nations" by the victory of Christ.[12] When Christ is preached to a listening congregation they are of course moved in a variety of ways. At times He is felt as the ideal course of action in a particular situation; at times He seems severe and aggressive. But His atonement cannot be exhaustively defined in terms of these psychological feelings which are merely part of a much greater fundamental revolution of the human condition. And this total transformation has its origin in the new thing that God has done in His humanity.[13]

In concentrating on the continuing work of Christ in baptism and preaching we are not simply speaking of His death but more particularly of His resurrection. But the important thing is to recognise that the resurrection is grounded in the crucifixion. The victory is achieved on the cross. The Evangelists

[12] Cf. Davies, *He Ascended*, pp. 177-179. In the doctrine of recapitulation in the early Church Jesus's struggle in His temptation on the cross and Christ's work in the Church are therefore regarded from a common point of view: throughout "man is recapitulated." For Adam, whose example Jesus had before Him in His temptations, fills the whole world; all men are "in him." But through His work in the Church Christ moves out among men who are in bondage with His gifts.

[13] Cf. Billing, *Försoningen*, pp. 66, 131.

affirm this note of triumph in Christ's passion not simply by recording the natural phenomena which followed the events at Calvary and which point in the same direction as, for example, the account of the stilling of the storm (Mk. IV.35-41).[14] They mark it as clearly in minor descriptive details which we hardly now associate with "dominion" and "rule," for example Jesus's treatment of the criminal on the cross beside Him who turned to Jesus as to a king who had "kingly power" (Lk. XXIII.42). There is nothing incidental in the account of the crucifixion, least of all the carefully etched words of those who surrounded this "king." It is significant that Christ can exercise His royal power on the cross itself and exercise it over a criminal when all the others have fled.[15] It is also significant that this other victim admits that he is suffering "the due reward of our deeds" (Lk. XXIII.41), and thus shows that he is a man under the law and wrath of God, waiting only for the word of Jesus. In this he represents the expectation of all mankind. In the scenes in which only Christ on the cross and a few others around Him take part we see already an enactment of what is going to take place when Christ comes to reign in His risen power. This applies also to His prayer for those who persecute Him, who "know not what they do" (Lk. XXIII.34). The prayer is repeated by Stephen when the first martyr was put to death, and later became a model in the life of the early Church (see Acts VII.60).[16] We are not to interpret Christ's prayer as a demonstration of His individual perfection —it can be a mark of utter egocentricity to "turn the other cheek." His prayer is for those who persecute Him. It is they

[14] In regard to Mt. XXVII.51, Lk. XXIII.45, see Cullmann, *Christ and Time*, p. 102. We find the same relation to external creation in Christ's resurrection, and to this we shall return later.

[15] It is also difficult (in spite of Dodd, *Fourth Gospel*, p. 428) to free oneself of the impression that there is some significance in the fact that John alone of the Evangelists puts Mary and the disciple whom Jesus loved beside the cross (Jn. XIX.26-27).

[16] On Mt. V.44 see Ethelbert Stauffer, *Theology of the New Testament*, 1955, pp. 179, 222-223. In martyrdom the early Church experienced what Christ Himself experienced before Pilate, though *after* Him, "in His footsteps" (I Pet. II.21). The young Church gave expression to its sovereignty in its sufferings. An example of this is to be seen in its prayer for the powers that persecuted it, and this prayer is directly related to its openness to "all nations." The Church lives for the sake of those outside it.

who are central. When Christ prays, "Forgive," He reveals His unbroken connexion with the God who forgives, the God of the Gospel, and therefore His prayer is an act of giving to those who persecute Him. But the prayer of Christ reveals no less *sub contraria specie* His dominion and invulnerability. He bows down to no part of creation. To receive from God, to give to men, and to exercise dominion are all connected, and on the cross are realised in a single act.

In the previous section where we dealt with Aulén's classical interpretation of the atonement we made the point that the early Christian doctrine of recapitulation requires a greater emphasis on the place of human nature in the work of Christ. It is not necessary to abandon this doctrine and adopt the so-called Latin type of atonement in order to justify our emphasis on Christ's humanity. The distinctive mark of the doctrine of redemption as the restoration of creation is that it begins with the prehistory of the Old Testament and the first article. When these are taken as the starting-point Christ's work of restoration consequently comes to be represented as an act done by man in face of the temptations of Adam with which Christ was also beset. At the same time, however, it is evident that this emphasis on humanity by no means diminishes the "continuity of divine operation."[17] God has a plan of salvation to accomplish through Christ. The first stage begins when Jesus after His baptism starts to preach the "kingdom." The second continues in what Jesus does on the cross to extend through His resurrection the operation of God to all nations. It is the same continuity of divine operation to which Einar Billing constantly returns whenever he deals with the atonement.[18] In Billing the humanity of Jesus is given far greater significance than in Aulén's treatment of the classical theory. His method is to trace the course of development peculiar to the life of Jesus, but the prehistory of the Old Testament is given no particular prominence in his theology. Billing takes Exodus rather than Genesis as his

---

[17] On the significance of this expression, see, e.g., Aulén, *Christus Victor*, p. 162.

[18] Apart from *Försoningen*, pp. 27, 94, etc., and especially pp. 100-101, on "world mission," see Einar Billing, *Herdabref*, 1920, pp. 39-40, and the same author's *I katekesundervisningens tjänst*, new ed., 1943, pp. 106-111.

starting-point, i.e. the emergence of Israel as a nation.[19] He sees the struggle and achievement of Christ as a continuation of the struggles undertaken and the achievements won by the prophets of Israel.[20] The forgiveness of sin corresponds to Israel's deliverance out of Egypt.[21] Our personal history in our earthly vocation is a microcosm of the history of Israel.[22] But of Adam there is little mention.[23]

At this point let us try to assess the positive contribution of Billing's method. For him humanity has a real contribution to make without thereby affecting the continuity of the divine operation. When present day scholars in Europe declare that the relationship between Adam and Christ and the central place given to the temptations of Jesus in the New Testament require us to define *the growth of Jesus as a man* in positive terms, it is a real loss that we do not have Billing's major work of biblical theology available in English. It is Billing who gives us in its original form "the idea of an inner human development" in Jesus.[24] He draws a parallel between Jesus and the prophets of the Old Testament, but these have previously been dealt with at length and interpreted within a vast biblical perspective in which God and His mighty works predominate. As Jesus develops He gradually comes to have an understanding of the new work of the Father which He has been sent to accomplish among men. As He—a *man*—attains to knowledge of God, in His very development He gradually comes to fulfil the purpose of *God*.[25] "Like the prophets before Him, Jesus has a task of God to fulfil, but with absolute power such as no prophet was ever given. He had full authority

---

[19] Einar Billing, *De etiska tankarna*, 2nd ed., 1936, pp. 81-83, on the "point of orientation."

[20] E.g. Billing, *Försoningen*, p. 97 and *De etiska tankarna*, pp. 295-296.

[21] Billing, *Försoningen*, pp. 22, 75.

[22] Billing, *Vår kallelse*, 2nd ed., 1916, pp. 52-56.

[23] It is significant that the text which is listed first on p. 145 of the index to Billing's *Försoningen*, and which is therefore the closest Billing comes to the first page of the Bible, is Ex. xx.2: "I am the Lord your God who brought you out of the land of Egypt." This is the point of orientation for *Försoningen* (p. 12) as well as *De etiska tankarna* (pp. 77-81). Billing does not come any closer than this to the prehistory.

[24] The expression is taken from Cullmann, *Christology*, p. 97. Cf. Hendry, *Holy Spirit*, pp. 112-113, Davies, *He Ascended*, p. 179.

[25] See Billing, *De etiska tankarna*, pp. 375-395, and *Försoningen*, pp. 85-99.

to act on the Father's behalf."[26] The difference between Jesus and any of the prophets must therefore come about gradually. Billing does define it at the proper place and time, but he does not include it from the beginning. He is free therefore, of the docetism which is to be found in so much modern theology. At the same time, however, he vigorously affirms that it is *God* who is at work in Christ. The resurrection is central to the New Testament and the key to everything, for it is Christ's continuation of the redemptive quest of which He became conscious in His temptation and death.[27]

Our difficulty with Billing's theology is not that he detracts from the humanity of Jesus or under-emphasises the operation of God in the atoning death of Christ. These two ideas, often kept distinct in other writers, are held together by Billing in a brilliant way. The problem is quite different. In his theology he sees only one divine function, which is to forgive, to seek, to elect, and to save. Nothing more needed to be said about what God is to do once Jesus as the last of the prophets had come to see more clearly what this function was.[28] This constant reference to the forgiveness of sins must, of course, imply that a different rule is in force, that there is a judge, and that the law holds sway. But Billing never defines positively this second factor to which the forgiveness of sins has reference. He never connects it with *God* or treats it as the activity of God in the world. If we begin with Exodus there is nothing that we can say about *all* human life independently of the preaching of the Gospel. God does nothing in creation or earthly government of any importance. In one particular nation, Israel, we see a masterly creative process, quite unlike the inner process of Greek philosophy, and the achievements for which it struggled benefit all men through the Gospel, the final stage of this process. But in a peculiar sense this Gospel stands alone. It does not conflict with any specific law. This exclusion of any universal law or judgment or wrath is not accidental in Billing but deliberate. Once he made Exodus as the basis of his theology

---

[26] Billing, *De etiska tankarna*, p. 376.
[27] Billing, *Försoningen*, pp. 24-28, 125-133.
[28] Cf. Bring, *Den systematiska teologiens uppgift*, VOL. I, p. 147, footnote 32.

he had inevitably to exclude the divine activity of judgment in the law.[29]

We have noted earlier that the idea of Adam's fall has no real significance in Billing's view of the atonement. And yet he does give human nature a central place. Jesus is one of the prophets of Israel and as such human. Having taken some time to discuss Billing's interpretation of the Bible we will not be surprised to find that in a similar way he connects the law with Israel and not with mankind. The sufferings of Jesus are an integral part of a large whole and cannot be put out of the reckoning, but they are not the judgment of God "under the law." The Crucified is free from the law in regard to His humanity. Billing is quite consistent in insisting on the inapplicability of the law of Christ at this point as elsewhere. Even in discussing passages such as Gal. iii.13 and Rom. viii.3, which speak of a judgment of God upon Christ, he draws his argument to a close by rejecting any idea of God passing judgment and stressing again that there is only one divine activity and it is not one of judgment.[30] The two essential features of Billing's theory of the atonement are expressed concisely in a work which he wrote for catechetical instruction. In this he asks, "How the work of Christ can mean at the one time a sacrifice made for man's salvation by divine love itself and the absolute assent of the only truly righteous man to the holy will of God."[31] *The* divine act is the outgiving love of God which is the Gospel. Jesus's task as a man is to affirm this gracious act and to bring it about. The most important consequence of Billing's Christology for our discussion of the relationship between the Gospel and the Church is that it may be quite possible to construct a theology of the *Church* on such a basis, but not a theology of human life. The work of Jesus continues in the Church, in infant baptism, and in the offer of grace.[32] But in Billing human life itself—birth

---

[29] This exclusion is of considerable importance for our evaluation of Billing's two concepts of vocation and folk church.

[30] See Billing, *Försoningen*, pp. 57, 63, 97-98.

[31] Billing, *I katekesundervisningens tjänst*, p. 84, and a similar definition on p. 87.

[32] Cf. Billing's *Herdabref*, pp. 57-59, and the whole of his *Den svenska folkkyrkan*, 1930. This has a breadth which is not often found in other writers of this period. But this broad concept of a folk church may also give rise to its opposite, a

and death—has nothing to do with God and His works. This restriction of God's dealings in the world is perhaps quite general in the theology of the twentieth century, but it has seldom been so emphatically bound up with the *Church* as in this writer. The real danger here as always is that of limiting God to the Church.

In our present discussion it is of importance to emphasise that any treatment of the atonement which has nothing to say about Adam or man's prehistory will tone down the idea of *wrath* in particular as an attribute of God. This can be seen not least in the interpretation of physical death. There is general agreement that in the Bible death represents the judgment and anger of God, but in our theology we shrink from this fundamental concept. Billing's doctrine of the atonement is no exception, and he nowhere treats death as a power of destruction and instrument of judgment.[33] This failure leads in turn to a kind of monophysitism in his view of the resurrection. Only when death is seen as something unnatural, a destructive power which does violence to our full humanity, can the resurrection of Christ be seen as the restoration of pure, uncorrupted humanity. Otherwise it is we and we alone who represent humanity, and the resurrection of Christ something exclusively superhuman, an expression of His divinity. The full range of the Christology of the early Church with its "true God and true man" can be seen in its insistence that God is at work throughout and yet at no point is the human factor excluded. Jesus is hungry and thirsty, is tempted, suffers, and dies. But always He is giving and obedient, guarding the image of God which has been destroyed in us. Since He does, death cannot hold Him. He is now "at the right hand of the Father," in the place

---

conception of the Church in which the law predominates. If God is bound to the Church, the Church's character of *Gospel* in the world of the law disappears. We must recognise that the law is operative in human life in order to keep our concept of the Church free from legalism.

[33] This is much more so than in the case of Aulén: see his *Christus Victor*, pp. 162-168. On the general problem cf. Cullmann, *Immortality*, pp. 28-30, and also Tor Aukrust, *Forkynnelse og Historie*, 1956, pp. 259-271, Adolf Köberle, *Der Herr über alles*, 1957, pp. 106-113, and, for a Roman Catholic view, Karl Rahner, *Zur Theologie des Todes*, pp. 31-51, and Robert W. Gleason, "Toward a Theology of Death," in *Thought*, 1957, pp. 39-68.

of power, still fully man. Christ rules the world in the fullness of His humanity. God has come down to earth to endure humiliation, hunger, and temptation, for it is on earth that Adam's life is to be brought back to its purity. This restoration is the work of God. But humanity—crucified humanity—is now through Christ in heaven. He did not put off His humanity when he ascended into heaven. But the humanity of Christ embraces the whole of humanity. He identified Himself with men in Gethsemane and on the cross, and He has not abandoned this identification, but still after His ascension gathers men into His Church through the Gospel.[34]

One might suppose that in this early doctrine of recapitulation the meaning of such terms as "man" and "humanity" would never remain constant. At times they refer to the human nature of Jesus. At the very next moment they are used to apply to the whole of mankind. When the same terms are consistently used to describe both it might appear that a substantial difference in meaning was involved. But almost immediately we find the same words used to refer to a state of wholeness in contrast to a less than human condition of which death and sin are integral parts. "Man" and "humanity" appear after the powers that destroy man have been defeated. Only this new extension of the meaning of the terms makes it possible for us to interpret Christ's work of restoration. To suggest that we should abandon the unity of terminology and use three different expressions for the three "distinct" connotations would be the same as to suggest that we do away with the doctrine of Christ's restoration of humanity. For this doctrine is based on the belief that Christ's humanity is the humanity of all mankind, restored in Him on the third day and raised up throughout all the world, at present through the word and sacraments and at the end in the life eternal.[35] There is no change in what is signified, nor is it two different things that are expressed.

Against this view we hear another voice raised in criticism.

[34] Cf. Davies, *He Ascended*, pp. 100-103, and 179 on Hilary of Poitiers. See also E. Thestrup Pedersen, *Luther som skriftfortolker*, 1959, pp. 180-181.

[35] Cf. Wingren, *Man and the Incarnation*, the references in the index under the heading "Recapitulation." The whole theme of the book is this single connotation of the terms "man" and "humanity."

Again it is Einar Billing.[36] In the general picture which we have
so far given it is *man* who is predominant. Salvation is the
restoration of a lost human purity. Even when this work of
recapitulation is interpreted as the elevation of man's original
condition and the enhancement of the life of creation, the
human aspect may still predominate. The difference between
the two is that whereas Adam's temptation and fall were still
ahead of him, once Christ had passed though the valley of
death His human nature was no longer liable to temptation.
It is this same humanity, no longer subject to temptation, that
Christ restores in those who are His own. This is eternal life—
freedom from the possibility of falling and a freedom from sin
which Adam did not have even in his innocence and purity.
It is still *man* we are dealing with in what we have spoken of as
the elevation of his original condition, and quite clearly it is
still man with whom we have to do even in the accentuated
demands which Jesus gave in the Sermon on the Mount.
These simply intensify a universal demand, heard even in the
world outside, that men should give to one another. When these
accentuated demands are obeyed, the old nature is gradually
put to death and the new brought to life. But the emergence of
the new man is the return of primal and uncorrupted man, while
the putting to death of the old is the uprooting of the sinful
will to oppose creation. But in essence it is still man we are
dealing with.[37] The danger of such an interpretation, as Billing
suggests in a different connexion, is that salvation will consist
in our coming in contact with man and not with God.[38] Man
is thus saved when he is "himself"! By emphasising this view
of man we shall open the door to a doctrine of redemption

[36] See the discussion in Billing, *Försoningen*, pp. 134-137, about the older ideas
of "Christ as the head of the new humanity" still current at the beginning of the
twentieth century.

[37] In Cullmann's *Christology*, in which the concept of "the image of God" is in
each instance used initially as a basis for both anthropology and Christology,
there is a much stronger emphasis on *divinity* in the "image," see, e.g., p. 192.
This avoids the danger of which we are here speaking. But in its place the danger
of monophysitism seems to be present.

[38] Cf. Billing, *Försoningen*, p. 136, footnote, where he speaks of the danger of
defining such a concept of grace that "it almost becomes the task of Christ to
bring other men into His own human life rather than bring them to God the
Father."

which is more germane to the fall and Adam's defeat in the face of temptation. The essence of such defeat consists in man's determination to live apart from *God*. The essence of man's primal righteousness consists of his unbroken fellowship with God, not in "works" or conformity to law. If redemption, therefore, is to be what it is, it must mean that in Christ we come face to face with *God*.

This is also an aspect which we have repeatedly emphasised. Up to this point, however, we have kept from putting any stress on the act of God in Christ, but in the chapter which follows next this now becomes an integral part of our construction. In making this new emphasis we do not give up any argument so far developed. God in Christ is Creator, and He renews His creation, human life, when He becomes man. But now we require to emphasise the divine nature of Christ, and this will bring the resurrection of Christ rather than the cross into the centre of our discussion.

CHAPTER III

CHRIST AND THE RENEWAL OF CREATION

God, Christ, and Man

IT HAS been a central affirmation of all anti-liberal theology since 1920 that God is the God who acts in Christ. In spite of its simplicity the affirmation is actually quite new, not in the sense that such a statement had never been made before (for there is hardly anything new under the sun in theology) but new in the sense that it had not been applied to the actual theological problems with which men were grappling. In the 1920s, however, it came to be applied indiscriminately to every conceivable problem—justification, love, the idea of God, and the concept of the Church. All alike were dealt with on the basis of this statement. The New Testament and the second article were regarded as a natural starting-point, while the Old Testament, the first article, and God's universal rule through the law were temporarily shelved.[1]

It is clear that in spite of its peculiar tendency to narrow the extent of God's activity in the world, theology since 1920 has made an important contribution in certain regards. It is also clear that reaction against this anti-liberal theology has already

[1] The similarities between the Lundensian motif-research and the dialectical theology of the Continent are striking at this point. Both developed in the years immediately after 1920. Einar Billing's theology belongs essentially to the period 1900-1912 and has a different structure. Its influence was felt later, coming notably through Aulén, in the Lundensian school of motif-research, but in Nygren's methodological writings of the 1920s we find no conscious connexion with Billing, but rather the new development of motif-research. What is of genuine importance in Lundensian theology is the development which it has made of Billing's insights. On the other hand the concepts which are lacking in Billing (e.g. the philosophical basis, or the idea of a basic motif) belong to the passing phase of the Lundensian school. As far as the dialectical theology of the Continent is concerned, Billing was almost entirely unknown.

69

set in, both in exegetics and systematic theology.[2] We are beginning to see what we lost in the years when opposition suddenly mounted against the so-called liberal theology. If the new reaction is not to be wholly misdirected and the results of theological study in the last twenty or thirty years thrown away, our present situation requires us to state in as vigorous terms as we are able, first, that the second article speaks of a *new* divine activity; second, that the New Testament gives us a new revelation of God which cannot be deduced from the Old Testament, but which must "take place" before it can be found "in the scriptures"; and third, that the universal rule of the law is done away with in the atoning death of Christ. The three things are connected. The basic affirmations of modern anti-liberal theology are not wrong. They can and should be stressed again today. Its error lay in its isolation of the second article, or the *agape* motif, or justification, etc. None of these are adequate starting-points by themselves, and they lose their significance if they are so isolated. But in the proper place to speak of what God has done in Jesus Christ is not only right and necessary, but quite central to our theology. This is the "Gospel," the word by which the Church will stand or fall.

God is then at work in Christ, dealing with us and raising up His Church among us through Him.[3] As we stressed in the previous chapter, man's humanity is restored through this work of God. But the restoration is brought about when Christ encounters *faith*. Faith listens to Christ as it would to God. It would not be faith without this listening for the voice of God from the lips of Jesus. In so listening man receives from Christ the divine restoration which He has been sent to being about. Humanity is thereby restored in man, not because he is looking for humanity, but because in Christ he encounters *God*. For even when He addresses men in Christ, God is the Creator God who makes all things new wherever He is. The word by which the world was made has now become flesh and thereby comes to refashion and restore man, whose will, opposed to God's,

---

[2] A study of the views of the dialectical theologians expressed in more recent years indicates that here we have a new situation. See, e.g., Karl Barth, *Die Menschlichkeit Gottes*, 1956, pp. 3-9.

[3] See Billing, *Försoningen*, pp. 30-32, Aulén, *Christus Victor*, p. 124, Nygren, *Christ and His Church*, pp. 89-93.

was formerly in conflict with the Creator. To say that God is at work in Christ does not mean that He is not at work apart from Christ. He is as much at work in external creation as He is in Christ. But since what He does apart from Christ is done to counter opposition to His will, His dealings with men apart from the humanity of Christ are in a double sense His "alien work."[4] In the first place God is dealing with men apart from Christ contrary to His innermost will. His purpose for man is to put to death the evil will which is in conflict with His own and which at the same time is destructive of man's life, for this evil will means death. The purpose of God is also to bring this man whose evil will He is putting to death to newness of life. But in dealing with the world by means of the law with its compulsion and revelation of wrath, God never brings this new creation into being. He prepares for the resurrection by dispensing death.[5] To speak anthropomorphically, He is less of a Creator than He wills to be. But in the second place there develops through this in the human subject an image of God which does not freely reflect God's own true nature. The image is not wholly untrue, for man in fact experiences God's dealings with him, even although it is primarily the works of the law that he encounters. But he is not aware of all that God is doing or of His innermost or "proper" work. He cannot, therefore, be a true image of God. Only when he has had experience of all that God does for him can he really be this image, and this means when death itself has been put to death (cf. Rev. xxi.4, 1 Cor. xv.26), i.e. in the resurrection of the dead.

The term "image of God" can easily come to be used in a wrongly objective sense to suggest that the activity of God which creates this image operates above and apart from purely human difficulties. The image of God is then a decree of creation for man which is realised in Christ whose image is bestowed upon him in baptism and imprinted upon him in the life eternal. If we hold to this objective view it is something quite different that we are discussing when we begin to speak of man's ideas about God or of his faith being clear or confused as the case

---

[4] Cf. Prenter, *Skabelse*, pp. 107-116.

[5] On the connexion between the first and second uses of the law cf. Ivarsson, *Predikans uppgift*, pp. 74-76, and Wingren, *Creation and Law*, pp. 174-197.

may be in his conception of God. But this formulating of a conception of God in man's own experience is also an aspect of God's work of creation. Only when we have introduced this apparently subjective factor into our discussion have we become free of a docetic view of the incarnation. To say that God is really at work in Christ means that He is really at work in *us*, such as we are. He is dealing with us in our own experience. When He renews His creation it is God, Christ, and ourselves who are involved. The "image" of God which develops within us in faith is the same image that is brought to fulfilment in the eternal life when we "shall see Him as He is" (I Jn. III.2) and have experienced all that God will do for us. At present this image has been brought to fulfilment only at one point in human life—in the resurrection of Christ on the third day. We do not attain the life of the new creation by disregarding the actual life of faith. It never pays to ignore a difficulty of faith in order to accelerate the process. This only debases faith and makes it another work of the law. Faith is faith in God only when it refrains from forcing its way through obstacles to faith and waits instead upon God. The incarnation means that faith will not have to wait in vain. The One who rose on the third day is described in the Gospels as coming to meet a variety of ordinary men in quite ordinary ways. God would not really be at work in Christ if we cut out all these passages from the Gospels and contented ourselves with the account of the resurrection. Faith receives what God is doing in Christ now when a man with a limited and inadequate experience of faith receives and takes into himself the picture of Jesus which such a commonplace account presents.[7] It is quite true to say that man is to grow to comprehend in himself the image even of the risen Jesus. But integral to this growth is his own death, and he has not yet come to the point when "the last shall be first."

[6] Cf. Phil. III.21 and Dahl in *Background*, pp. 441-442.

[7] "Demythologising" in imitation of Bultmann generally takes its starting-point in a proclamation of the crucified and risen Christ. Behind this choice of a starting-point lies the long held scepticism of form critics in regard to the historicity of the events described in the Gospels. A much simpler form of demythologising appears automatically as soon as we accept that the Synoptic narratives describe events which have actually taken place. Cf. Julius Schniewind, "A Reply to Bultmann," in *Kerygma and Myth*, pp. 45-101.

The Gospel contains statements about the resurrection of Christ, and these statements speak of it as an event. When the soldiers said, "His disciples came by night and stole Him away while we were asleep," their words also spoke of an event. But they abolish the word of the Gospel. A Gospel which can be abolished by a description of a purely external event is *itself* an account of external events. This part of the Gospel cannot be abandoned, but the account offered by the soldiers of what had taken place at the grave was not intended to offer life or salvation to those who heard it. In contrast the Gospel of the resurrection of Christ is nowhere referred to in the New Testament without this particular claim being included in the account of what had taken place. To affirm in any age what ^X the New Testament says about the resurrection is to *preach* the word, otherwise the affirmation has nothing to do with the New Testament. To preach, quite simply means to recount the events which mean life and salvation for those who hear them. For the New Testament such preaching is itself the form in which the risen Christ lives and is at work in the world (cf. Acts, xxvi.23).[8] But Christ continues to have dealings throughout the whole life of those who hear the word of the Gospel, and only when they have attained the resurrection is His activity at an end. The account of the resurrection includes all this in all its literary forms, however brief certain passages in the New Testament may be. We do violence to a passage and make no attempt to examine its historical content if we wrest it from its total context. Thus the resurrection accounts speak of an event which is essentially unique and which happened only once to the one man who is the restorer of humanity. They also contain a promise about new things which will come to pass for those who hear the Gospel. But no^X less do they imply a word of judgment, for they presuppose that man is in bondage.[9]

This Gospel about Christ, however, is something that is

[8] See also the typical affirmations about the presence of the Lord when the kerygma is preached after the resurrection, e.g. Mk. xvi.20, Mt. xxviii.20, II Cor. v.19-20. It is on this that Bultmann builds. Cf. his "New Testament and Mythology," in *Kerygma and Myth*, pp. 38-43. In the New Testament an account of Christ's resurrection generally speaks of His *sending* those who are His witnesses.

[9] Cf. Richard Niebuhr, *Resurrection and Historical Reason*, 1957, pp. 176-177.

F

preached. The significance of this is not always clear to those who
do preach. The object of preaching is not to obtain intellectual
assent to what is proclaimed. It is to bring about the death and
resurrection of those who hear the preaching. It has the same
object as baptism. This death and resurrection may be brought
about when a man intellectually assents to everything included
in the account of the resurrection. But what happens if a man
does not believe what happened on the third day, but does
believe in and live by other things that are told about Christ,
e.g. the events at Gethsemane or Golgotha? Here we are coming
to look at temptation in a new way and from a different angle,
and again the temptation is to "grasp" at something for
oneself. It is our firm suspicion that in the last twenty or thirty
years the Churches in Europe which have espoused this anti-
liberal attitude have bred this way of thinking—these innermost thoughts a man has when he goes into his room and shuts
the door—and that this has obscured the *incarnation* in favour
of a docetic Christ whose divinity never comes to face doubt
or a sense of forsakenness.[10] The object of preaching and
baptism is the fashioning of men in the image and likeness
of Christ, i.e. to make them truly human. But we cannot
conceive of this being done without trial and difficulty. If those
in the Church who are fashioned to this image and likeness
never know the depths of doubt but cling instead to doctrinal
certitude in order to still their own uncertainty, then the
opposite happens to them and they are refashioned in the
image and likeness of Adam. This occurs, moreover, within the
Church itself, even perhaps under the guise of an intense
allegiance to the Church. If enough of them in a Church are
involved, everything that that Church does is affected, which
means in turn that the Church has become separated from
humanity in its need, i.e. from the humanity which the Church
exists to serve. Luther's well-known words about the faith
which cleaves to "crib and cross" has something to say to our

[10] The strength of Wilhelm Hermann's opposition to forced faith lay in his
ability to take Luther's criticism of the view which made the works of the law the
basis of salvation and apply it in a new situation, in which "faith" was in danger
of becoming something offered to God. This legacy of Hermann's has now fallen
to Bultmann. Cf. Otto Schnübbe, *Der Existenzbegriff in der Theologie Rudolf Bult-
manns*, 1959, pp. 23, 57-58, 139.

generation and not least to our modern preaching of the word of the resurrection and of what God has done in Christ.[11] It was no mere chance that the early Church brought together with great care the accounts of the life of Christ on earth which fill the Gospels.[12] They are an essential part of the Gospel. Faith is pure only when it clings to God's act of deliverance in Christ and accepts it as a gift without violating its intellectual integrity. The inclusive and varied character of the Gospel narratives serves to give us a true picture of Christ. The crowds about Him are an aspect of the incarnation. For all time to come as long as Christ is preached they are the objects and recipients of the divine activity, and those of every age who hear the Gospel can identify themselves with them— Zacchaeus, the centurion, the Canaanite woman, the rich young ruler, the thief on the cross, and so on.[13] To treat these passages methodically and trace fundamental ideas in them is to fail to see their significance. Their point is that they are part of the narrative pure and simple and their proper place is preaching. This is where we see the true representation of Christ—it is *here* that these passages do what they are intended to do in the dealings of Christ with the individual. There are many different individuals and many different pictures of Christ. Faith draws from the riches of the Gospels what it needs in order to live. It is pointless to give instructions to faith or prescribe what it is to do, for then it ceases to be faith and what God has done in Christ is changed back into the same kind of judgment and constraint which men already find in the world around them. But God has done something in Christ that is wholly and completely *new*. It already brings the future to the man who hears the Gospel and opens up prospects of still further gains to come when he acquires increasingly the full picture of Christ and is increasingly refashioned in this image. We cannot stress enough that the death of this man is part of this future. It may well be the opposite of faith to insist that a doubting and uncertain individual should believe in the

[11] See the many variants in Sigfrid von Engeström, "Människan Jesus såsom utgångspunkt för Luthers teologiska tänkande," in *S.t.k.*, 1929, pp. 17-19.

[12] Cf. Schniewind in *Kerygma and Myth*, pp. 97-98.

[13] Cf. Ebeling, *Evangelienauslegung*, p. 444, also Ivarsson, *Predikans uppgift*, pp. 48-50.

resurrection of Christ. This may mean that such a person is grasping after a likeness to God which he has not yet been granted and clinging to this prerogative rather than living in the condition of abasement which is involved in "obedience unto death."[14] In our modern civilisation this latter state may have more faith than we know.[15]

Only a Church which is entrusted with the task of proclaiming the resurrection is able to be tolerant, i.e. able to deal patiently with the varied reception men give to the Gospel and the extent to which they accept it. Baptism and preaching are based on the word of the resurrection and both point forward to a future development towards which man is struggling. Even the liberal theology with its interest in a life of the historical Jesus, now the object of scathing criticism on the part of the demythologising school, has contributed its share to our picture of Christ. Here is a real task for the ministry of our churches to debate—how can we preach the whole of the Gospel without excluding the resurrection or misconstruing it, but at the same time trying to allow for the different reception which will be accorded to it, so that we do not exclude anyone who is still perhaps clinging only to a fragment of the synoptic Jesus? This is a particular question for ministers of the word and sacraments, and may indeed be the greatest single problem of the ministry.[16] To be concerned solely with ecclesiastical solidarity without showing forbearance towards growth is to turn faith into a work of the law. Faith then ceases to be faith in God, and when the Church demands that something shall be done, it has taken the place of God and become an idol.

The entire life of Jesus from "crib" to "cross" has therefore a place in what we have to say about the work of *God*. In the

---

[14] It must be remembered that Phil. ii.5-11, which speaks of Christ's refusal to count equality with God a thing to be grasped and His choice of self-emptying in pure obedience unto death, is a passage which urges the *imitation* of Christ. He is our example.

[15] Much of Dietrich Bonhoeffer's difficult writing from his later years points in this direction. See *Die mündige Welt*, 1955, especially pp. 76-78.

[16] See Billing, *De etiska tankarna*, pp. 406-409, 430-435, where the passages about the growing seed and the unfruitful tree (Mt. xiii.24-26, Lk. xiii.6-8) are discussed. The "doctrine" of the reception which men accord to the Gospel, says Billing, is a special one for the *apostles*, not for those who receive it. Even though his exegesis is untenable in its details, this view of the ministry is of abiding importance.

previous chapter we discussed what it means to say that Christ is under the law. We first examined the connexion between Adam, Christ, and ourselves and dealt with the whole of Christ's humanity from the aspect of temptation. The following section on the cross maintained that the death of Christ was a culmination of His temptations and not something which was incidental to them. So now in our discussion of the work of God in Christ it is possible for us to trace in every part of the Gospel which comes before the resurrection the redemptive activity of God which is visible to faith in every age. The resurrection is not a miraculous event appended to a tragic life which bore no trace of having been used by God. It is a culmination of the new creation which was continually going on even in the humiliation of Jesus. And if we would trace what part of His earthly life pointed forward to the resurrection, it is important that we look in the right direction—not to His mighty acts so much as to His *forgiveness of sins*, the most astonishing of all His acts to His own age. If we keep this firmly in mind we shall also see the resurrection in its true perspective. For the resurrection means that forgiveness of sins is now offered through all the world. It means that Christ is now dealing with every single man and woman among the "nations" in the same way as He dealt with those He met in the course of His life on earth.[17] Since this gospel is at the heart of what He now does in His risen power, the Church must proclaim not only the risen Christ but also the *earthly* Christ and tell continually how He comes to meet those who are burdened by guilt.

The story of the paralytic (Mk. II.1-12 and parallels) is very suggestive in this connexion. However we may interpret the passage we cannot fail to note that the man's healing is subordinated to the forgiveness of his sin. The first thing Jesus does for him is to forgive him, and according to the verdict of those who were present to *forgive* means to put oneself in the place of *God*. It is to do something here on earth which only God can do. "It is blasphemy! Who can forgive sins but God

---

[17] This, too, is a key point in Billing. See *Försoningen*, pp. 75-77, *De etiska tankarna*, pp. 393-395, *I katekesundervisningens tjänst*, pp. 72-74, 99, and also *Herdabref*, pp. 42-43.

alone?" The story concludes with the healing, but this is done so that it may be seen that Jesus has power, power, that is, to forgive sins (Mk. II.10, Mt. IX.6, Lk. v.24). This is His ἐξουσία. The doctrine of recapitulation in the early Church was able to explain the healing miracles to a greater extent than the exposition of the Gospels which has prevailed in recent years. These miracles, it argued, were a foretaste of Christ's resurrection and the resurrection of the dead, and they were a witness to the truth that the Creator was in Christ, renewing His creation. It is, however, incorrect to say that the Gospel of the forgiveness of sins or justification disappeared from the total picture. The first task of the Church in the present time is to preach the Gospel—to speak a word to those who are guilt-laden which will lift that burden from them.[18] This in itself is the renewal of creation. Forgiveness—the removal of sin— is the beginning of wholeness for the body. And it cannot be denied that much modern psychiatry agrees with this constant theme of the early Church Fathers. In the prehistory of the Old Testament, sin came first, followed by death (cf. Rom. v.12). In the account of the healing of the paralytic the same sequence occurs. First comes the forgiveness of sins. This is the priority which concerns the whole Church. The task which it has received from the risen Lord is to preach the Gospel. There is great eschatological significance in the addressing of a word of forgiveness to the guilt-laden. The body in the meanwhile waits for life though it is still at present paralysed (cf. Rom. VIII.11, 23).[19]

The offer of forgiveness which is made not only to the Jews but to all nations in the apostolic preaching (cf. Lk. XXIV.46 f.) presupposes that the law, wrath and judgment of God have been

---

[18] On Irenaeus's use of the passage about the man who was sick of the palsy see Wingren, *Man and the Incarnation*, pp. 56, 128, footnote 40, 151, and also *Living Word*, pp. 176-180. Christ's divinity as the forgiver of sin and as risen Lord is the *same* reality. Those who question the possibility of the resurrection ought also to ask whether it is likely that Christ's forgiveness removes guilt, or whether it is not more likely that sin remains unforgiven. If we consider this a meaningless question, we may also consider that the resurrection is meaningless, even if "historical investigation" should prove that it did take place—or, more correctly, we give it the same significance we should give any other miraculous rising from the dead in ancient texts. Even if these did take place, they have nothing to do with *us*.

[19] Cullmann, *Immortality*, pp. 38, 56-57.

revealed to all men (Rom. 1.18-32). The acts of God described in the second article of the Creed are not what He did first. They are *new*, and all part of a single redemptive act, a continually renewed offer of forgiveness which brings His judgment to an end and thereby recapitulates creation and restores its purity. The new character of this offer which God makes through Christ is also to be seen in the heightening of His command that men should give to their neighbours with a deeper and greater liberality. The law confronts a barrier of opposition and even when it succeeds in forcing men to give to one another their giving is poor and meagre in comparison with the pure and undestroyed creation. But in Christ and the forgiveness which He offers the barrier has been broken down, which means that the impulse to give overflows the confines of the law. When Jesus accentuates the command in the Sermon on the Mount, not only does He accentuate the Jews' rule of life but the kind of love which the Gentiles display in their dealings is taken as an example of what the disciples are to do, but in a heightened way, in loving their enemies (Mt. v.40 f.). When the barriers are broken down in lives which display such freedom and overflowing generosity, we are still doing no more than the sun and rain are already doing (Mt. v.45). Nature itself is purer than man.[20] It is man who is impaired and man who must be healed, for judgment and wrath have prevailed against him. The heightened demand is at the one time both old and new and the tension between newness and continuity belongs to the nature of this accentuation.[21] In the natural law God opposes murder, and His purpose is fulfilled even when we do no more than promote friendship among neighbours and fellow workers.[22] In love and forgiveness of one's enemies He breaks down much more of men's opposition. But in these new acts of God in Christ also there is

[20] It is possible that this is something peculiar to Matthew. Cf. Günther Bornkamm, "Endwartung und Kirche im Mattäusevangelium," in *Background*, pp. 233-234. Closely related to this, however, is the passage in which Paul speaks of the groaning of creation, Rom. viii.19-22. See also Rom. xiv.14, Tit. 1.15, and Jesus's important word about where defilement is to be found, Mk. vii.14-23.

[21] Cf. Erling Eidem, *Det kristna livet enligt Paulus*, VOL. I, 1927, pp. 313-341, and also Richardson, *Introduction*, pp. 49-53.

[22] Cf. Helmut Thielicke, *Theologische Ethik*, VOL. I, 1951, pp. 687-706.

presupposed a continuing opposition on man's part, otherwise there would be nothing to forgive and no enemy to love. Complete freedom from evil will be found only in the life eternal when there will be no more temptation or possibility of falling. This will be the restoration of the primal purity—and yet it will be something "more" than that (cf. II Cor. IV.4-6, Rom. V.12-21).[23] For the purity of the primal creation could be lost, but not eternal life. On this last day the law will cease to be valid, for then the last judgment of all will take place. Until that time the law is in effect.

But the new creation, by which everything will be changed, is already going on in the world where guilt prevails and the law still holds force. The form which this new creation takes is the Gospel, the word about the forgiveness of sins. This word is *new* in comparison both with the Old Testament and God's universal rule of law. It totally alters man's existence under the law. Since the one who forgives is the Creator, the promise of freedom from death is embedded in forgiveness as such: "Where there is forgiveness of sins, there is life and salvation." When God, the Giver of life, enters into fellowship with man, death cannot hold him.[24] But for the sake of clarity it is important to look first only at forgiveness, the point at which the new creation comes to man in his bondage. *If Christ's humanity is to be seen in the fact that He is tempted and alone, His divinity is to be seen in His offering men the forgiveness of God.*[25] The solitariness and temptation of Jesus culminate in the cross. In the cry "Why hast thou forsaken me?" He faces the God of wrath, alone in His solidarity with all mankind. His willingness to give and His offer of forgiveness culminate in the resurrection. In His risen power Christ is sent to all mankind with the word of forgiveness, united as He is with God. But the God who speaks

[23] On the exegesis of these and similar passages, see Dahl in *Background*, pp. 429-442.

[24] Cf. Aulén, *Faith of the Christian Church*, pp. 288-290.

[25] Cf Billing, *De etiska tankarna*, pp. 313-314. Jesus breaks away from the typical prophetic approach by not, like them, pointing to God's acts, but instead by offering forgiveness in His own words, i.e. by offering fellowship with God. This is why there is no doctrine of forgiveness in Jesus: He Himself forgives. In Paul, on the other hand, there is a doctrine of forgiveness or justification: he points to Christ and interprets something which has already been done. Cf. Billing, *Försoningen*, pp. 52-55. See also David Bosch, *Die Heidenmission in der Zukunftsschau Jesu*, 1959, pp. 60-64, and also the summary on pp. 193-195.

His word of forgiveness in the Gospel was no less present *incognito* in Christ's identification with all mankind on the cross, i.e. in His very cry of forsakenness. For if Christ's divinity consists in His offer of forgiveness, He is no less divine when, in His solidarity with all mankind, He prays for forgiveness for those who crucify Him. God Himself has known these depths and puts an end to His own wrath by suffering to overcome the hostility that is opposed to Him.[26]

The situation of those who are burdened by guilt is wholly transformed by the word of forgiveness, and when this word takes away all their guilt it is of necessity a *divine* word. No one can really address a word of total forgiveness to another without doing so in God's name. If we leave God out of our reckoning, a word which forgives men all their guilt becomes irrelevant. We cannot say whether it is true or false. It corresponds to no verifiable reality. If a sinner knows that the word of forgiveness which he hears comes to him from God, it has a particular meaning for him, but he can never verify its truth. This is the point of correspondence between the word of forgiveness in the Gospel and the word of judgment in the law. Those who are aware that they are guilty in the sight of God are well aware of their guilt but have no way of proving that God condemns it. If they had, God would not be the God He is, concerned as Creator with the *whole* man with all his thoughts and feelings. In the same way we have no means of proving that the Gospel is true when it says to a man that his sin is forgiven. He may accept it in faith or reject it in unbelief, but there is no third possibility. If he is conscious of sin the Gospel will seem to him to be incredible and this will make him reject it—every man is accountable for his own life! But in so rejecting the Gospel he is turning from the relationship to God brought about by forgiveness but not from the relationship to God itself. He has simply entered into a different relationship to the Creator who surrounds him on every side. For to assume responsibility for one's life and to carry the burden of sin alone is a typically

---

[26] Christ's attitude to the soldiers who crucified Him and to the thief on the cross beside Him is one aspect of His dominion. In this He is already exercising the dominion which He will one day exercise "everywhere" in His risen power, the dominion of the Gospel and forgiveness.

religious attitude even when a person never uses the word "God." Only a man can ever think this way, for only man is appointed to rule over creation and only he can make an idol out of it.[27] To be accountable for one's life and to be aware of one's guilt is in fact to be in a relationship to God, though a relationship of wrath. It is a relationship which may be unpleasant but which cannot be evaded. The biblical view of the *Word* as a word addressed to the captives can be understood only from this aspect.

If the Gospel had to do with matters which were independent of it, plainly its veracity could be established. But it would not then be a *creative* word. A word which creates and which poses the reality of which it speaks cannot be verified. Such a word calls for faith, and faith can increase in the present as it did in the past through the widespread effect of the spoken word. But even though it increases, it remains faith. This is primarily because man's bondage in sin, though broken by the word, is not done away with, but recurs again and again. His freedom from sin which he finds in the Gospel is not a demonstrable fact.[28] The life of faith is something continually received from God, not a possession. As long as man's freedom from death is still to be attained, i.e. as long as man lives by hearing the word of the Gospel without seeing God face to face, the freedom from sin which is bestowed by the Gospel retains its eschatological character. *When we speak of the forgiveness which is given through the word we are speaking of the resurrection of Christ on the third day.* Forgiveness is proclaimed and freedom from sin offered by the One who on the cross attained such freedom from sin in His final temptation, and who therefore is also

[27] Hence the Gospel is not preached to nature but to man. Only *man* is brought in to the Church. We have given too little consideration to this truth. Cf. Cullmann, *Königsherrschaft Christi*, pp. 38-39.

[28] *If* the reality of the forgiveness of sins independently of the Gospel could be demonstrated, it would necessarily be something *other* than the forgiveness which is communicated in the Gospel. The same thing is also true of the resurrection of Christ. The attempt to authenticate it scientifically implies that we are including it among other comparable phenomena—this is what Eklund does, e.g. in his *Tro*, pp. 188-191. But if we do this, we lose sight of what the New Testament regards as the essential truth of the resurrection, viz., that the risen Christ is now at work in the preaching of the Gospel. See K. H. Rengstorf, *Die Auferstehung Jesu*, 2nd ed., 1954, pp. 28-29.

free from death. What lies in the future for those who live by faith is a present reality in Him. And it will come to them only as He is present with them. But this presence of Christ is nothing other than the Gospel. The specifically new event which takes place after the resurrection is the coming of the Gospel to "all nations." The visions in which the witnesses of the resurrection see Christ are granted to them to appoint them to their mission. He shows Himself only in order to send them out.[29] There is no available eye-witness account for those who have questions to ask about the historical accuracy of the resurrection other than the single source of the Gospel accounts. This says something of great importance to us about the possibility of verifying the resurrection. We have no greater possibility of proving this than we have of proving forgiveness.

This means that to state that Christ has risen is to preach Christ. In so far as theology enters into the picture at this point, we must content ourselves with the negative statement that theology cannot dispute the resurrection without thereby destroying the Gospel which it is charged to interpret.[30] It is impossible to examine scientifically the veracity of the message of the resurrection. In this context to assent to such a statement means nothing more than that it is plausible that a dead man can come alive. But to say such a thing is to go against what the New Testament teaches us about Christ's resurrection. The New Testament has several passages which speak of dead persons coming alive (e.g. Lk. vii.11-17, viii.49-56), but these persons do not become the objects of *faith*. Jairus's daughter does not bestow forgiveness of sins, and the son of the widow of Nain does not send men out with the Gospel to all nations. The uniqueness of Christ's resurrection is not that a dead man comes alive.[31] It is that Christ is now "in all the world," continuing the word which He began during His

---

[29] See Mt. xxviii.9-10, Mk. xvi.14-15 (cf. Mk. xvi.10, 13), also Lk. xxiv.31-47, Jn. xx.17-18, 21-23, 29 (and cf. here Dodd, *Fourth Gospel*, pp. 185-186, 443), Jn. xxi.14-16, in which the kernel is the commissioning of Peter to the pastoral ministry, and Acts i.4-8, and the three very important accounts of Paul's journey to Damascus, Acts ix.15-20, xxii.10-15, xxvi.15-17.

[30] Cf. Gustaf Wingren, *Theology in Conflict*, 1958, p. 149.

[31] Sven Wermlund's conclusions in *Det religiösa språket*, 1955, pp. 84, are highly debatable.

life on earth, *and this work is unique.* The divinity of Christ is not to be seen primarily in His triumph over the grave but in the fact that while He was on earth He put Himself in God's place and forgave men all their sin. His resurrection on the third day means that He still continues to forgive. A historian looking for tangible evidence has no other fact to go on than this world mission of Christ which in less than a generation speedily extended by means of the preaching of the Gospel into all the world.[32]

The trouble today, however, is that whether or not the resurrection is regarded as true it is cut out of this Gospel in which forgiveness of sins and the resurrection form a single unit. This usually indicates that the resurrection is regarded as a proof of the existence of a God. If it could be shown likely that the resurrection did take place, then the existence of God could also be shown to be credible. The assumption in such an argument is that the world in which men are born, love, work and die has no connexion with God. God has nothing to do with such a world, or at least if He has, His activity is confined solely to an act of raising a man from the dead. The only conceivable point at which the "existence of God" could be demonstrated is the new divine activity referred to in the second article of the Creed, when God puts an end to the judgment that hangs over man. All such arguments are thoroughly theological, but they have a Barthian accent! This is what modern theology characteristically is saying. But it becomes difficult to gain a true understanding of what the New Testament means by the resurrection of Christ when modern theology disregards the first article and God's dealings with men by means of the law, or when we wind up every discussion simply by asserting that Christ has risen. Any such acknowledgment may easily bring the narrative of the resurrection of Christ down to the level of other passages in which the dead are miraculously brought to life. But the New Testament manifestly does not do this, and if we do, we are thereby robbing the narratives which speak of

---

[32] Without any doubt Bultmann is right in this basic thesis. The strength of his theology lies in the clear connexion which he makes between resurrection and kerygma. Cf. Billing, *Försoningen*, pp. 100-101, and his relationship to Kähler. But it does not follow that the logical conclusion is demythologising.

Christ's resurrection of their characteristic as *Gospel*, and they cease to speak to us of the forgiveness of sins.[33]

The question which concerns us here is one of methodology: how can we get closer to the biblical material in order as far as possible to be able to keep from altering its meaning by the manner in which we put our questions? The Gospel ceases to be Gospel if it is not allowed to speak of a new activity on the part of God who is active in all human life from birth to death. The New Testament ceases to be "new" when it becomes the basis and starting-point of theology rather than the basis of the second in the series of the articles of faith. It would seem necessary for us to have this double starting-point, so that from the first we leave room both for the work of God in all human life and for His work in the Gospel. And it seems necessary also that from the first we consider that the word of the Gospel is the preached word, i.e. that we begin not with a book but with the event of preaching. In this double phenomenological starting-point of the preaching of the Gospel to men nothing is assumed which cannot be seen by all. But such a starting-point keeps the theological question open, and this is the main thing. The word spoken in the prehistory of the Old Testament about all men and the word spoken in the Gospel of the New Testament about the death and resurrection of Christ fit together easily in this methodological framework.[34] The Gospel is turned outwards to "all nations" and those who come to hear this word in preaching always have this prehistory, their own history, behind them.

The Resurrection

The discussion in the previous section has made it quite clear that the passages which describe the resurrection of Christ in the New Testament are different from those which describe the restoration to life of other persons. To exclude at this point the Gospel declared by the risen Christ, through which He continues in all the world the same unique activity which was

[33] Cf. Koch, *Auferstehung*, pp. 180-181, 242-243, etc.

[34] Cf. Wingren, *Creation and Law*, pp. 186-193, in which the consequences of the double phenomenological starting-point are more fully developed. Method exists to serve content and has no independent significance. See also Prenter, *Skabelse*, pp. 29-36.

formerly restricted to particular individuals, is to cut the nerve of the New Testament message of the resurrection. We cannot say, "Christ is risen," as the New Testament means this without proclaiming Christ as Saviour. Now, however, we turn to discuss the other side of the question. To say that Christ is risen implies the inescapable conclusion that Christ has passed from a real death and from the grave into life. To declare that he is risen is also to insist that His resurrection has actually taken place. In preaching of salvation it would be intolerable to say, "His disciples came by night and stole Him away," for this would mean the end of the Gospel. In this regard the message of the resurrection is not different from other events in the life of Christ which are described in the Gospels—the nativity, the temptation, the meeting with publicans and harlots, the night in Gethsemane, etc. All of these describe something which actually took place. The Gospel is destroyed if this human life was not a reality. But each of these events has something to do with the new thing which God brought about in the whole of Christ's human life. John makes use of a highly significant literary device throughout His Gospel when he shows how throughout his ministry Jesus was surrounded by people who saw and heard all He did without understanding any part of it.[1] Both aspects are important— the Gospel claims to describe something which actually took place, but what took place is described in the *Gospel*, i.e. in a message which declares the new thing that God is doing with those who hear it in every age.[2]

[1] Cf. Ethelbert Stauffer, "Agnostos Christos," in *Background*, pp. 293-294.

[2] Wermlund, *Det religiösa språket*, p. 84, clearly implies that a scientist's statement that Christ rose from the grave would have the same meaning as the declaration of the New Testament that Christ rose from the grave. The whole of our discussion in the preceding section should have made it clear that we cannot make this identification. But this does not lead us to the distinction made by Nygren and Bring between "religious" and "theoretical." Here, too, it would be fruitful for us to examine Einar Billing's theological method. His main proposition has to do with the part played by ordinary external history in the biblical writings, from the Red Sea to the events of Easter Sunday. But these events are preached in the Church and have a specific meaning for faith. Billing is not, therefore, concerned to speak in general terms about "religion"; he limits himself to a systematic interpretation of biblical history. Methodological uncertainty certainly does not express itself in such obvious unwillingness to put theology into a philosophical framework—quite the reverse. Cf. Gustaf Wingren, "Einar Billing's teologiska metod," in *Nordisk teologi*, 1955, pp. 279-292.

In the Gospel of the resurrection the term "Christ" bears a significance quite different from that of the phrase "son of the widow" in the passage about the miracle at Nain, Lk. vii.11 ff. It does not simply refer to one individual, but includes the whole of Christ's unique work as the bestower of God's forgiveness and therefore as the one who raises fallen humanity. This means that the whole of the Church that was still to come is included in the term. If, however, we submit the account of the resurrection to historical research the word "Christ" will no longer retain this meaning, for we change the meaning as we pursue our research. If we want to find a phrase which can be used both in scientific research and in the preaching of the Gospel and mean approximately the same thing in both places, then we must choose one which does not mention Christ. We could say, for example, "the grave was empty." It is hardly possible that a historian would overlook the empty grave, for to do so would require fuller explanation than to account for it. But this historical phenomenon is open to painfully obvious explanations which inflict a mortal blow on faith.[3] At the same time it constitutes an inseparable part of the proclamation of Christ's resurrection, and it is the part of our subject to which we now give our attention.[4]

This brings us back to the "three relations" which we are to take into account in our description of the bondage in which man is held and of Christ's descent into this state of bondage to end it. The man who in his acquisitiveness has made himself independent of God and thereby forfeited life inevitably becomes acquisitive in regard to his neighbour. He cannot now give to others and comes instead to bow down to the creature and cling to it rather than rule over it. These three forms of man's evil form an indivisible unity. They constitute a single sin, seen from the three aspects of man's relation to God, to his neighbour, and to creation. No one can be in this condition without experiencing the wrath of God and being under the law. But by coming

[3] Hans von Campenhausen, *Der Ablauf der Osterereignisse und das leere Grab*, 2nd ed., 1958, pp. 42-45.

[4] Cf. also Wolfgang Nauck, "Die Bedeutung des leeren Grabes für den Glauben aun der Auferstandenen," in *Z.NT.W.*, 1956, pp. 243-267, and also Harald Riesenfeld, "Evangelieforskningen som historievetenskapligt problem," in *Annales acad. reg. scient. upsal.*, VOL. III, 1959, p. 63.

into this very condition Christ has put an end to it. His purity
is expressed in all three relationships, though His victory is
concealed on the cross. He does not make Himself independent
of God, but is obedient to Him. But since obedience involves
self-giving and death His cleaving to God is concealed in the
dread which He feels there in the presence of God. He does not
make Himself independent of other men, but identifies Himself
with the whole of mankind. Since, however, those to whom
He gives life are in Adam's state and He alone is not, He must
die, without any relationship to His fellow men, who either
flee or revile Him. On the cross He bows down to no part of
creation and clings to no prerogative, but since He kept Himself free from idolatry even in this last temptation which meant
His death, His dominion over creation even at that point was
not apparent. These three aspects of His purity constitute a
single, indivisible unity through which He attained His victory.
We find the same indivisible unity in His resurrection. Christ's
unbroken communion with God is to be seen in His continued
willingness to give to men through the preaching of the Gospel,
and this preaching which is proclaimed to "all nations" witnesses to the dominion which He has been given: "All authority
in heaven and on earth has been given to me" (Mt. xxviii.18 f.).
All is still concealed, but it is now concealed in "the word."
No proof is offered. Instead, the word is preached.[5] And yet
new aspects of freedom have emerged—Christ's humanity is
no longer liable to temptation and no longer is He rewarded
with abuse or desertion. Now He finds faith in the Church
and—supremely—there remains the mysterious outward sign
of His dominion over creation—the empty grave.

This outward sign is the guarantee that the *body* has part in
redemption. The one who rose at Easter is the same as the one
who was tempted and who "suffered under Pontius Pilate,
was crucified, dead, and buried." Thus the connexion between
Adam's life, i.e. our life, and Christ's is retained even in the
resurrection. When the believer looks forward to His own death

---

[5] The account of the empty grave is *not* intended as a proof, as Nauck clearly
shows, *Z.NT.W.*, 1956, pp. 251-259. Eklund, *Tro*, pp. 136-148, maintains that in
the New Testament it is a question of proof, and consequently he rules out any
idea of the resurrection culminating in preaching.

he does not see something incidental to redemption. The grave too is part of recapitulation and of our burial with Christ in baptism (Rom. vi.4, cf. 1 Cor. xv.4). Baptism extends through the whole of the Christian life. To speak of the resurrection without mentioning the body or the grave often indicates a failure to discern how God deals with the body in other ways. But if human birth is a divine act of creation and if God's government is expressed in human society in the coercive power of the law which we experience concretely in the sweat of our face, then God does not cease having to do with the whole man at the moment of his death. The Gospel account of the Easter event and the relationship which the sacraments have to the body in water, bread, and wine, confirm the peculiar promise which is implicit *sub contraria specie* in the disciplining and chastening of the body.[6] The Christian experience of what happens in the sacraments also indicates a remarkable convergence of two lines. In a situation of difficulty (in a purely external sense) divine worship is frequently filled with a joy which is quite beyond explanation. In this we see the connexion between the sacraments and worship and ordinary human life. The Gospel and the sacraments do not bring man into contact with a new divine purpose which is unknown to him in the rest of his experience, but communicate something new which is done for him by the God whose loving discipline is experienced in the whole of life. The whole of human life is death and resurrection. In a situation which is fraught with "death," i.e. outward hardship, this peculiar character of human existence is lit up for us by shafts of joy from the sacraments which hold out resurrection to dying men. Worship means that the resurrection of the dead is already taking place in the offering of praise.[7]

The empty grave thus points to the continuity between the work of the risen Christ in the present and His humanity. But it tells us nothing of the kind of body which Christ now has. When we ask this question the New Testament points us back to the outward signs given by Christ to those who were

---

[6] Cf. Prenter, *Skabelse*, pp. 539-542.

[7] On the connexion between resurrection and worship see Koch, *Auferstehung*, pp. 330-338, 240 f.

G

witnesses to His resurrection—the word of the Gospel, baptism,
and the Eucharist. Faith does not come from the empty grave
but from preaching (Rom. x.17).[8] Any investigation of what
these witnesses saw, heard, or experienced, brings us back
again to these same external realities. The whole point of the
passages which deal with the experiences of such witnesses
is that they were sent to bear witness and to preach the Gospel.
We have a concisely expressed illustration of this in Acts x.40-
43, which culminates in the offer of the forgiveness of sins.
When Matthew, Mark, and Luke recount how the risen Christ
showed Himself to the eleven, their conclusion is the same in
every instance—He sends them out to preach and to baptise
(Mt. xxviii.16-20, Mk. xvi.14-20, Lk. xxiv.33-49). The
Emmaus narrative indicates that the breaking of the bread is
the place where the Lord is to be known (Lk. xxiv.30-33).
When John's Gospel tells how Jesus came to the apostles
through closed doors, it also records that they were sent out
with the word of forgiveness (Jn. xx.19-23). The same Gospel
also contains an account of an appearance at the Sea of
Tiberias, the core of which is the transmission to Peter of the
pastoral ministry (Jn. xxi.14-17). In addition, this Gospel
records the appearance of Thomas, the central point of which is
the words "Blessed are those who have not seen and yet
believe" (Jn. xx.24-29). The meaning is plainly that the period
of sight comes to an end with the sending of the apostles, after
which faith is based on the word and not on sight.[9] Finally,
each time the book of Acts describes Paul's encounter with the
risen Christ on the road to Damascus the conclusion is the
same: "Depart: for I will send you far away to the Gentiles"
(Acts xxii.21, cf. ix.15, xxvi.17). This interpretation which we
find in the New Testament of the presence of Christ is well
expressed in the first chapter of Acts, where the apostles enquire
about the time when the kingdom is to be restored. In answer
to their question Christ sends them out as His witnesses "to the
end of the earth" (Acts 1.3-8).[10] This is how the kingdom is

[8] See N. A. Dahl, "Der historische Jesus als geschichtswissenschaftsliches und
theologisches Problem," in *Kerygma und Dogma*, 1955, pp. 123-124, and Nauck
in *Z.NT.W.*, 1956, p. 259, and von Campenhausen, *Ablauf*, pp. 52-53.
[9] Cf. Dodd, *Fourth Gospel*, pp. 441-443.
[10] See also Cullmann, *Christ and Time*, p. 162.

to be restored. Christ lives on in preaching and the sacraments.[11]

Some of these descriptions of resurrection appearances include reference also to the ascension (Mk. xvi.19, Lk. xxiv.50, Acts i.9). Others record how He gave the apostles the Spirit without mentioning the ascension as a separate event (Jn. xx.21 f., cf. Gen. ii.7).[12] Paul receives the Spirit (Acts ix.17) and begins to preach (Acts ix.20) after he has seen the bright light from heaven on his way to Damascus (Acts ix.3, xxii.6, xxvi.13). The Pauline Epistles and the Gospels of John and Matthew do not refer to the ascension as a separate event, but they clearly assume that when Jesus showed Himself in His risen power, He did so in order to send His apostles out, i.e. to cease His appearances in that particular form and to be present instead through the word which the apostles preach.[13] Together with the word the apostles go into the world with baptism in order to draw those who have gone astray in Adam into Christ's work of restoration. It is quite apparent that the breaking of bread also belongs here. When the Emmaus narrative speaks of the breaking of bread as the place where the risen Christ is known (Lk. xxiv.30 f., 35), the reference is not simply to a meal once held in a village outside Jerusalem, but to a meal still continued in every congregation.[14] The few variations which we find in the resurrection appearances coincide in this regard that they speak of something which is still going on and which constitutes the Church, viz. preaching and the sacraments. This activity is accorded a particular place in the third article of the Creed, which refers to the Spirit. The work of the Spirit begins after Christ has completed what He had to do on earth, and always the Spirit takes

[11] As regards the Pauline epistles cf. W. T. Hahn, *Das Mitsterben und Mitauferstehen mit Christus bei Paulus*, 1937, pp. 124-126. Also of interest is John A. T. Robinson, *Jesus and His Coming*, 1957, e.g. pp. 135-137, where the idea of a "return" of Christ is regarded as a late product (see the summarising passage, pp. 182-185). The consequence of this, of course, is a strong emphasis on the presence of the risen Christ in the Church.

[12] On Jn. xx.17-28 as a Johannine variant of the ascension and Pentecost, see Dodd, *Fourth Gospel*, pp. 429-450, 442-443.

[13] See also Davies, *He Ascended*, pp. 27-68. Cf. Robinson, *Jesus and His Coming*, p. 135.

[14] See Nauck, in *Z.NT.W.*, 1956, pp. 258-259. Cf. Richard Niebuhr, *Resurrection* pp. 180-181.

from the completed work of Christ and gives to men.[15] The resurrection culminates in the outpouring of the Spirit and the upbuilding of the Church. When the Spirit takes what is Christ's (Jn. xvi.14 f.) it sets its seal on all the outward marks of which we have been speaking. Baptism, preaching, and the Eucharist, as we stressed earlier, are wholly "epic" in character. Always they set forth Christ. In precisely this way they restore the image of God in those who receive what they offer. The whole Church is the recapitulation of creation and the restoration of man's wholeness.

Since the dominion which death exercises over man is unnatural, the victory of life in the resurrection means the restoration of wholeness rather than the gift of something "supernatural." The healing miracles in the Gospels—the raising of Lazarus and of the son of the widow of Nain, and so on —reveal that the salvation which is bestowed by Christ is wholeness. The restoration of Lazarus and the widow's son to life does not mean that they are given divine life but simply human. Though restored to life they do not forgive sins or send out apostles "to the end of the earth." What we speak of as biological death, common to man and beast alike, is hardly ever referred to in the Bible. On the other hand, however, reference is very frequently made to man's special place in creation and his appointed dominion and rule over the rest of creation (Gen. 1.26-28, 11.19, ix.1-7). A subjection which is natural for the animal creation is unnatural for him, and therefore death's dominion over man is unnatural. The prehistory of the Old Testament speaks of man's downfall, the Gospel of his rehabilitation. Surrounded as He was by the blind, the lame, the deaf, and the dumb, Jesus restores them to wholeness and to what is natural to man, not supernatural.[16] But of course the act of giving life is quite different. This is something which belongs to the Creator and not to the creature. It is again the creation of life from nothing. Man can never create, even in his state of purity. All he can do is to receive and pass on what the Creator bestows on him. There is, therefore, a vast difference between Christ's resurrection and all other

---

[15] See Hendry, *Holy Spirit*, pp. 21-23, and also in this connexion Jn. xvi.7, 14.
[16] Cf Köberle, *Der Herr über alles*, pp. 105-107.

healing miracles of the Gospels. The two are quite different, even though these other miracles mean that the dead receive life. For to receive life simply means to be human. But to give life or to create is a divine activity. And we see this divine activity, i.e. the divinity of Christ, most clearly even before His resurrection in His forgiving men their sins. In this He attacks death at its root, viz., sin (Gen. ii.17, Rom. v.12, vi.23). Christ puts Himself in God's place by forgiving sins (Mk. ii.7). But the resurrection once and for all puts Him in God's place, and therefore the resurrection is the starting-point of the Gospel which is preached in all the world (cf. Acts xxvi.23). Christ is at work in the world of death as the giver of life by continually giving to men the Gospel, forgiveness, baptism, and the Eucharist.

This explains why it is proper to discuss these outward signs by which the Church is built up under the heading of "Resurrection" and also the more inclusive heading of "Christ and the renewal of creation." The arrangement which we have followed in the present work will also consciously emphasise that the Church is to be included in Christ and the Gospel.[17] Even before coming to the second part of this book, in which we shall speak of the Church, we have been compelled to deal at length with the elements by which the Church is built up, for these are involved in Christ's own activity. And the organising principle which underlies them all is the *Gospel* as the forgiveness of sins.[18] The Church comes into being when the Gospel is preached in the world or to the nations. The Church, therefore, is governed wholly by the Gospel and is therefore included in the outward movement of the Gospel through which the Church came into being and which continues through the Church. We cannot explain the relationship which the Church has to Christ if we do not also speak of its relationship to the world. For the line goes from Christ's resurrection to "all the world," since in His resurrection He has attained a dominion which embraces more than the Church (Eph. i.19-23, Col. i.13-20).[19] When He exercises this dominion the Church comes into being, for He exercises it through the outward signs

[17] Cf. Nygren, *Christ and His Church*, p. 90.
[18] This was Billing's main concept throughout his writings and dominated both his *Försoningen* and his volume of essays, *Den svenska folkkyrkan*.
[19] Cf. also Heb. i.1-3, ii.8, 1 Cor. xv.24-28, Phil. ii.8-11.

with which He sends His apostles into the world, and by them His Church is built up. But it is important to observe the order: first comes the resurrection of Christ, then the mission to all the world, and finally the Church (Eph. 1.22 f., cf. Col. 1.17-22). In this order we see that the Church is included in Christ's own movement outwards to all the world and to all the nations (Mt. xxiv.14, xxv.32, xxviii.19, Lk. xxiv.47, Rom. xvi.26).[20] This outward movement belongs to the very nature of the Church, and if it is abandoned the Church ceases to have fellowship with *Christ*.

There is an intimate connexion between all this and temptation. Again the temptation is to grasp at likeness to God and cling to it as a prize without sharing it or passing it on to others. In His own temptations Christ did not seek a position of security or shun suffering. On the contrary, He emptied Himself. This is the real significance of the various temptation narratives (Mt. iv.1-11, Mk. viii.32, Mt. xxvii.40): victory lies in giving, defeat in keeping. Being now raised from the dead, Christ is free from being tempted. The cross was His final test. But His Church is still tempted, and its chief temptation is also of a religious nature—it is the temptation to cling to its divine attributes (cf. Gen. iii.5) without serving others in doing so. Such a self-seeking Adamic attitude cuts the Church off from Christ, for even in His risen life He does not cease to enter into the depths of human sin by means of His outward gifts. He gives to men the gift of His divinity which is the forgiveness of sins. The Church exists to advance this mission of Christ. The eternal life which is bestowed in preaching and the sacraments cannot, if it is a life in Christ, be something that the individual seeks for himself apart from the "unsaved" who do not have it. In fact the most difficult task in eschatology is to be able to speak of an eternal life received in joy which is still not an egoistic prize to be grasped.[21] One sometimes has the impression that

[20] Passages such as Eph. iii.10 and Heb. x.12-13 are part of this missionary perspective. If the cosmic perspective is lacking, missionary activity becomes a concern of the missionary society alone. But in the early Christian period the Church *is* mission.

[21] This is the problem in the "Jenseitseschatologie" which is described in Hans Grass, "Das eschatologische Problem in der Gegenwart," in *Dank an Paul Althaus*, 1958, pp. 67-69. Interesting suggestions are made by Gleason in *Thought*, 1957, pp. 49-51, in regard to French existentialism.

theology succeeds in combating the desire for salvation for oneself alone at point after point only to be defeated at the last point of all when it comes to the question of heaven and eternal life. If in the life eternal anything is to be put to death, it must be the old acquisitive Adam. But we can speak of heaven in such a way as to make it the very place where this Adam is found. There are two things which will help us to correct such an error—one is fellowship and the other praise, i.e. divine worship. For worship is common praise, eternal life in the present time.[22]

Since it is the Gospel which issues from Christ's resurrection, it may be appropriate in dealing with the resurrection, with which we conclude the first part of the present volume, to try to summarise all that we have so far said. The main theological problem which has concerned us in the same form in each of the four preceding sections has been the relationship between Christ's divinity and His humanity.

As man Christ stands under the law. Under the law and under wrath Christ lives the life of Adam, i.e. our own human life, which means that He is tempted. His temptations come to a climax in Gethsemane and on the cross. In His temptation He is divested of His divinity in such a way that to the end it is His dread in the presence of God which binds Him to God. But the humiliation is really a victory, for it represents the opposite of Adam's attitude. When Christ refrains from seeking to be like God, and rather empties Himself, taking the form of a servant, He in fact achieves the image of God, i.e. true humanity. When Adam—man—destroyed human life, what happened was that he wanted to become "like God" and avoid the form of a servant. In the life which He lived as a man Christ succeeded in rendering obedience, even though He had "emptied Himself." And this obedience broke the power of the law and did away with wrath. The uncorrupted life is free from the law and therefore from death. But this life has been realised only in the resurrection of Christ. Humanity is to be found only in the one who rose on the third day, and if we would attain humanity we must seek it from Him.

As God Christ is at work in begetting and creating in others

---

[22] Cf. here Peter Brunner in *Leitourgia*, VOL. I, 1954, pp. 168-170, 248-250.

the life which they themselves do not possess. Adam did not have the power to create even in his God-appointed state of purity. Since the dominion of death and the destruction of human life arose in man's disobedience and yielding to temptation, Christ brings His creative power to bear at the critical point when He forgives sins. His divinity was to be seen in His earthly life in His forgiving men their sins.[23] This completes the circle, for we have just defined His humanity as His submission to the law. And it is manifest that His offer to forgive sins annuls the judgment which the law passes against man. *But He began to break the power of the law even before His death, and in this we see His divine nature revealed.* Now that He is risen He continues this same divine activity among all men through the Gospel which comes from the empty grave into all the world. His resurrection has an added factor which marks it off from the resuscitation of others who were dead, viz. the offer of forgiveness. This is the heart of His resurrection.

Once we interpret human and divine nature in this way, we see that both come to their highest point and both stand revealed in one and the same event. Otherwise God and man will frequently be defined in such a way that their unification in Christ becomes an impossibility, and the two natures become mutually exclusive. Thus if God is predominant, Christ's humanity appears a sham, whereas if His humanity predominates it will seem that God has been put out of the picture. But if we define the divinity of Christ as His forgiveness of sin, then this divinity is increased on the cross when He prays for the forgiveness of those who crucify Him, and increased in the one who is burdened with anxiety. According to the Lutheran doctrine of the *communicatio idiomatum* Christ's divinity "communicates" His attributes to His human nature.[24] The power of His divinity to destroy the dominion of the law is effective even in His humiliation, for His humiliation

---

[23] It is one of Einar Billing's strong points that he sees the divine work in this and also in the resurrection. But he does not speak of Christ bearing the law and wrath. See his *De etiska tankarna*, pp. 375-395, and also *Försoningen*, pp. 123-133.

[24] Cf. Herbert Olsson, *Grundproblemet i Luthers socialetik*, VOL. I, 1934, pp. 134-136, and Paul Wilhelm Gennrich, *Die Christologie Luthers im Abendmahlsstreit*, 1929 pp. 60-62.

is obedience and this obedience puts an end to the law and to wrath.

God's freedom from the law and His power to create are not therefore in effect apart from Christ's human conflict. The sphere in which these attributes apply is a human life lived under the law and subject to temptation. The extraordinary thing about the Gospel of the *resurrection* is that it contains all these human accounts of the temptation in the wilderness, the agony of Gethsemane, the cross, and so on.[25] It would not be a Gospel of the resurrection, in other words a Gospel for the tempted and the dying, if it did not also show Christ *under the law*. For all those to whom the Gospel is proclaimed stand under the law. And if the Gospel did not depict man's own desperate need when it set forth Christ, it would never assure him that the activity of God which he experiences as wrath in his present life can come to be experienced as *life*. But the Gospel proclaims the lowly humanity of Christ, and therefore it is filled with promise. This is a point of great importance for our discussion which follows of the humanity of the Church, and therefore gives it particular emphasis.

By submitting Himself to temptation Christ has identified Himself with all who stand under the judgment of the law. His baptism in the Jordan meant that He put Himself where He did not properly belong: He submitted to "a baptism of repentance for the forgiveness of sins" (Mk. 1.4-11). He there made Himself one with all men and did not stand aloof from them as He might have done. The temptation in Gethsemane and on the cross likewise imply His identification with humanity. He shared in men's alienation from God when He cried from the cross in His own forsakenness. The conception of God which He knew at this time was no delusion, for this is what God is really like—He does condemn man. But it is this self-same God who does something new and He does it in the one who cried aloud at Calvary. The "obedience unto death" of the Crucified is God's own triumphant act by which the whole of creation will be renewed. The new relationship between God and men established through the resurrection is brought about through means which can neither exist nor continue if there are

---

[25] See also Schniewind in *Kerygma and Myth*, p. 98.

none to be benefited by receiving them.[26] A meal is not a meal unless there is someone to eat and drink at it; the same is true of baptism or of preaching, though the significance for theology of this latter point does not yet seem to have dawned on us. Preaching implies a congregation—the word is to accomplish its purpose among those who hear it. This brings us to the critical point—when a man hears the word or receives the sacraments he does not then encounter God for the first time. All men have experienced the operations of God through the very lives which they live. Every day they receive life from Him and are disciplined by Him in the demands which their neighbours make upon them. But of the new relationship which is established through the death and resurrection of Christ they have had no experience before. The Church has a specific function to fulfil in the world which, apart altogether from the Church, is governed by God, the *deus absconditus* who has dealings with men and constrains them to do His will without disclosing to them His inner reality. If the Church is unable to discern this universal rule exercised by God through the law or to make it clear to men how God is already at work in all the world apart from the Church, it will inevitably lose sight of the Gospel which is its special responsibility. The Gospel is Gospel by virtue of the fact that it sets itself against the law.[27]

There is, however, a further matter of equal importance to be considered. The relationship of "wrath" which all those who hear the Gospel preached have already experienced in their daily lives is the same as that which Jesus Himself endured in His life. In Him, however, this "alien work" of God has passed into His "proper work." Since it has, Christ is now preached to us. Our very lives make us subject to the alien work of God. Every man has the prehistory of Genesis behind him. If God's alien work in us is to issue in life, Christ must come into our being. If He does, it is inevitable that the alien work will then be transferred. This is what underlies the peculiar fact that to preach the humanity of Christ is to preach His resurrection. Simply to declare from the pulpit that Christ is

[26] This was a key point in the analysis of preaching and the sacraments in the first chapter of the present work.

[27] The connexion between righteousness and Christ's resurrection is emphasised by Rengstorf, *Auferstehung*, pp. 87-89.

risen is often to say nothing at all. The early Church which lived in the first flush of wonderment that followed the resurrection carefully drew together all the stories which had been told of the human Son of man who had "nowhere to lay His head" and whose very humanity as revealed in His agony was a scandal to some.[28] To preach His resurrection biblically means taking the four Gospels seriously at this point. In our own age in particular, when theology is a closed door to many people, it is a great gift to be able to preach Christ in His humanity in simple, graphic terms and to proclaim Him as a member of the human race. It is sometimes destructive of faith to bombard a man with the repeated assertion that Christ is risen and leave it at that. His resurrection and our restoration to the likeness of God are grounded in the fact that He is preached and that it is His image which is set forth in preaching. The dogmatic assertion that He is risen may with advantage be set a little to one side in favour of a more general presentation in preaching which speaks of His whole actual life. Any preaching which concentrates on pure doctrine without speaking—as we have called it—"epically" of His life is docetic, even though it may speak of the incarnation in the correct doctrinal and indeed antidocetic terms.[29]

The new thing that God does in the death and resurrection of Christ is new in relation to an "old" which is also from God and which we experience in the simple, elementary fact that we live together on the earth. Theology cannot depict the character of this new activity of God if it does not outline God's universal role through the law. And this in turn cannot be described as long as the first article is played down or given its place after the second article and the New Testament alone taken as the basis of theology.[30] When they are, this is a sure sign

[28] On the interpretation of Mt. viii.20 see Cullmann, *Christology*, p. 162.

[29] Cf. Østergaard-Nielsen, *Scriptura sacra*, pp. 109-120.

[30] From one point of view we can say that both Bultmann and Nygren represent a double aim. The former is concerned with the kerygma of the New Testament, the latter with the early Christian agape-motif. Each combines this attempt in his own way in historical material with a philosophical outlook. But it is typical of both that the historical material which each employs comes from the New Testament. Thus in both writers philosophy comes to occupy the place which properly belongs to the Old Testament. Since the subject of the New Testament is the Gospel, it follows further that both writers represent a methodological combination of

that it is our own quest for knowledge and not the acts of God that has become determinative of the structure of theology. What is the solution to this complex difficulty in modern theology? It is quite apparent that we must face up to a discussion of theological method and procedure. But this will reveal that the heart of the problem concerns the proper methodological starting-point. All the deviations in the content of theology which we have mentioned above—the dichotomy between creation and law, the neglect of the Old Testament and the concentration on the New—are to be explained by a peculiar methodological feature which we find in modern theology, viz. the determination to adopt a single point of departure in explaining what Christianity or the Christian message means. *But the message of the Gospel springs from the resurrection of Christ and comes to men who by the life they live are already implicated in the "old" work of God, in submitting to which Christ suffered on the cross.*[31] This can be made clear only by taking a *double* starting-point for our theology: by taking, that is, first the Christian proclamation, and second, the community of those who accept this word but who are still affected by the law. The best methodological starting-point is to begin

---

philosophy and the Gospel—in neither does the idea of the law as regulative of *all* human life play any essential part in the formation of theological method. If the theological content is to be preserved intact and undamaged by the method adopted, a combination of philosophy and *law* is to be recommended. There is no hiatus between law and promise: at this point the philosophical framework and theological content should combine without conflict. On the other hand there is a real hiatus between Gospel and promise, as between Gospel and law. A theology which does not encounter conflict at this point generally loses something of the content of the Gospel. The thought of a methodological combination of philosophy and law is by no means as absurd as it may appear at first. Cf., e.g., K. E. Løgstrup, *Den etiske fordring*, 1956, pp. 17-19, and Axel Gyllenkrok, *Systematisk teologi och vetenskaplig metod*, 1959, pp. 96-98. The attempts made by Løgstrup and Gyllenkrok to set forth a purely human ethic are of much interest from the theological point of view, and can lead to other conclusions than the authors themselves draw.

[31] These two divine acts, one in which Christ suffers and one which He discloses in His victory, have been combined in Billing's theology to form a single operation, that of the Gospel and the forgiveness of sins. This is so marked in his conception of atonement that Christ's subjection to wrath and law is changed into a single divine act which Christ perceives and effects. See e.g. Billing's summaries in *I katekesundervisningens tjänst*, pp. 84, 87. In Billing's concept of a folk church we find the same thing in a different form—the forgiveness of sins offered to the nations dominates his whole picture, but he lacks a doctrine of the law.

with the preaching of the Gospel in a society in which the actual demands made by the law are determinative.

This will allow the first article, the law, and the prehistory of the Old Testament, which are otherwise pushed to one side, to fall into their proper place. When they do, something else happens—*the Church comes to be governed wholly by the new reality, i.e. by the Gospel.*

PART II

THE CHURCH

CHAPTER I

THE SPIRIT AND THE WORD

The Gospel in the World of the Law

WE HAVE concluded our discussion of the second article of the Creed and the finished work of Christ and now pass to the third article which deals with the Spirit. The Trinitarian Creed, at least in the form adopted at Nicaea, lists in the third article the Church, baptism, the forgiveness of sins, and the resurrection of the dead. From this point onwards we shall now deal only with this third article.[1]

As we have already seen, the exaltation of Christ after His crucifixion is manifested in His continued giving of gifts to men. Some passages describe the ascension as one particular event (Mk. xvi.19, Lk. xxiv.50 f., Acts 1.9 f.) which was climaxed by the commission given by Jesus to His apostles to go out into the nations. This they did after the descent of the Spirit (see especially Acts 1.8–ii.11, cf. Mk. xvi.20). In other passages (see especially Jn. xx.21 f.) Jesus is represented as having given the Spirit to His disciples when in His risen power He sent them out into the world. While they are still behind closed doors and before they have even met the "men from every nation under heaven" mentioned in Acts ii, Jesus gives them the Spirit.[2] In each case, however, the gift of the Spirit is connected with the sending of the apostles, and, most importantly, with their commission to bring the *Gospel*

---

[1] See here in particular Hendry, *Holy Spirit*, pp. 11-13, on the neglect of the third article. In recent theology the second article has come to push out not only the first article but to a certain extent the third as well. It seems, however, that the number of those who would like to repair the damage done to the third article is larger than the number of those who are ready to treat creation and law. This latter theme has been politically compromised in Europe during the twentieth century, and this, of course, acts as a deterrent. Ecclesiology, on the other hand, has received increasing attention recently.

[2] Cf. Dodd, *Fourth Gospel*, pp. 429-430, 442-443.

to the world. This Gospel, taken into all the world at Pentecost, comes to men who have fallen into temptation and whose broken and fragmented lives are lived out among the many nations of the world. Out of this hostile and divided humanity Christ creates "one new man" through "one Spirit" in "one body" (Eph. II.14-18). This is the work which Christ does through the Spirit for man and by which the Church comes into being. The Church in turn exists to promote this work of Christ among men, and where it does the law disappears and the Gospel stands supreme. Christ has abolished the law of commandments and ordinances (Eph. II.15) and in His risen power has Himself come and preached the Gospel to men (Eph. II.17).[3] The man of whose fall the prehistorical narrative in Genesis speaks lives in every nation under the judgment and wrath of God. There is no possibility of peace for such a man until this relationship of judgment is ended. This is why the Gospel, which the apostle refers to as the proclamation of peace (Eph. II.14-17), is continually to be brought to the world of the *law*. When the Gospel is proclaimed and the Church comes into being, the dominion of the law and the relationship of wrath are ended. Where this work of recreation continues, the Spirit is present in the preaching of the word.[4]

It is important to emphasise that the word addressed to the nations at Pentecost was a *preached* word. Had the work of the Spirit been primarily the composition of sacred writings, the outpouring of its power could just as well have been expressed by getting chosen witnesses to undertake the writing of sacred books. But this is not what happened. When the Spirit breathes on men, they begin to *speak* and their words go out to every nation under heaven. They do not simply speak to the converted. Thus the kerygma can actually be the means of restoring a fragmented and disintegrated humanity.[5] Man is created anew and brought into unity in the body of Christ. The ideas of

---

[3] See Richardson, *Introduction*, pp. 216-217, 243-244. It is clear that in several passages in the New Testament Christ is regarded as the real subject in missionary preaching: it is He who preaches. Cf. Acts xxvi.23, II Cor. v.20. Eph. II.17 also belongs here. On the Gospel of Mark see Willi Marxsen, *Der Evangelist Markus*, 1956, pp. 87-92.

[4] Cf. Hendry, *Holy Spirit*, pp. 73-74.

[5] See Zimmerli, *I Mose* 1-11, VOL. II, p. 232-234.

a new creation and the outpouring of the Spirit are closely connected, and this latter concept in turn is related to the idea of being born of the Spirit (Lk. 1.35, cf. Mt. 1.20). The emphasis as always is on man's total dependence on the intervention of God, and at no point is this new gift or creation guaranteed or validated by lineal continuity or by making a human institution the channel of divine power. Theories of apostolic succession inevitably assume that the Spirit can be confined within some lineal succession that is subject to human control. In consequence these theories betray an inner hesitation about the power of the preached word. Then where there has been some disruption of the lineal succession, e.g. through failure to consecrate a bishop or by being out of communion with the Pope, the *word* has ceased to be regarded as being able to *create*.[6] The relative indifference shown by the Lutheran Reformers to this method of guaranteeing historical and humanly regulated succession is connected with their view of the word as the creative and life-giving word of God. The ministry is principally a preaching ministry and as such is subordinate to the Gospel. The outpouring of the Spirit at Pentecost, expressed in the preaching of the Gospel to the nations rather than in the composition of sacred writings, corresponds in the period of the Reformation to the fact that the Lutheran confessions do not discuss the inspiration of scripture but treat the doctrine of the Spirit in the articles which deal with the ministry. "The Holy Spirit, who calls forth faith in those who hear the Gospel, is given by means of the word and sacraments."[7]

Thus the sphere of the Spirit's activity is not confined primarily to the middle-ground between a sacred author and an empty page, nor is the work of the Spirit to be defined primarily in terms of the writing down of holy words in a book. The sphere of the Spirit's activity lies rather between the mouth of the preacher and the heart of the listener, and the work of the Spirit is to bring faith and life to birth there. Before the Gospel comes, a man's heart is not just an empty vacuum. It is already filled—but with unbelief and death. This means

---

[6] Cf. Persson, *Romerskt och evangeliskt*, pp. 32-49.

[7] Article 5 in the Augsburg Confession. Cf. Hendry, *Holy Spirit*, p. 74.

that the wrath of God and the law that condemns there hold sway. But life is the opposite of death, just as judgment is the opposite of forgiveness. In spite of this, however, there is in a real sense a continuity in the divine activity, though this continuity is *sui generis* and not to be restricted to the ministry of the Church, but is compatible with faith in the mighty act of God's new creation through the word. God has not rejected mankind. Even in man's disobedience His "strange" work on behalf of rebellious man continues unceasingly and culminates where the cross comes to its climax in the Gospel. From creation onwards God has never ceased to work for man, but this work is always expressed in the expulsion of evil and the establishment of good. It is, in other words, a work of death and resurrection throughout. It begins at creation and continues through the fall, the life, death, and resurrection of Christ, to the last day itself, and all mankind is implicated in it. Since God from first to last is the gracious Creator, any theory of a purely ecclesiastical continuity constitutes an attempt to eliminate God, for then any idea of a new and unexpected intervention by God is put out of consideration.[8] Only a theory which leaves room for such a mighty and unconditional intervention from God's side can be said to express a *divine* continuity. The doctrine of an apostolic succession satisfies neither the first nor the second requirement. In the first instance it guarantees continuity of the divine activity through the rites of the Church, so that God is bound and no longer sovereign and free in the preaching of His word.[9] In the second place—and the two are connected—it confines the idea of a continuity of operation to the sphere of the Church when this continuity is actually much wider.

Here again we see the inner connexion between mankind and the Church which we have already discussed more than once. The Spirit is not a power that can be channelled through the Church from generation to generation by means of an unbroken line of episcopal consecrations. If it were, we should be able to think of the Spirit in isolation from the preaching of

[8] Cf. also Gustaf Aulén, *Reformation and Catholicity*, 1962, pp. 158-159.
[9] For a criticism of the ideas of succession see also Oscar Cullmann, *Die Tradition als exegetisches, historisches und theologisches Problem*, 1954, pp. 32-34.

the Gospel to the nations that are under the law,[10] and should fail to see that the Church cannot be so separated from the rest of mankind who have not yet been baptised. When the Spirit was poured forth at Pentecost the risen Jesus was heard speaking "in all the world." Christ is alive and at work wherever the Gospel comes to confront the humanity that is "in Adam." But to be in Adam is not the condition and mark only of the vast majority of mankind who are outside the Church. We are all "in Adam" (cf. 1 Cor. xv.22). Wherever the Gospel is proclaimed life comes to the old Adam and the old fallen nature, and this means that a new work of creation is coming into being in the face of death. This work of creation, moreover, is the converting work of baptism which continues each day in those who are baptised, and comes to its appointed end in the resurrection of the dead. The gift of the Spirit which comes to us in the Gospel is not simply the actual coming of the Gospel to men. We may think that it is if we treat the imparting of knowledge as a separate function of the Gospel. But the Gospel is primarily *resurrection*. (The resurrection of Christ is manifested in the preaching of the Gospel in all the world, while the resurrection of those who hear the Gospel arises from their hearing and believing.) But the Spirit manifests itself no less strikingly in the contrary work of putting to death the old, though this too is bound up with the resurrection. Hence the second use of the law, the pricking of the conscience, is referred to as its spiritual use, *usus spiritualis legis*.[11] In the demands and accusations of the law which "put to death," the Spirit is at work. As the Spirit drove Jesus out into the wilderness "to be tempted by the devil" (Mt. iv.1, Mk. 1.12, Lk. iv.1), so it is also the work of the Spirit to accuse those who are under the law and bring their guilt home to them.

[10] This preaching of the Gospel and the baptism which is annexed to it would not in this case by itself mean that the Spirit was given and the Church a present fact. In the first place it would represent a special qualification of the ministry guaranteeing that the Church is in fact present in the full sense of the word. Where this ministry does come about (through succession), its primary and proper task is not the preaching of the Gospel. It is concerned, rather, with the exclusive sacrament of the Church and the ordinations by which this restrictive Church propagates itself.

[11] Cf. Arvid Runestam, *Den kristliga friheten hos Luther och Melanchthon*, 1917, pp. 159-160.

The sphere in which the second use of the law operates is the same as that of the first use, viz., the external world and human relationships. Since faith in God has been disrupted, man in his idolatry cleaves resolutely to the things of creation and is incapable of sharing them with his fellows. Therefore he hears the voice of law and judgment speaking in the cry of human need around him and in his own despair at the transience of his idols, the pleasures in which he delights. The sin which is uncovered in the second use of the law is the sin of the human heart in the presence of God, but this disclosure is made plain in the relationships of the external world even before the last judgment. An uneasy conscience for ever calls to remembrance actual deeds, often insignificant, but always indicative, which reveal the nature of the human heart. Uneasiness of conscience is a prelude to the final judgment, for this last judgment of all is always depicted in the New Testament as a summons to appear before God or Jesus Christ. But it is men's works that will then show what men have been, simple, everyday acts and their behaviour to "the least of these" brethren of Christ (cf. Mt. xxv.31-46, II Cor. v.10).[12] The second use of the law does not need to wait until the Gospel is preached in order to do its work. Judgment and wrath operate wherever men live together. But when the Gospel is preached it brings this judgment to a head. When Christ is set forth before men, their lack of purity is disclosed in clearer detail than at any other time, for now they see before them the one who is the "image of God" and who exhibits perfectly the generosity of giving which they no longer possess.[13] It is only in the light of the Gospel that men come to see that the old Adam in them is indeed old, for by this light the new being comes to life in them. In its second use the law reveals that it has failed to do what it ought with man and that it now serves the other purpose of being a "tutor" until Christ comes again (Gal. III.24). The law was able to put to death but not to give life. But this work of putting to death, which negates the function of the law for

---

[12] See Wilfried Joest, *Gesetz und Freiheit*, 2nd ed., 1956, pp. 165-169, 176-185. Cf. Mt. xvi.27, Jn. v.29, Rom. II.6.

[13] Cf. Wingren, *Creation and Law*, pp. 181-195. See also Arnold B. Come, *Human spirit and Holy Spirit*, 1959, p. 83.

its own purpose, is its "spiritual" use. When the law assumes
this function, the Spirit is at work in the midst of death.
Anthropologically, this death corresponds to Christ's death
on the cross, for under the veil of the death and frailty which
we see at Calvary there lay both victory and life. The
difference between Christ and ourselves is that His victory
was won through obedience even to the death of the cross,
whereas ours is won through the coming of the word of the
Gospel.

This Gospel is the kerygma which was preached in all the
world after the resurrection, and for those who hear and accept
it, it is both life—resurrection—and death—the putting to
death of the old nature. This kerygma comes to the nations of
the world among whom fallen Adam still exists, but it is also
preached to the household of faith where the same old and
fallen man has still to be confronted by the word of the Gospel.
The Spirit is at work in putting to death the old and in giving
life to the new.[14] When the Gospel comes into the world of the
law the consequence is always the same for the new convert
or for the believer of many years—Pentecost and the world
mission of the Church cannot be separated, and always while
the old is being put to death the new is being brought to life.
The Gospel as the good news of the forgiveness of sins is a word
preached in the face of sin and the dominion of law throughout
the world.[15] Much of the discussion about "earthly government" and the articles of the Creed in the last generation or so
has arisen from a peculiar interpretation which has treated
each article as a doctrinal proposition and has derived political
ethics or the doctrine of civil government either from the first
or from the second article of the Creed according to its particular predilection. But earthly government is only one aspect
of the larger issue of God's continuing activity in the world as
Creator and Judge. God continues His work for the whole

---

[14] Cf. further Ivarsson, *Predikans uppgift*, pp. 134-139, in which, however, the
argument is affected by the specific distinction which this author makes between
law and exhortation.

[15] Cf. Gerhard Ebeling, "Erwägungen zur Lehre vom Gesetz," in *Zeitschrift
für Theologie und Kirche*, 1958, pp. 305-306. Ebeling is critical, however, of the
Reformers' widening of law in a universalist direction, a deviation, he feels, from
the Pauline, more purely "Jewish" concept of the law (see pp. 300-302).

world through His particular and unique work in Christ and the Gospel, and when this latter begins and the former is shown to be "old" and "former," the old is suddenly seen in a new way—it is a preparation for what is to come, something that passes away, but that passes away with a promise.[16] The earthly government is universally binding on "Adam," even where the name of Christ has never been heard of. But when the Gospel comes, the breath of the Spirit moves over all the recalcitrant world, putting to death the old and bringing to life the new. Even where the world lies under judgment, the Spirit is still able to use the constraint and force of this judgment for its purposes. Death then becomes death in Christ, simple physical death. The second article no less than the first and third refers to human life and daily work.

When civil government or other earthly authorities are regarded in this way as having the responsibility of administering the wrath of God, it is quite clear that the New Testament does not assume that the demands made by them should at all times be just or reasonable.[17] The Book of Revelation depicts the state as corrupt and reprehensible, but even so it still does not cease to be an instrument of the wrath of God in the world (cf. Rom. XIII.4): "The destructive fury of Rome and of the nations is one of the signal effects of the operation of the divine ὀργή as the end approaches" (see Rev. XI.18).[18] It is misleading to set Romans XIII and Revelation against one another at this point. If the earthly government is regarded as of God only when its demands are held to be acceptable even from a Christian point of view, but is regarded as something wholly apart from God when these demands are improper, we are then deriving the law from the Gospel and have come

---

[16] Cf. August Strobel, "Zum Verständnis von Rm. 13," in *Z.NT.W.*, 1956, pp. 90-91.

[17] Cf. also Wilder in *Background*, pp. 531-536.

[18] Richardson, *Introduction*, p. 78. Cf. Is. x.5. If we see the crucifixion of Christ in this light, it is not unreasonable to interpret even Pilate's unjust judgment of Jesus as an expression of God's hidden will, a will which aims at final victory over evil—see Acts IV.26-28. On the problem of "wrath" in Paul, cf., Eidem *Det kristna livet*, VOL. I, pp. 83-84. The idea of wrath plays a central role in Luther, cf. Ragnar Bring, *Dualismen hos Luther*, 1929, pp. 264-265, 316-329.

back again to the formula of "Gospel and law."[19] Even if
parents abuse the responsibility which they have towards
their children, this does not prevent them from being used by
God despite the error of their behaviour. We encounter the
Creator in our relationships with other people even when they
are evil. The preaching of the Gospel in the world of the law
makes it possible for us, however, to discriminate among the
multitude of demands made upon us by those among whom we
live and releases us from the obligation to do what is requested
of us, ostensibly because love of our neighbour requires it but
in fact because such demands have been prompted by lust for
power or wounded pride. It would actually be unloving on our
part to assent to such demands. Someone always gets hurt
when we begin to make terms with those who are greedy for
power. We shall return shortly to discuss this discrimination
or "sifting" of the demands which are made of us. At present
we are still concerned with something far more fundamental
and therefore more easy to overlook—the law unceasingly
and in constantly varying forms presses its claims upon us even
in the wrongful demands of those among whom we live.

What in present day terms are these powers which hold men
in bondage under the law? (See Gal. iv.3-11, Col. ii.8-20.)
To define them in terms of the actual historical situation which
lay behind these passages would make it only too obvious that
they are almost totally remote from our day. The law then
comes to be thought of as a purely Jewish phenomenon belonging to a bygone age which has no connexion with modern life.[20]
In the meanwhile modern man is disturbed to read about some
particular "complex" in a book influenced by psychology
and at once recognises it as a description of his own symptoms.
In a similar way he recognises his own bad qualities as a parent
when he learns how the children of maladjusted parents behave,
for he is well aware that his own children are like this! His

[19] On this formula see Karl Barth, *Evangelium und Gesetz*, 1956, pp. 11-12, and
N. H. Søe, *Kristelig etik*, 4th ed., 1957, pp. 13-19, and, in regard to the state,
pp. 380-382.

[20] If we adopt the definitions of the law which belong to the period of the
Reformation, the result will be essentially the same: we shall get a good picture
of the sixteenth century world of ideas, but those who hear the law spoken of will
fail to recognise that they also are subject to it. Cf. Wingren, *Theology in Conflict*,
pp. 66-82, 159-160.

various phobias, insomnia, feelings of inadequacy and fear of death all combine to taunt and accuse him and instil anxiety in his innermost being. If only he could escape it all and become what he ought to be and live up to his idea of what a free man should be! In some such way as this the law continues to operate in our own day. Now as always it insists that a man does something or makes particular efforts to secure health and wellbeing. If today the Gospel is not being preached against *this* law then we have no Gospel, for the Gospel always offers men freedom from the law which actually burdens them.[21]

This makes preaching a difficult thing. But perhaps at this point it should be stressed even more that this makes faith a difficult thing. The despair which a man feels under the law is made more terrible by the conditions which the law demands. *If* only he could fulfil the law, then he would be acceptable to God and belong to Jesus Christ. Therefore, *if* only he could do all that the law requires, i.e. be free of his complexes and anxieties, etc., that he could be a real Christian. This epithet "real," so beloved in our time, in fact connotes a legalistic confidence in works and therefore a wrong belief, for it robs God and Jesus Christ of the power to enter into fellowship with the sinner. The law operates today as it always has, though in different ways, in the multitude of the demands which it lays down as the conditions of securing health and security. Justification by faith does not mean that the law ceases to have any effect, but that it is limited, as Luther emphasises, to the "world," while the conscience is freed through the Gospel.[22] The law will effect changes in family life, e.g. in the relations between parents and children and all other human relationships. It is good that the law should judge us in these areas. But the law has nothing to do with salvation and our relationship to God.[23] We shall have to translate into modern terms what Paul says in Rom. viii.38 f. about our freedom from "angels," "principalities," "heights" and "depths," and apply such passages to the contemporary forms of the

---

[21] *Theology in Conflict*, pp. 101-102, and the whole discussion of the double phenomenological starting-point, pp. 161-164.

[22] See, e.g., W. A. xl. 1. 469 (the Larger Commentary on Galatians, 1935).

[23] Cf. Olov Sunby, *Luthersk äktenskapsuppfattning*, 1959, pp. 60-62.

bondage from which we are now free through faith. Complexes, anxieties, apprehensions, phobias, the fear of death and inability to sleep cannot today separate us from the love of God which is in Christ Jesus. Salvation is not to be found apart from these things but in the midst of them. When the Gospel which speaks to us of the victory in Gethsemane and at Calvary is preached in the world of the law, it gives the conscience an inward freedom. These modern principalities and powers still threaten us, but their sting has been drawn (1 Cor. xv.56 f.) when they can no longer condemn us before God or separate us from Christ. The power of the Gospel is revealed in man's acceptance of his fears in faith and his willingness to put to death his old egocentric nature, a death which is exercised by these agonising powers in the service of the Spirit.

This acceptance of their fears is possible only where men have come to see the eschatological significance of the simple events of daily life and have recognised that eschatology has something to do even with ordinary human need, so that each day becomes a "last day." No one, confronted by the inevitable fact of death, can make long-term self-improvement a condition for receiving the Gospel. The Gospel is received as a free gift, and the fact that death continues its work of destruction in the individual who receives the Gospel does not prevent him from receiving it. On the contrary, the forces of destruction are pressed into the service of the new life which comes into being and which has a future as yet undisclosed.[24] It is more difficult to relate this radical acceptance of which we have been speaking to such moments when one has still a great "length of days" to fulfil on earth. It is especially difficult in an age which has much to say about eschatology but in which those who talk about it plan their future far in advance, as though this life were all. There are times when eschatology comes to be regarded as little more than some doctrine or theory that has to do with the Church or the sacraments but not with daily living. The actual, concrete form which the law takes in every human life and the uniquely individual character of the cross of suffering which each of us has to bear makes it a proof of faith to apply the Gospel to one's own personal problems. It is

[24] Cf. Prenter, *Skabelse*, pp. 218-220.

much easier to detach faith from one's own personal situation and alter it into mere intellectual assent to certain dogmas, and lose oneself in the anonymous crowd of a congregation, and think of eschatology only in terms of the collective future of the Church. If we begin to "believe" in this depersonalised way, it becomes even more difficult to relate the sacraments to daily life and work, for we have then all unconsciously adopted a theory of the sacraments which breaks the connexion between baptism and human life and between the Eucharist and daily work—no longer do we think of the work of the Spirit being continued in the ever new encounters between the Gospel and the world of the law. Instead we think of the Spirit being channelled through the Church and having no relation to the struggles of daily life.[25] Our failure to think of the Spirit as active in the world contributes to this narrow view of the work of the Spirit and further separates it from those areas in which the Gospel comes to the individual in his burden of guilt.

The power of the law is in fact an integral part of the message of the Gospel. For the Gospel is a word that is addressed to a responsive subject, and of this subject we read in the Genesis story of the creation and fall. The Gospel is the word with which the Spirit comes, the redeeming word which is addressed to the Adam who still lives in those who hear it. The work of the Spirit in conversion consists in both putting to death and annihilating the old and raising to life and increasing the new. Once we see the law and Gospel in this way we discover that a

---

[25] See also Hendry, *Holy Spirit*, pp. 55-67, 72-75. The interpretation of the Spirit as canalised in the ministry of the church is often found in Protestant churches as a swing of the pendulum in a hierarchical direction towards a position hotly denounced by enthusiastic revivalist movements. In the sectarian view the Spirit is conceived as a personal possession of the converted or regenerate, a condition which is independent of outward means. The ministry and Church order are therefore set against this spiritualising interpretation. Once these two attitudes become fixed there is generally no understanding on the part of either side of what is meant by the preaching of the Gospel in the world of the law as the unchanging power by which the Church is daily created. The preaching of the Gospel, like baptism, becomes for both sides a "starting-point." After baptism the revivalist groups concentrate on subjective development and sanctification, the hierarchical groups on the consecration of the Eucharist by the ministry. Neither side realises that sanctification is the daily death and resurrection which take place when the Gospel comes again and again to men who are under the law, and which are a continual working out of baptism.

divinely ordained rule of law, wrath, and guilt holds sway when the Gospel comes, and that this rule is to be found even when those above or around us—government, parents, neighbours, or social groups—abuse or selfishly use the power entrusted to them.[26]

The demands made upon us which we find irksome do not mean that our fellow-men are good, yet God still comes to us through these demands. When, therefore, the Gospel is preached and faith comes to birth, this means that we now have a new opportunity of critically examining these demands which are made upon us, and the duty of sifting among them to determine which to accept. The freedom of the Christian from the law implies also freedom to choose between the multifarious demands made by those among whom we live.[27] It is certainly no mark of love, for example, to weaken in one's resistance to despotic or tyrannical power, for love itself is quite capable of standing against force and thwarting it. In regard to what we have called "sifting" between demands it will be instructive to pay heed to Luther. For the Reformer there were three facts to be reckoned with. First, he was confronted with a universal rule of law in the world into which the Gospel comes to men as the word of forgiveness. There were also the earthly authorities which were the instruments of that law but which were also liable to a criticism which accepted some of their demands but rejected others. Third, he had the task of preaching Christ as the example of men's works.[28] But we do not need to go to Luther. The Biblical writings themselves deal with the same three things.

When modern theology tries to demonstrate the validity of a "radical moral requirement" on a purely human basis and without reference to the preaching of Christ's finished work,

[26] On the exegesis of Rom. 11.14-15, which is of importance in this connexion, see Günther Bornkamm, *Studien zu Antike und Urchristentum*, 1959, pp. 93-118, where Bo Reicke's interpretation, among others, is justly criticised (pp. 102-104).

[27] Cf. Wingren, *Theology in Conflict*, p. 76, and also, in fuller detail, *Creation and Law*, pp. 93-94, 143-144, 157-159, 165, 189-190 (and see further the references cited under "demands, evaluation of," in this latter work).

[28] He does not, however, refer to this preaching of Christ as example and image as the preaching of the *law*. See Ivarsson, *Predikans uppgift*, pp. 134-144. Cf. Edmund, Schlink, "Gesetz und Paraklese," in *Antwort*, 1956, pp. 333-335 (quoting Paul, Luther and even Calvin against the one-sided interpretation of Barth).

it is generally dealing with a demand which has nothing to do
with what the Reformers understood by the first use of the law,
and which does not take its point of departure in the proclamation of Christ in preaching. In the 1930s Friedrich
Gogarten's remarkable work, *Politische Ethik*, exercised considerable influence and its publication at that date was significant. What Gogarten calls the "man tut das und das" demand
perhaps corresponds most closely to what Luther calls the
"civil use" of the law,[29] while his radical "du sollst" demand,
which cannot be fulfilled and which addresses man as evil
and not as good, corresponds to Luther's "spiritual use" of
the law. At the same time, however, this latter demand in one
respect resembles the Gospel summons to imitate Christ, a
summons that is grounded in the proclamation of His death.[30]
But Gogarten is unwilling to accord this commandment, which
he calls "absolute" and which he sharply distinguishes from
moral "conventions," the power to differentiate between
demands made in the political realm. Indeed, he explicitly
excludes this discriminatory function.[31] In an era which found
no relationship between earthly government and the will of
God it is easy to see how a theologian such as Gogarten was
thus forced to stress as his sole contention that even the earthly
government belongs to God, and how in so doing he lost sight
of the freedom to criticise political values and norms. But all
this brought him no closer to the Bible or to the Reformation.

Twenty-four years after Gogarten's book first appeared in
German the Danish scholar K. E. Løgstrup published his *Den
etiske fordring* ("*The Moral Imperative*") which dealt with the
same general theme but made not a single reference to the
earlier work.[32] Like Gogarten, Løgstrup too dealt with the
periodic changes in conventional morality and spoke also of a
radical demand for love of one's neighbour.[33] This radical
demand arises from the very fact of human life, but at the same

---

[29] Friedrich Gogarten, *Politische Ethik*, 1932, pp. 9-11, 62.
[30] See *ibid.*, pp. 11, 62, 115, etc.
[31] Cf. Gunnar Hillerdal, *Gehorsam gegen Gott und Menschen*, 1954, pp. 154-163.
[32] The relationship between Løgstrup on the one hand and Bultmann and
Gogarten on the other is in the main a positive one. See, e.g., Løgstrup, *Den etiske
fordring*, p. 127, footnote.
[33] *Ibid.*, pp. 56-125.

time it is identical with the commandment of Jesus.[34] As in Gogarten, Løgstrup's argument is opposed to that type of "Christian ethic" which looks to scripture for its precedents in preference to becoming really involved in the problems of society where the well-being of one's neighbour is always paramount.[35] Since this is the point at which he has chosen to do battle, Løgstrup rejects the idea of a specifically Christian order of society and at the same time describes in detail with examples from family and economic life how moral and social conventions change from generation to generation. Strangely enough, however, the preaching of the Gospel is not related to the circumstances which bring about a new development in the pattern of human behaviour or cause an old and outmoded pattern to disappear. We do not find the positive relationship between the Gospel and faith on the one hand and the critical sifting and differentiating between the pressing demands made upon us in human society on the other.[36]

One important reason why both these important ethical studies have misrepresented in this way the critical function of the Gospel vis-à-vis the prevailing order of society is that they have confined their interest to legislation and the political sphere and so on. Both writers are eager to avoid the mistake of turning faith into an ideology peculiar to Christians but not found among others. In such a case the Christian faction would bring to the task of law-making a set of assumptions which would prevent them from having any unrestricted discussion with the others or undertaking a genuine examination of all relevant facts in a particular case. If the Church and Gospel are understood to be a regulative factor in this sense, then Gogarten and Løgstrup are quite right to reject such an interpretation. But a study of the Lutheran Reformation will show us that we have also to deal with the no less significant category of "misuse," likewise a universal phenomenon. Every human being is thus surrounded by neighbours whose welfare is to be

---

[34] *Ibid.*, pp. 9-11, 125-126, and especially 220-233. Cf. Gunnar Hillerdal, *Teologisk och filosofisk etik*, 1958, pp. 162-172, but Hillerdal's criticism of Løgstrup is rather narrow.

[35] Løgstrup, *Den etiske fordring*, pp. 125-132.

[36] Cf. also Løgstrup's essay, "Lebensanschauung und Recht," in *Die Freiheit des Evangeliums und die Ordnung der Gesellschaft*, 1952, pp. 24-28.

promoted but whose demands are nevertheless to be treated critically. The believer who comes to faith through the Gospel does not acquire a new ideology but faith, and this faith means the restoration of humanity, i.e. a new means of forming a true judgment.[37] There are good grounds for the assertion that man in the Church is not different from man in *creation*, but now restored to his free dominion over everything that God has created good and to the free service of his neighbour. The work of the Gospel is to heal the creature who has gone wrong, viz. man, and enable him to live in his proper place in the world which God has created. The Church is this open community, living under the word and sacraments, and when it ceases to be open it ceases to be the Church. The freedom of the Christian consists in his sovereignty over rules and conventions. But this simply means that the Gospel gives him the power to discriminate among the demands with which he is beset, and the sphere in which this power operates is the Church which stands under the rule of the Gospel.[38]

We have noted above a tendency in modern theology to think of the Spirit as being channelled through the apostolic succession. This in turn leads to a refusal to accept that the Church properly functions only when the Gospel confronts the law which holds men in bondage, and that the ministry is primarily a preaching ministry. Corresponding to this restrictive Church is the restrictive society in which service is certainly rendered to the needy but which has not yet been opened to the Gospel. In each case the tendency is to think in terms of a collectivism either in regard to the Church or to the political sphere. It is not unlikely that both these contradictory tendencies may be the expression of a common, underlying temptation, typical perhaps of our day, to lose sight of the individual—to evade the real difficulty of dealing with the solitary, tempted soul who lives in the midst of social problems which make personal to him the constraint of the law, and also of explaining how the Gospel and the sacraments at precisely

[37] See Paul Ramsay, *Basic Christian Ethics*, 1953, pp. 63, 75, 153-190, 349-351. Cf. also Ragnar Bring, *Förhållandet mellan tro och gärningar*, 1933, pp. 202-205.
[38] Cf. also Hillerdal, *Teologisk etik*, p. 292, Ivarsson, *Predikans uppgift*, pp. 113-133, 158-163, Sundby, *Luthersk äktenskapsuppfattning*, pp. 290-291, footnote 13. The continuing discussion of this point is of great importance.

the point of this earthly need communicate the death and resurrection of Christ to those who receive them. The spiritual government and the earthly government are quite distinct. This is admitted. But they do not exist in a vacuum. They are governments which are exercised over men, and very often they touch the same man whose old nature is put to death in this clash between the two at the same time as new life is brought into being.[39] In this acutely personal event the Spirit is at work.[40] If the doctrines of creation and the Church are not therefore related to one another and seen to have their point of intersection in the individual, they both lose their true significance.

[39] See also Peter Brunner, "The Christian in a Responsible Society," in *Lutheran World*, 1958, p. 246-248. We shall return to the question of sifting the demands made upon us in our discussion of "the new activity" and "freedom and the law" below.

[40] And in the event *baptism* is fulfilled. A renewal of the third article will not ignore this point. Cf. J. E. L. Oulton, *Holy Communion and Holy Spirit*, 1951, pp. 185-188.

The Ministry

When the Gospel has been brought to bear upon the guilt under which man labours, the Spirit is at work. The purpose of the ministry is to bring the word of the Gospel to this point in every human life. When this word does come to guilty man, as we saw in our previous discussion of the meaning of Christ's resurrection, it is Christ Himself who comes to man.[1] It is primarily Christ who is sent, and He was sent when He was "born of a woman, born under the law" (Gal. iv.4). The transmission of the Gospel is grounded on this first mission of the Son, and, as we have also seen previously, is connected with the outpouring or "sending" of the Spirit (cf. Gal. iv.6). This relation is clearly stated in the Johannine version of Pentecost where Jesus says to His disciples: "As the Father has sent me, even so I send you" (Jn. xx.21), then gives them the Spirit (Jn. xx.22) and bestows upon them the power to forgive sins (Jn. xx.23).[2]

[1] Cf. Marxsen, *Der Evangelist Markus*, pp. 90-92, 99-101.

[2] The insufflation of the Spirit in Jn. xx.22 is a parallel to Gen. ii.7; it is a new creation. Cf. A. M. Ramsey, *The Resurrection of Christ*, 2nd ed., 1946, pp. 86-87.

I

The one who is sent fulfils his mission when he carries out the command of the one who sent him. He is, as it were, a mouthpiece, speaking a word that is not his own. Christ, who is sent by the Father, can at one time speak about God as though He were someone other than Himself, but He can also turn to men with something to offer them, and speak to them as though He alone were God. So it is with those who are sent out. The Old Testament gives us many illustrations from daily life: Jephtha's messengers are Jephtha himself and Joseph's steward Joseph himself (Judg. XI.12 f., Gen. XLIV.4-10).[3] The Father's sending of the Son and the Son's sending of the Gospel through His apostles means that God is at work in Christ whenever the ministry of preaching or of the Gospel is exercised. But this direct divine activity in the ministry does not prevent the minister as a man among men from speaking of God as a man would speak of a father who was far away or out of sight. Jesus Himself in His temptation was in a certain sense separated from God. The strong emphasis on the ministry which in anti-liberal theology of different hues has come to take the place of the uncertain and tentative approach to matters of faith at the turn of the present century tends to lead to a "monophysitic" view of the ministry as wholly divine. This view corresponds to a similar movement in Christology towards monophysitism. The divine aspect of the ministry is sharply distinguished from the human. It is, however, important to understand not only that the minister as a private person is human, but also that the ministry itself is human in nature. It can be exercised only in solidarity with men, and this also means in solidarity even with those who show some interest in Christ but who have real difficulties with what the Church teaches about Him. This is the biggest problem of the ministry: how can it proclaim the Gospel about Christ crucified and risen without diminishing it, but how at the same time can it deal patiently with the varying reception which it receives and with its slow growth among men?[4] None should be excluded from the Christian

[3] See Aubrey R. Johnson, *The One and the Many in the Israelite Conception of God*, 1942, pp. 9-10.
[4] Cf. Billing, *De etiska tankarna*, pp. 406-409, 430-435. In his highly original exegesis of the parables of the seed and the hidden growth Billing maintained that the apostles (precisely because they were charged with the responsibility of

community who has even the slightest grasp of the Gospel, but correspondingly those who have no more than a passing acquaintance with the Gospel have no right to affect or alter the greater part of the whole, for this greater part, the whole Gospel, belongs to the Church and not to individuals within it. This is, then, the central problem of the ministry in our time, and all other questions are minor in comparison.

God deals with the whole human race in Christ, and therefore the ministry, which bestows the benefits of Christ's finished work, is a ministry of the Gospel for all mankind. If the mighty act of God in Christ is interpreted in such a way that Christ's temptation and passion, that is, those situations in which Christ Himself is under the law and sees His will in conflict with God's will, are no longer regarded as having anything to do with the divine work of recapitulation, theology will come to feel a little bit uneasy about what we may call "the human nature of the Church."[5] It becomes more difficult to see how Christ has anything to do with the hesitant and doubting. Rather than try to find a point of contact in the predicament of seekers and doubters, the Church comes to concern itself with a theory about "faith," which cuts short the questions of the perplexed, and holds the door open only to those whose faith is "mature." The rapid conversions in our day, for example, from atheism to a wholesale acceptance of every doctrine in the new faith, are a typical phenomenon. They are conversions without intermediate halting-points. But it is a mistake to suppose that such conversions are typical in our day of the inward and hidden life of faith of the individual. We each have all kinds of intermediate halting-points, and the uncertainty of the individual in regard to separate points of doctrine is as strong today as it was at the turn of the century. Conversions from the total denial of a doctrine to a total acceptance of it are typical rather of the Churches of today and of their theories about themselves. While these

---

sowing and distributing) required a doctrine of human growth, unlike the people to whom they preached. It is difficult to do justice to this side of the ministry— that part which has to do with men's reception—when the humanity of Christ is pushed out to the periphery of Christology. This isolates the divine action in our doctrine of the ministry.

[5] Cf. Welch, *Reality of the Church*, pp. 42-73.

sweeping conversions are to be found in a limited number of cases, another group increases quietly and without publicity. This is the group of the spiritually homeless, who do not feel at home in the Church, but who still live by the "likeness" of Christ, though admittedly only by a fragment of that likeness. In connexion with these the ministry and the ministers of the Church have an enormous task to accomplish. If our theory of the ministry accentuates only the divine nature, then when this ministry has to deal with the situation in which the Gospel is received listlessly and with reservations, in practice it is incapable of uttering a word. The practical difficulties which the Church experiences in a situation such as this are due generally not so much to its lack of practical training as to its lack of adequate theory. Monophysitism, that is to say, is an unsatisfactory theory, and its inadequacies increase when expressed in a doctrine of the ministry.[6]

It is difficult to make a comparison between the ministry as it existed in the Church of the New Testament period and our modern equivalent. There is a strong tendency in a number of present-day denominations to focus their attention solely on one particular ministry of early Christianity, the apostolate, despite the fact that the apostolate was a unique phenomenon and limited to this foundation period. Cullman has good grounds for his argument that the apostolic ministry in our day is not the responsibility of any successors to the apostles, but is still exercised by the apostles themselves, and that the instrument through which the original and unique apostolic ministry is continued today is the writings of the New Testament. These alone speak to us with apostolic authority, and our ministry is merely a ministry of expounding and interpreting them, a ministry subordinate to the word of scripture.[7] But the difficulty of making any comparison between the ministry of the early Christian Church and that of the present day is complicated by a second factor, namely the change in attitude to world mission. Each of the four Gospels ends with the command to

---

[6] In Prenter, *Skabelse*, pp. 399, 440, where a line is similarly drawn from Christ-ology to other doctrines, the term "monophysitism" is used in a more restricted sense than here.

[7] See Cullmann, *Tradition*, pp. 33-35, in reference to Gal. i.12 and Jn. xvii.20.

evangelise. The Gospel was to be brought to those whom Jesus Himself had never met, and to the parts of the earth on which He had never set foot. However we may regard the historic accuracy of this command to evangelise, the historian can at least assert as an indisputable fact that the mission was fulfilled by the first generation. The Acts of the Apostles and the Epistles are in agreement to this extent, that they show us an apostolic ministry in action. The ministry of the apostles was in every respect a missionary activity, carried on throughout the Mediterranean area in regions where Jesus had never been, and is a graphic illustration of the discharging of the mission of which each of the four Gospels speaks.[8] In our own time, however, the ministry is restricted geographically to particular congregations in which it is difficult to see immediately the missionary aspect of the work of the ministry.[9] Those in our day who go and preach the Gospel to the heathen are often men and women outside the ministry, and the question of ordaining or setting them apart does not usually give rise to any heated arguments. Passions are aroused only when we come to deal with the ministry of those who work in one particular geographical situation. All of a sudden what the New Testament has to say about apostles comes to have particular importance!

There are, of course, historical reasons for this comparatively recent concentration on the ministry when bound to a particular local congregation and this indifference to missionary activity overseas. Fairly early on the monarchical episcopate made the city the ecclesiastical centre for the surrounding area.[10] After the Middle Ages the development of the parochial system divided the greater part of Europe into local congregations gathered around a parish church with its parish priest. The task of evangelising the nations of the world who had never

[8] Cf. Gustaf Wingren, *Kyrkans ämbete*, 1958, pp. 17-19.

[9] On closer examination we can, of course, see this missionary aspect quite clearly. For the old nature which remains in the baptised is essentially the same as that of the pagan. The old Adam lives in "all nations" and his influence is at work whenever even a mature Christian yields to temptation. In this sense Sunday preaching is missionary preaching. Cf. Karl Fezer, *Das Wort Gottes und die Predigt*, 1925, pp. 98-99.

[10] Holsten Fagerberg, "Biskopsämbetet och andra kyrkliga tjänster i den gamla kyrkan," in *En bok om kyrkans ambete*, pp. 75-77.

heard the Gospel gradually became a peripheral activity of the Church, and in many instances was wholly lost sight of. When it was recovered in the eighteenth century and in the nineteenth became more firmly established, it was generally undertaken by a missionary society whose character it bore. Even when the Churches of Europe themselves officially assumed the responsibility for mission, missionary service remained as something optional and amorphous, and bore no imaginable resemblance to the ministry, fenced around as it was with much stricter traditions, and to the proclamation of the Gospel in the parishes of western Europe. If tradition is our authority, there is no doubt at all that those ministries which have to do with local parishes but which have no specifically missionary character are in a class by themselves, and are much more strictly regulated than those appointments which are clearly missionary in character and which make men in every nation under heaven the offer of baptism and the Gospel. The difficulties begin when we refuse to treat tradition as an instructive norm and instead make a direct comparison between early Christianity and the present time, and then apply only *biblical statements* to the present day ministry. For it then becomes clear that the distinctive feature of the early Christian apostle, that is, the thing that makes him distinct from a modern bishop or parson, and the distinctive feature of a modern missionary, are in many ways very much the same.[11] We see this very clearly in the service of the commissioning of a missionary, in which passages from Christ's own command to evangelise are often included in the prayers and addresses given to the candidates. But in the New Testament there is not a single line which speaks of a commission given by Christ to preach the Gospel to the nations which does not also refer to the person sent out as *eo ipso* an apostle. The charge given by Christ to preach the Gospel is quite clearly an *apostolic* commission in the New Testament. To allude to such passages from

[11] Roman Catholic theologians are better off since for them, as for the Anglicans, tradition has a greater independent importance. They do not have to argue on the basis of *biblical texts alone* in asserting that the Pope or the episcopate, as the case may be, is essential for the ministry. The writings of the early Church have also independent value as evidence. With regard to the Roman Catholics cf. Oscar Cullmann, *Peter*, 1953, pp. 213-215.

the New Testament in the course of the commissioning of a missionary implies that the apostolic task is now being given to some other person. This should not distress us. According to the New Testament, baptism, the preaching of the Gospel, and the Eucharist, are all functions which Christ uses as the means by which He gives salvation to men. They have been entrusted, the writers of the New Testament state, only to the apostles, but the same writings quite clearly state that all of them administered by persons other than apostles, though the New Testament does not tell us how these functions passed from the apostles. The pastoral Epistles, and particularly the Epistles to Timothy (see 1 Tim. IV, 14; II Tim. 1.6, cf. 22), witnessed to the fact that fixed regulations developed little by little, but they tell us no more than this.[12] There are many other developments in the early period which are referred to in the pastoral Epistles, for example, the treatment of the widows of the Church. Were we to take these Epistles as our principal authority for the outward ordering of the Church in our own time, we should have to treat all that they say with similar respect. But if on the other hand we pick and choose among the regulations of these Epistles, and regard as regulative for our own practice the trend towards a monarchical episcopate and an ordered succession such as followed in the post-apostolic period, while on the other hand we dismiss as of no consequence features which disappeared, then the principle of selection of biblical passages is determined by the early Church and not by the Bible itself.[13] But if this is the case we should admit that the norm and guiding principle of the Church today is tradition. If on the other hand we persist in maintaining that it is the Bible and in this particular case the New Testament that is normative for us, we immediately

[12] See also Tit. 1.5. Cf. Hans von Campenhausen, *Kirchliches Amt und geistliche Vollmacht in der ersten drei Jahrhunderten*, 1953, pp. 169-170.

[13] This selective factor, drawn from outside the Bible, is apparent in Harald Riesenfeld's essay, "Ämbetet i Nya testamentet," in *En bok om ämbetet*, 1951, pp. 53-63. Cf. Fagerberg, *ibid.*, pp. 108-112, and also Gärtner in *Svensk kyrkotidning*, 1956, pp. 291-292. It is even more astonishing that all three of these writers find the three-fold ministry of "deacon, priest and bishop" in the New Testament (Riesenfeld, p. 54, Fagerberg, pp. 73-74, 107-108, Gärtner, p. 291). The Anglican Church, of course, regards the three-fold ministry as the ideal. See in this connexion, e.g., Ragnar Askmark, *Ämbetet i den svenska kyrkan*, 1949, pp. 241-243.

find ourselves in difficulties. For since the general responsibility for missionary endeavour was turned over in the nineteenth century to men and women alike, while in the local Churches of the West the ministry of the Churches which sent them was restricted to one area and more significantly was restricted only to men, the defenders of the traditional order of the ministry have felt it necessary to turn to biblical arguments to prove that the minister of a local congregation has an apostolic ministry, while his companion on the mission field has no such apostolic ministry. The more we attempt to wrest passages from the Bible to support this quite ridiculous position, the further away from the Bible we get.

This whole misunderstanding of the ministry, the Gospel, and the missionary task, is connected with the common tendency to reduce baptism and the preaching of the Gospel to little more than a preliminary act, and to make the administration of the Eucharist the specific function of the ministry.[14] From the very first, however, the Eucharist was the lesser of the two sacraments. New members were incorporated into the Church not through the Eucharist but through baptism. (Acts II.41). When, therefore, the apostles were sent out into the world, they were not commanded to celebrate the Eucharist, but to preach and to baptise—the two activities which are open to the Gentile world (Mk. XVI.15 ff.). When converts have been brought into the congregation through baptism, which takes place once for all, the Eucharist binds them together as a congregation. Since it is founded upon baptism and can never be put in front of baptism, the Eucharist is an exclusive activity of the congregation, continually repeated.[15] If we take our starting-point in baptism, as the early Church did, the exclusive nature of the Eucharist presents no problem, and this exclusiveness does not mean that the church is less conscious of the fact that it has been sent. The "primary" sacrament, baptism, is together with the preaching of the Gospel the Church's point of orientation, its mission to the world continues

---

[14] 1 Cor. XIV.34 has thus been used in more than one instance as a means of excluding women from the right to celebrate the Eucharist, though for long they have preached and taught in the Church.

[15] Cf. Moule, *Sacrifice*, pp. 30, 42-43.

each day, and its doors stand continually open. The Eucharist is the prayer and praise of the redeemed as they await the coming into their midst of new members, whose entrance into the Church is by way of baptism, and whose life thereafter is the life of baptism. This is the life of death and resurrection, and it is nourished by the constantly repeated Eucharist in which the crucified and risen Lord comes to those who await the final death and resurrection.[16] But one of the most disastrous changes in the history of the Church is the reduction of baptism to a mere formality, the dropping of world mission, and the development of a purely local Western Church. This automatically forces attention on the more exclusive sacrament of the Eucharist, which tends to become the point of orientation when we look at the ministry. The distinctive feature of the minister is his power to celebrate the Eucharist.[17] The specific attribute of the ministry is no longer the task of evangelising the nations for which the apostles were sent out, but comes to be an introverted, exclusive, and wholly ecclesiastical activity.

This declension from the idea of the ministry in the early Church has led to various theories of aspostolic succession and to a view of the Spirit as a power guaranteed by ministerial succession and restricted to the Church. The sphere of the activity of the Spirit ceases to be regarded as the encounter between the Gospel, through which the risen Christ comes to men, and the separated nations of the world in whom we see fallen Adam in bondage. The continuity in God's dealings with men is no longer the continuity between His work in creation and what He does in the Church, but is limited to the Church and extends from the apostles to the present time, and is guaranteed by unbroken episcopal succession.[18] While recognition is accorded to the baptisms of such Churches as lack the apostolic succession as well as to their preaching of the Gospel, it is not accorded to the Eucharists of these bodies, and it is the Eucharist which is the central point of debate. But this

[16] Cf. Davies, *Spirit*, pp. 123-124.

[17] Cf. Persson, *Romerskt och evangeliskt*, pp. 55-57.

[18] In one way this means that the Church itself is subject to the law. Cf. T. F. Torrance, *Royal Priesthood*, 1955, pp. 50-62.

means that baptism and the Gospel, the two responsibilities with which the apostles were sent out into the world, are no longer regarded as capable of bringing the Church into being and communicating the Spirit to men. The point of orientation by which the early Church was led to undertake its mission and the situation which prompted it to assume Christ's own ministry and brought it to suffer and to be put to death for men—all this remains unchanged, but it ceases to determine the conception of the Church and becomes instead peripheral. In this new situation the Church inevitably turns in upon itself. The distinctive feature of the ministry which sets the minister apart from the congregation is the ability to celebrate the Eucharist, which has been fenced around from a very early date.[19] This shutting off of the ministry from its primary object produces an acute and rapid introversion which is all the harder to reverse when the number of those outside the Church is increasing, as it is in Europe. "Outside" the Church baptism continues to be administered as infant baptism in a national Church: increasingly it becomes a formality while the Eucharist increasingly becomes an esoteric gathering.[20] The responsibility for evangelism grows greater but the introversion does not change. Only a new awareness of the meaning of baptism could effect such a change. And this in turn would throw the whole question of the ministry into a totally different light.

This recovery of the meaning of baptism will have two consequences. First, it will enable us to see that the ministry has to do primarily with what lies beyond itself. It is this that gives it its direction, and this objective that stands out in utter clarity when we get down to the basic question of what the Gospel is. It is the "word to the captives." Such a recovery will have the further effect of subordinating consecration or ordination to those mighty acts of redemption in which *all* who are in the Church have part. The ministry exists to dispense and administer these redemptive acts, and those to whom they are administered come to participate in the same salvation as the minister himself. But his participation in this salvation is

---

[19] Cf. Elert, *Abendmahl*, pp. 64-86.
[20] Cf. Oulton, *Holy Communion*, pp. 187-188.

attributable not to the fact of his ordination but of his *baptism*. Ordination bestows upon the minister the responsibility of administering the means of salvation. But should he come to have doubts about his own redemption, his only refuge and stay is the forgiveness of sins, but it is through the means of grace that he has access to this comfort and not by virtue of his ordination.[21] Nothing can be added to baptism, and all that we receive after baptism is the means by which the work of baptism is continued. From the moment of its administration baptism, as we have seen, is an act of God which bears on the whole subsequent life of the baptised—his temptations and trials, his victories in times of temptation and his physical death. When we think of the Spirit being mediated through an ordained ministry, we no longer retain this profound view of baptism. It makes no difference to plead, for example, that this unbroken continuity of ordination gives baptism its deep significance, for baptism has never in the history of the Church been exclusively reserved to the ministry. Other acts have been, but never baptism, which in fact can be administered by any Christian, independently of ordination, and which is still today accepted across denominational lines.[22] To accept the Gospel and baptism as the basis of the Church means that we must reject any idea that consecration or ordination constitute the Church. The ministry is charged rather with the administration of the acts of redemption, i.e. of the means of grace. Conversely, the moment we introduce a doctrine of succession into our view of the ministry, we cease to regard the Church as grounded on baptism and the Gospel. One view is opposed to the other.[23] We have to choose between them.

[21] Cf. Davies, *Spirit*, p. 176.
[22] On the ecumenical consequences of this cf. Torrance, *S.J.T.*, 1954, pp. 267-269.
[23] The term "vestigia ecclesiae" is sometimes used even in the ecumenical writings of the evangelical churches to denote preaching and the sacraments. If the means of grace are only "Notes" of the Church, the basis of the Church is clearly something other than the means of grace. It is strange that the Churches which sprang from the Reformation can accept this terminology. On the other hand it is quite natural that Roman Catholic theologians should rejoice to see the evangelical Churches accept it. Cf. Gustave Thils, *Histoire doctrinale du mouvement oecuménique*, 1955, pp. 143, 147, 183-197.

The early Christian Church clearly made its choice and subordinated even the apostles, viz. the highest ministry they knew, to the higher authority of the Gospel. The conflict between Paul and Peter at Antioch was a conflict within the Church between two apostles and could not thus be resolved by reference to apostolic authority. At Antioch Peter had kept the Gospel from coming to the Gentiles, for by withdrawing himself from fellowship with the uncircumcised he had made circumcision and not baptism or the Gospel constitutive of the Church. In so doing he had gone against the "truth of the Gospel" (Gal. II.14), and in consequence was forced to yield, not because Paul was an apostle, but because the Gospel had been proclaimed to the Gentiles and customs such as circumcision, which Christ and all His apostles had observed, had now disappeared.[24] It was not circumcision that had been taken into all the world. It had a place, but not in the redemptive act accomplished and instituted by Christ, and, therefore, it was not included by Him in His command to take the Gospel into the world. From this it is quite clear that circumcision is not essential for the Church, that is to say, it is not necessary that this particular practice of the early Church should also be found in the Church today. Any exegesis that looks at early Christian custom and usage and automatically assumes that the same usage should be found in the Church today loses the very point of what the Church meant to early Christianity. The Church is founded on the fact that it has been *sent*, and it exists to bring salvation to the *nations*. Those functions through which salvation is brought to men have to be performed by someone, and the Church confers this responsibility on whom it will, but it is free to choose the ways in which this necessary task is done, and in so doing renders obedience to Christ in freedom.[25]

Since in the New Testament the Gospel has clearly authority over the apostles, any question of continuity in regard to ordination is out of harmony with the general drift of the New

[24] On Gal. II.11-14 cf. also Ragnar Bring, *Commentary on Galatians*, 1961, pp. 78-85.

[25] Cf. Hans von Campenhausen and Heinrich Bornkamm, *Bindung und Freiheit in der Ordnung der Kirche*, 1959, where the former deals with the early Church (pp. 5-25) and the latter the Reformation (pp. 26-48). See also Ramsey, *Ethics*, pp. 75-76.

Testament. Indeed, we notice as soon as we turn to the New Testament how reserved it is in regard to the whole problem, and how general its references are to the laying on of hands. While there are great passages which state in detail the meaning of the Gospel and connect redemption with the Gospel and with baptism, there is not a single verse in the New Testament which ties salvation to rites of ordination in which a ministry is transmitted from one office-holder to another.[26] We can also understand why there is this comparative indifference. No one can become more than an apostle through such ordination. But even supposing that ordination were to make a man an apostle, such a person would have no authority in the Church whatsoever if he went against the Gospel. He would be in the same position as Peter when he tried to restrict his dealings to the circumcised. We are therefore forced to look beyond the question of ordination to the means of salvation with which Christ sent His apostles into the world after His resurrection. It is clearly these means, wholly regulated and governed by the Gospel, which have the real authority for all who are apostles and all who are ordained.

This authority is different from worldly authority. It does not seek to grasp or to possess. The Gospel, the word of forgiveness, baptism, and the Eucharist are gifts which have been given "for the forgiveness of sins," and Christ Himself continues to give gifts to men by means of them. Our difficulty in forming a true picture of the early Christian ministry in its conjunction of fixed patterns and lack of consistency is related to a gradual disappearance of the idea that the Church is to confront the world around it in an attitude of generous and creative giving. And then the ministry may come to be regarded as a *privilege* for its possessor, a might and power which the minister has in distinction from those who do not have such authority.[27] This idea of privilege which is frequently introduced into the concept of the ministry comes more from an emphasis on a continuity of ordination which is quite foreign

---

[26] See the summary in Campenhausen, *Kirchliches Amt*, pp. 331-332.

[27] See, however, on the other side the strong emphasis on ministry as *service* on Olof Linton, "Kyrka och ämbete i Nya testamentet," in *En bok om kyrkan*, pp. 114-115, 125-131.

to the New Testament than from anywhere else. It also makes it easier for us to understand why such a view of the ministry should be attractive at a time when the Church is weak and particularly among the ordained clergy themselves. But to understand this will not keep us from a theological examination and criticism of such a view.[28] The problem of correctly interpreting the Gospel and the sacraments in our day is a difficult one, and the answer is perhaps not made easier but rather more awkward when those who preach the Gospel and administer the sacraments have a conception of the ministry which from a human point of view can be understood in psychological terms, but which does not conform to the specific and particularly exacting task, entrusted to these persons, of displaying a disinterested generosity rather than an acquisitive self-centredness.

This brings us back to what we called the "greatest real problem" of the ministry: how are we to administer the gifts which Christ has given to men without growing impatient at the slow response or at the fact that frequently only fragments of His gifts are received? What would happen if we began to read the New Testament from this point of view? It would mean that we should see Christ continually at work with His apostles, who time and time again misunderstood Him. This in fact is the normal order of things when the Gospel comes into the world. It would also mean that we should see in the New Testament Epistles the same process operating between the writers of these letters and those to whom they wrote, the constant return to the elements of the faith, the struggle against wrong interpretations, apostasy, the works of the law, and, last but by no means least, the constant

[28] It must be understood, unfortunately, that in Sweden New Testament exegesis can not only fail in its critical task at this point but also at times defend obvious misinterpretations with exegetical arguments. Every exegete knows that the idea of the minister in the Christian Church, cherished by certain Churches, as a counterpart to the priest of the Old Testament has no basis in the New. The term ἱερεύς is used in the New Testament of Christ (Heb. v.5-10, vii.17-28) and of all Christians (Rev. 1.5) but never of the ministers of the Church. In spite of this, Riesenfeld in *En bok om kyrkans ämbete*, pp. 68-69, draws a parallel between the Old Testament and New Testament ministries. He explains the universal priesthood in the New Testament as the product of a process of democratisation. Our starting-point is to be a "special" New Testament ministry. The serious thing in all this is the context of which the whole of this argument is part.

encouragement in suffering. This is the normal life of the congregation, and this is the normal business of the ministry.[29] But it is even more important that the minister himself is in the same situation. The encounter between "the old Adam" and Christ, "the new Adam," is not limited to the mission field, but takes place whenever the Gospel is preached. The death of which baptism is the sign takes place afresh in every victory over evil, for then the old is put to death and the new raised to life. The tendency to monophysitism in the ministry does not, of course, mean that those who espouse such a view are blind to this slow growth. It is a fact of everyday experience. But it does mean that they regard the situation as inconsistent with true faith. Faith for them should be "evident," mature, and in a higher class than that of the missionary situation. It should not have to endure having the Gospel and baptism proclaimed as *news*, but should be moving on to some further refinement with its "point of departure" well behind it. We have seen that a monophysitism such as this becomes awkward when confronted with the humanity of Christ, His agony in Gethsemane, His temptations, His references to God as someone distinct from Him and even as the God who forsakes Him. The modern emphasis on the divine nature of the Church and ministry is merely a consequence of the same tendency in Christology. There are many reasons for this, but perhaps at the very bottom it is a reaction to liberal theology and an unresolved and unsettled conflict in the sphere of the interpretation of scripture.[30]

There is no doubt that the most important event since the Reformation has been the emergence of biblical criticism. Any idea that this development can be reversed is quite unrealistic. It is obvious to all those who are theologically literate—among whom in particular we should include the ministry of the Church in the West—and increasingly to others

[29] The actions of the ministry—the distribution of the means of grace—do not presuppose that "faith" is a static possession on the part of the recipient, but aim at *eliciting* faith. In this regard the period of the Reformation is classical. On worship as "Reizung zum Glauben," see Vajta, *Theologie des Gottesdienstes*, pp. 224-230, Ivarsson, *Predikans uppgift*, pp. 35-68.

[30] See here Gergard Ebeling, "Die Bedeutung der historisch-kritischen Methode für die protestantische Theologie und Kirche," in *Z.T.K.*, 1950, pp. 1-46.

who have even an ordinary school education, that the Bible is a literary product with a simple account of human origins, the investigation of which requires no more than accepted rules of procedure. But only to a very limited extent has this insight made any impression on the preaching or teaching of the Word, so far as such preaching or teaching is carried out by the ministry of the Church. The form of preaching in our day is determined by norms which were established before the emergence of biblical criticism, and attempts to give a fresh interpretation to preaching generally look back to the period of the Reformation or to some earlier event in which the problems raised by modern study of the Bible were unrecognised. The consequence of all this may well be the emergence of a type of ecclesiastical speech that lacks elementary honesty. One of the strengths of the generation which witnessed the triumph of historical criticism was that many of its leading exponents, in Sweden notably Einar Billing, tried to exploit its positive achievements in the preaching and teaching of the Church.[31] But the anti-liberal theology which followed the First World War did not exercise itself unduly on this task. This undoubtedly explains the monophysitic character which, as we saw above, marks this school of theology at certain points. Inevitably the harvest of such a distortion is a loss of contact with those who hear the Gospel, and an inability to enter into dialogue with the man who has doubts and reservations in matters of faith. But those who make the humanity of Christ a living reality for the people to whom they speak are able to incorporate the findings of biblical criticism into the ministerial acts of the Church. To suppose that this will make us lose sight of the divinity of Christ indicates that we have failed to accept that the incarnation ever took place at all.

Baptism and the Church

In early Christianity baptism was clearly regarded as the door of the Church. Once the baptised had passed this door,

---

[31] One example is Einar Billing's address to the Swedish Bible Society, printed in the annual review of the Society for 1922 under the title, "The Wonders of God's Law," and published in 1923; see especially pp. 25-30. Cf. also *Herdabref*, pp. 45-52, and another work, *Universitet och kyrka*, 1923.

however, many other opportunities were provided to allow the new life which had been received in baptism to develop, and apart from these such growth was not possible. This same general view prevailed during the Lutheran Reformation, at which time baptism was regarded as in one sense extending to every part of the Christian life, but for this very reason was not completed with the liturgical act (then almost always infant baptism). We assume that all this is generally understood.[1] The problem with which we shall deal in this section relates to the consequences of this basic concept in our present situation where we have national Churches which are based on infant baptism, but once this baptism has taken place, there is no further development in the spiritual growth of the baptised. What does this mean for our view of the Church? There are particularly good reasons, as we shall see, for including the present section in the chapter which deals with Spirit and Word.

Our insistence on the openness of the Church has been a major point in the argument above. The Church is based on a commission, and since this commission extends to "all nations," it will not be fulfilled until it reaches to the furthest corner of the globe. Each new birth continually increases the humanity which is the object of Christ's seeking and coming, and therefore a national Church which baptises infants is continually in a missionary situation and is already obedient to the summons to evangelise within its own land, independently of any "foreign" mission which it undertakes.[2] But this openness is only one side of the matter. Though baptism is the first sacrament, it should not be the last. It is followed (in the case of infant baptism) by instruction which leads to the second sacrament and to the Lord's table. If confirmation precedes first communion, neither this confirmation nor this communion should be the last, but on the contrary, if baptism is the door of the Church, it is the entrance also into a continually new

[1] Cf. Cullmann, *Early Christian Worship*, pp. 82-83. In regard to the Reformation see Luther's interpretation of baptism in the Larger Catechism of 1529.

[2] The folk church, according to Billing, is therefore world mission as such. See, e.g., his *Herdabref*, pp. 68, 93-94, also Oscar Krook, "Kyrkobegreppets förnyelse i svensk teologi," in *En bok om kyrkan*, pp. 251-254, and Billing, *I katekesundervisningens tjänst*, pp. 143-144.

K

hearing of the word, renewed study, renewed communion, and renewed prayer and praise day by day.[3] If openness towards mankind is one aspect, *fellowship within the congregation* is the other. The communion or koinonia of the baptised is an indispensable part of life in the body of Christ (1 Cor. XII.12 ff.).[4]

Openness towards men and the nurture of the Spirit within the fellowship of the congregation are theoretically easy to combine, and in the daily life of the national Churches of the eighteenth and nineteenth centuries in particular such a combination was regularly found. These huge, all-inclusive national Churches were, however, incapable of keeping their many members close to the means of grace which follow baptism and are intended to complete the work of baptism in the daily putting to death of the old and resurrection of the new. The aspect of communion, on the other hand, i.e. common prayer, confession, praise and mutual discipline, was frequently taken over by sectarian groups, but these had lost sight of the openness of the Church which was based on Christ's death for the *world*. The increasing numerical and spiritual emptiness of the national Churches and the emergence of free Churches were both signs of the times. Oddly enough, the two circumstances were related to one another, and the cause in each case was a minimising of the significance of baptism. In the national Churches baptism ceased to have any meaning since the baptismal act was not followed, at least to any great extent, by other new works of Christ which are essential to the understanding of baptism. In the free Churches a great deal was said about conversion, regeneration, adoption as sons, and so on, but there was a failure to connect all these acts with baptism; and where baptism was practised, it was hardly ever regarded as an act of God involving the baptised, and mostly as a confessional act on the part of the person baptised.[5] It is perfectly evident that in the twentieth century a period of reappraisal is necessary for these two distinct Church types,

[3] Cf. Lampe, *Seal*, pp. 304-305, in regard to the connexion between infant baptism and the work of catechising in the Reformation.

[4] Cf. Anders Nygren, "Corpus Christi," in *En bok om kyrkan*, pp. 20-23. The exhortations in Rom. XII.4-21 are also of importance in this connexion.

[5] Cf. Anders Nygren, "Dopet i ekumenisk belysning," in *S.t.k.*, 1959, pp. 220-221.

each by itself one-sided. The national Churches are aware that they have lost the communion aspect of their life in the body of Christ, and the free Churches that they have closed certain windows to the outside world which ought to have been kept open. The period of ecumenical awareness, to name one factor, is heavy with possibilities for the future.[6] It is of particular importance to us in the present discussion that this awareness should not be translated into practical action too quickly but confined to the studies of the theologians. Our major task, therefore, is to analyse the problem theologically.

One of the benefits available to the baptised after baptism is the frequent celebration of the Eucharist and in particular the most important benefit of all—the continuing service of divine worship. There are, however, other aspects of the Church's life which should be mentioned here, e.g. church discipline. Mt. xviii.15-17, a passage which records Jesus's own words about discipline, refers quite clearly to expulsion from the fellowship of the Church. Indeed, the total subordination of the Church to the Gospel is also expressed in the New Testament writings in terms which suggest that the very *expulsion* of a notorious offender from the Church is taken to be a "judgment" passed on the guilty person in advance before the last judgment of all, in order that he may thereby be saved at this last judgment (1 Cor. v.5).[7] We get on quite the wrong track, therefore, when we isolate Church discipline from its direct connexion with the preaching of the Gospel, and turn it instead into a special *nota ecclesiae* which is added to preaching and the sacraments as a third sign by which the Church is to be recognised. Here as always Luther is instinctively right in his interpretation of the Bible.[8] He speaks in positive terms of Church discipline as a proper and useful ordinance, but he does not include it among the essential marks of the Church.

[6] See also the well-known discussion of the "ecumenical triangle" in Lesslie Newbigin, *The Household of God*, 1953, pp. 30-31, 94-98, 111, 131-134. The three sides of the triangle are "Protestant, Catholic, and Pentecostal."

[7] Cf. 1 Cor. xi.28-32. On the use of Matthew and Paul in the early period, see Elert, *Abendmahl*, pp. 71-88.

[8] See Gösta Hök, "Luther's Doctrine of the Ministry," in *S.J.T.*, 1954, pp. 16-40. Bengt Hallgren, "Luthers syn på kyrkotukten," in *Svensk missionstidskrift*, 1955, pp. 225-227, and also Ivarsson, *Predikans uppgift*, pp. 108-109.

When later theologians did, their concept of the Church of necessity became legalistic. It has been sometimes held that Calvin was the source of this more legalistic line in the Reformed tradition, but this view has no historical basis. In his doctrine of the marks of the Church Calvin followed Luther and the Augsburg Confession.[9] The addition of "la discipline ecclésiastique" to the Gospel and sacraments as a third "marque de l'Église" was indeed to be found quite early in some of the Calvinist Churches, but it was never universally accepted. The Reformed Church in France, for example, rejected it.[10] In the revivalist movements of the last century, on the other hand, Church discipline as a visible mark of a true and pure Church was often strongly emphasised, quite independently of the old confessional boundaries. At times the controversies about Church discipline and the purity of the Eucharist stimulated the establishment of free Churches in this period, including some which broke away from Lutheran national Churches.

To say that it is theologically untenable to make Church discipline a third sign of the Church does not mean, however, that there is no longer any need for discipline in the huge, all-inclusive national Churches. The opposite is true. At the present time Church discipline is compromised chiefly by the reasons which are mainly advanced to justify it. A minister who automatically refuses to remarry divorced persons is generally acting on the basis of an insufficiently considered concept of marriage as an unrepeatable sacrament, and is consequently operating with a crypto-Roman Catholic concept which has no basis in the Bible. If at the same time he fails to exercise discipline where it is proper and where he can do so without going against ecclesiastical or civil law, e.g. among those preparing for confirmation, his immediate and automatic severity in regard to marriage helps to make it more difficult to maintain a sound and reasonable position in questions relating to Church discipline.[11] The primary aim of Church discipline in our time should probably be to define what is the irreducible minimum

---

[9] See François Wendel, *Calvin*, 1963, pp. 297-298.
[10] Cf. René Voeltzel, *Vraie et fausse Église*, 1956, pp. 100.
[11] On the question of marriage cf. Sundby, *Luthersk äktenskapsuppfattning*, pp. 255-301.

of actual participation in the life of the congregation which is required for election to or service in any office in which *decisions of vital importance for the spiritual life of the Church are made.* In this matter it is incumbent upon the Christian Church to claim certain privileges from the state and any other secular authority. Such a claim does not imply any drift towards legalism, but on the contrary is *a safeguard of the Gospel* as the ground and source of the Church. We have frequently stressed above that it is difficult at times to discern the implications of the Gospel and to see in what direction it summons the Church to move. The Church maintains its vitality only when individuals within it come to understand what this difficult decision involves. No one can understand what he has not personally experienced in the Gospel. The situation becomes abnormal if national Churches include the few who are part of the inner life of the local Church, but who on account of their smallness of numbers are not able to influence decisions affecting the Church at large, and also the majorities who are permanently outside the worshipping community and yet on account of their numerical strength direct the internal affairs of the local Church. This is a disciplinary problem of supreme importance in our time. We shall go astray if we make the question of Church affiliation central. The real problem is different, and concerns election to positions in which decisions about the spiritual life of the Church are made.[12]

Baptism we have said, is a door into the Church. The practice of infant baptism in national Churches, however, is open to serious question. For in the case of infant baptism instruction must follow. If it can be shown that instruction does not in fact follow, the time has come for a critical examination of infant baptism. On the other hand it cannot be seriously disputed that we cannot continue the practice and at the same time employ a concept of membership which excludes the baptised from the Church and treats them as outsiders.[13] Even those who linger on the fringes of the Church—those who have theological difficulties, or hardly ever come to worship, or have known only

---

[12] Cf. Wingren, *Living Word*, pp. 183, footnote, and 189-190, and the same writer's *Kyrkan och samhället*, 1958, pp. 15-18.

[13] Cf. Oulton, *Holy Communion*, pp. 127, 186-188.

a fragment of the picture of Jesus which we have in the synoptic Gospels—these too have all passed into the Church through the door of baptism. The operative principle for the Church at this point is that of patience, for involved directly or indirectly in this situation is a pastoral concern for all, even if they have no contribution to make and as far as worship, confession and the Eucharist are concerned, are merely onlookers. But on a different level these persons have part in the decisions made by their Churches in which the very cup of salvation which the Church holds out to men can become subject to legislation through change in ritual, Church order, or handbooks of instruction. All these may be freely changed, but the purpose of any change must be to further the Gospel.[14] But those who have not experienced the Gospel for themselves cannot discern this purpose. Baptism is the entrance to this life which is lived each day in the strength the Gospel, for the life of baptism is life under the Spirit and the Word. The attitude of patience in a local parish situation which involves the pastoral oversight of individuals is a protection for the Gospel against the law, except when decisions are reached in Churches by persons whose indifference to the Gospel is plain and yet who also seek to govern the Church as a whole. In this situation patience ceases to be patience and becomes instead mere carelessness. Those who feel that they are incapable of anything but the most nominal commitment to the Gospel need not on that account be excluded from the fellowship of the Church. But none of those who are nominally committed have any right to demand that their minimum commitment shall suffice for all others. No one person embodies the totality of which each has a part. The whole Gospel belongs to the Church, and the Church must insist that its treasure is safeguarded in its entirety. This is a problem of Church discipline which is subordinate to the Gospel and therefore to the only authority which the Church has.

The other traditional expressions of Church discipline are also important in their place. Each is a corollary of the basic requirement that the Gospel which is given to the Church

---

[14] See von Campenhausen and H. Bornkamm, *Bindung und Freiheit*, pp. 24-25, 38-48.

may not be offered to those who are notorious sinners and consequently refuse to put the old to death. They refuse, that is, to apply to themselves the significance of baptism (the putting to death of the old and the resurrection of the new) and so cannot receive what follows after baptism in the Church (absolution and the Eucharist).[15] Here again we see that the whole of the Christian life is included in baptism and all that follows it merely unfolds what is given in baptism.[16] To be baptised means to submit to a conversion of Adam's fall and to be refashioned in the image of Christ. The movement in Adam's fall is from life to death and it cannot be altered unless the contrary and painful movement is made from death to life. The image of Christ exhibits both the cross and the resurrection, and man is refashioned in His image when he takes up his cross and turns his eyes towards the eternal life which is yet to come. And the cross which we take up is always some concrete reality of our daily existence which points us to a journey that will end in death. All that the individual experiences in the Church after baptism takes place within his actual existence and assists him to fulfil his baptism. At the same time those among whom he is set share the same experiences, hear the same lessons in the course of the Christian year, receive the same word of forgiveness and taste the same bread and wine. But their problems and difficulties and the "ways" which they must travel are quite different. The doubt and temptation in which baptism comes to its fulfilment in the life of each believer is so much hidden from sight that any growth in holiness is concealed, even when it occurs in full view of men and in the midst of the workaday world in which, to all outward appearance, men's lives are wholly interwoven, and all is open to view.[17] This fellowship in the body of Christ with its vast individual differences is the Christian Church. Daily life must keep going if the fellowship of believers is to be preserved from artificiality. Taking part in the life of a religious group

---

[15] Church discipline does not by any means "purify" the Church, for the worst sins in God's sight are not the open and obvious ones, but will be hidden until the last day. Cf. Prenter, *Skabelse*, pp. 568-569.

[16] Cf. also Davies, *Spirit*, pp. 123-124.

[17] None has rivalled Luther in his discussion of this invisible aspect of sanctification in daily life, generally in a bitter attack on the monasteries, in which the

which meets in a place apart from where we work or dwell is helpful from time to time, but it is not the same thing as the Church, which is a territorial community comprising those who live in its vicinity.[18]

Here we come to the heart of the meaning of communion or koinonia. No external expressions of fellowship are so liable to corruption as the highest. The lower forms of fellowship are usually fenced around by so many protective devices that attainment of the highest type of fellowship in them is precluded, but in return they cannot easily be wholly destroyed. There is, however, a constant danger that even the highest social groups of home and family, which are capable of providing an inexpressibly rich fellowship in which the integrity of each individual is respected, may become totally corrupted. In the history of the Church the local congregation is one such outstanding expression of koinonia, and even to this day an occasional example is to be found in Europe—perhaps a parish church whose life is interwoven with that of its district, in which no clear line is drawn between the life of the congregation and the life of the community. But in many other places local congregations are mere skeletons without any real koinonia, and what fellowship there is flourishes in religious groups apart from daily life and work, though often in a sedate and peculiarly vapid form, lacking the firmness which the skeleton gives to the body.[19] We have shown above that the modern

---

aim was to make sanctification visible by escaping from daily life, but from which the real mortifications have in fact been removed. If there are mortifications in the monasteries, Luther says, there is no possibility of being sanctified by them. Our burdens are laid upon us in the world outside, among those whom we consider to be wicked. See, e.g., the remarkable passage in *De votis monasticis*, 1521, W.A. VIII.588, 10-32.

[18] See Billing, *Den svenska folkkyrkan*, pp. 62-65, and the interesting reference to Schlatter's thesis about the natural relationships of life as an aid to the fellowship of the Church. The connexion made by the territorial Church between human and Christian is in fact a fruit of the *incarnation*: through Christ the divine nature has been poured out into human nature and can no longer be separated from it.

[19] This is the problem dealt with by Einar Billing in his writings on the concept of the Church. He tries to solve the problem by operating with different "circles" within the territorial Church, concentric circles around the means of grace, among which the circle of those who partake of the Eucharist is the innermost and least numerous. See Billing, *Den svenska folkkyrkan*, e.g. pp. 9-14, where he speaks of breaking through the circles by means of intercessory prayer. Cf. also Billing's *Kyrka och stat i vårt land i detta nu*, 1942, pp. 25-27.

tendency is to think in terms of the group, and Church and sacraments are nowadays discussed in such a way as to neglect individual problems. It is not made clear that the Gospel is always addressed to the individual in his guilt—never to a group, but always to the individual who is in bondage to the law and upon whom is laid the pressure of his own troublesome local situation, which is expressed concretely in his working relationships with his fellow-men and involves particular attitudes and associations. The old nature is given individual expression in every man, and its features are recognisable from his own conflicts long since past; and yet this old nature is the Adam of prehistory, who is still tempted every day in a thousand little ways, and if he yields to his temptations, they banish faith and love. But now Christ Himself, who proved victorious in the most strenuous temptation of all, enters in the Church into all the problems of these different individuals through the Gospel which is offered to all and the Eucharist which is given to all. Everyone gets the *same* gift from the means of grace, and yet what each gets is *different*.[20] The outworking of baptism means that individual expressions of the old nature are put to death and individual expressions of the new brought into being. All this takes place on the level of daily life and in man's actual existence, and yet it is a fruit of word and sacrament. *This is communion*.[21] It is a fellowship which is too deep for words, and can be articulated only in the common prayer and praise of the Church.

Such is the nature of this fellowship that it becomes pointless to ask whether it is fellowship with God or with our neighbour, with Christ in His Church or our fellow Church members. It is basically fellowship with Christ, participation in His body, and our growing into His death and resurrection.[22] But the one thing that dislocates the fellowship which we have with other men is the continuing vitality of our old nature and the absence of the new, and also, of course, the presence of the

[20] Hugo Odeberg, "Den nutida individualismen och kyrkotanken i Nya testamentet," in *En bok om kyrkan*, pp. 71-73.

[21] Cf. Aulén, *Eucharist and Sacrifice*, p. 73, Richardson, *Introduction*, pp. 376-377, on fellowship and communion.

[22] Cf. Come, *Human Spirit*, pp. 82-83, 121, for a discussion of "image and likeness" and the Spirit's renewal of man.

old nature and the absence of the new in them. Our relationship to God and to our neighbour is the same reality, seen from
two aspects. Christ's coming to the Church and to all these
different individuals within it and their incorporation into
Him involves therefore a process of disciplining and putting
to death those forces which are destructive of fellowship in
society. It also involves a regenerative process through which
something comes into being which is one with God and which
in consequence can unite men and incorporate them into a
single body.[23] The word "body" is used here to mean both the
body of Christ and the body corporate of the Church—its
members are different from one another and each has a different
task, but the same blood circulates through all of them.[24] Self-
examination to seek out the unseen temptations which burden
every man is a work of the Spirit through which Christ
triumphs over the ancient enemy against whose temptations He
struggled in the wilderness and on the cross. His triumph allays
the points of conflict in human relationships, takes away the
spirit of pettiness, and causes generosity to prevail even where
judgment must be passed upon the erratic ways of a fellow-
being, since it would be even less kind to be lenient. In this
critical self-examination the old nature is put to death and
thereby the work of baptism continually repeated, just as its
work of regeneration is fulfilled in daily obedience, trust,
and joy. This is what Luther means by being "clothed in our
baptism." The other sacrament, repeated over and again
unlike baptism, is the coming again of Christ to clothe us once
more in our daily garb and to safeguard the work of baptism
until the final death and resurrection.[25] This connexion between
the sacrament and daily life *can* be maintained even in a church
where worship is poorly attended, and there is no need to
adopt a purely sectarian view of the sacraments or one influenced by a doctrine of Eucharistic sacrifice. At this point
the number of those taking part in worship is irrelevant. The
determining factor is what kind of *theology* we have.

[23] Aulén, *Eucharist and Sacrifice*, pp. 69-79., properly refers to Luther's sermon
on the Eucharist of 1519.

[24] Cf. John A. T. Robinson, *The Body*, 1952, pp. 46-48. See Eph. ii.14-16.

[25] Cf. Prenter, *Skabelse*, pp. 508, 587. See the conclusion of the fourth section
of Luther's Larger Catechism.

In His command to evangelise Christ speaks of baptising and preaching (Mk. xvi.15 f., cf. Mt. xxviii.19). Neither one, however, is an end in itself; both have a permanent function to fulfil, so that the Church continually comes into existence through baptism and the preaching of the Gospel, just as each individual believer turns back each day to his baptism and the Gospel.[26] None who is living the Christian life can ever come to a point ahead of the Gospel and baptism before the final death. The events which follow baptism and the first hearing of the Gospel take place in order that what is promised and bestowed in the Gospel and baptism may be developed to the fullest extent, for not everything can happen on the day of our baptism or of our first hearing of the Gospel. The perspective which is opened out on the day of baptism includes everything that will take place before the eschatological consummation. We see this most clearly in the exhortatory passages of the New Testament and the many admonitions and commandments which were intended to regulate the conduct of the baptised between baptism and physical death. As Jacob Jervell has shown conclusively, at least as far as Paul is concerned, the New Testament is to an astonishingly great extent "baptismal exhortation." That which has taken place once for all in baptism is the basis for what is done—or ought to be done—afterwards in the whole of the Christian's daily life.[27] Only in the resurrection of the dead and eternal life will we fully see what has been given in baptism.[28] The old is put aside in baptism and the new is given, and the old must be resisted and put aside in the daily moral struggle in which the new man is formed in conflict with temptation. But in the eternal life there will no longer be any temptation to combat, for then all things will be new (Rev. xxi.9) and the last judgment will have been passed over all that is old (Rev. xx.10–xxi.4).[29]

The Church is therefore continually in a missionary situation. There never comes a time in the Christian life when we cease to live by the Gospel and live instead by commandment or instruction, for commandments and admonitions are

---

[26] Cf. Hendry, *Holy Spirit*, p. 73, Marxsen, *Der Evangelist Markus*, p. 92.
[27] See Jervell, *Imago Dei*, pp. 231-256.
[28] *Ibid.*, pp. 256-284.   [29] Cf. Richardson, *Introduction*, pp. 244-245.

themselves instruments for the outworking of baptism and the Gospel. The view that baptism and the Gospel are to be confined to some initial period, after which the Eucharist or commandments or something else takes their place, is a deviation from the Gospel and is to be attributed to the strange disappearance of *anthropology* which is a characteristic of modern anti-liberal theology.[30] This missionary situation is permanent, since the fallen Adam of man's prehistory is to be found in "all nations" and is the object of the world mission of the Church which originated in the resurrection of Christ and the subsequent descent of the Spirit. It is still present even in the Church and among the baptised, and will continue to be present until the "old Adam," as it used to be called, returns to the dust in physical death. Each Sunday when the Gospel is preached the Spirit is again present, as at Pentecost, and the Gospel is again preached to the pagan world in which law and guilt hold sway. Exhortatory precepts follow the Gospel and originate in the constantly renewed preaching of the Gospel,[31] and are in fact demands for a daily "conversion," and therefore for daily obedience to the summons of the apostolic Gospel to the Gentile world (Lk. xxiv.46 f., Acts ii.36-41, x.39-42, xiv. 15 f., xvii.26-31).[32] Those who have received the once for all baptism are nourished in the repeated Eucharist which is given to the members of the Church to revive the communion which they have with one another. But it is baptism that is brought to fulfilment in the Eucharistic meal. The true baptism is the

---

[30] The "commandment of Christ" is then conceived to be especially related to matters of Church order, and Church order separated from the preaching of the Gospel. As a result it loses its flexibility—it is no longer an *instrument*. The Eucharist also loses its connexion with the Gospel, with the result that the distribution of the elements (communion) is pushed out to the periphery, while other aspects of the liturgy become predominant, notably the offering or presentation of the elements to God. Both "commandment" and "Eucharist," if understood in this way and separated from baptism and the Gospel, can be fitted remarkably well into ideas of succession in the doctrine of the ministry. Missionary preaching, that is, is not a privilege of the ministry, and baptism has been administered by all Christians from the earliest times. The attempt to orient the concept of the Church around baptism and the Gospel is consequently regarded as a threat. *Hinc illae lacrimae!*

[31] In regard to Luther see Ivarsson, *Predikans uppgift*, pp. 113-133.

[32] Cf. Dibelius in *Coniectanea*, NO. XI, 1947, p. 52, also Hägglund, in *Studier*, pp. 78-88.

death and resurrection of Christ, and the benefits of these are given to men through all the means of grace. None of these acts of the Church adds anything to baptism or the Gospel, and what is done after baptism and the preaching of the Gospel merely unfolds new aspects of what was given at the first.[33] This is why it is so important that the legislative bodies of the Church, which have the power to change the external ordering of the Church, should consist of people who look at the questions with which they are confronted from the point of view of the Gospel. It is not, for example, "popular vote" that is the decisive thing. *The Gospel is sovereign authority in the household of faith.*

The purpose of the Church's ministry among men is that salvation shall come to those who accept what it has to offer. Even those acts which involve judgment, e.g. the withholding of the word of forgiveness or of the Eucharist, as well as the word of direct rebuke (i.e. any acts of ecclesiastical discipline) have the object of saving those at whom they are directed. We become members of the Church through the basic acts of baptism and the Gospel named by Christ in His command to evangelise. Once we have passed through the door of baptism into the fellowship of the Church, we enter into "the acts which follow," among which the Eucharist is the most important, but in all of which we see the continued nurture of the Spirit brought to us in different forms of the word. The whole activity of the Church in relation to God and to our fellow-members— prayer and praise to God, mutual service and encouragement— all this is part of the fellowship which the Church enjoys and passes on to its members old and newly admitted alike. The ministry exists in order that baptism, preaching, the Eucharist, and the word of forgiveness, may continue to be heard and administered, and is thus the servant of those acts which are set above the ministry. These acts do not derive their validity from the ministry but from the risen Christ Himself who now lives in them through His word, for no ministerial act is

[33] This holds good *even of Church discipline* and of *the power to bind*; indeed it is true of expulsion from the congregation (1 Cor. v.5). Luther is in the line of the New Testament in this. See Hök, *S.J.T.*, 1954, pp. 26-34. When the Church does something for men in its ministry, what it does aims at their *salvation*. This is true without exception. Hence all that the Church does is subordinate to baptism and the Gospel.

performed which is not accompanied by His word.[34] The ministry is subordinate to Christ's own personal acts through which He comes to men offering the redemption which He has obtained. It is a serving or distributive ministry and cannot bestow power but merely passes on that which in itself already possesses power by virtue of Christ's word. The object in ordaining ministers, consecrating bishops or commissioning missionaries is that Christ's work of redemption may be extended, since the acts for which these persons are responsible are Christ's own redemptive acts. Those who are called to a particular ministry seek to make all that they do a means by which the acts of Christ may come to men, and through this ministry with its offer of forgiveness new advances are made in reaching men. *But ordination itself is not a redemptive act for the ordained*, and if the ordained have doubt concerning God's adoption of them and their salvation, it is to their baptism, to the Eucharist, and to the Gospel, that they must turn for help. It is of no benefit to fall back on consecration or ordination.

The Anglican, J. G. Davies, expressed the same thought in carefully weighed words: "Orders cannot be regarded as a *sacramentum evangelii* since they have no direct bearing on the salvation of the recipients—ordination cannot be said to be the means of conveying to the candidate the fruits of God's graciousness, of His saving activity."[35] This statement is of considerable importance for our interpretation of baptism and the Church. In defining the relationship between Christ and the Church we tend to interpolate the ministry between the two. But this is to set the clergy or ministry above the Church, and implies that Christ's first act was to appoint ministers, and that only after these had begun to function did the "Church" come into being. In this case the true Church is the priesthood, episcopacy, or papacy, for on this view ministers mediate between the Church and God. But the ground of the Church is in fact baptism and the Gospel which were given by Christ (they are expressly mentioned in His command to evangelise), and since they were *given*, there were at the beginning "apostles," i.e.

[34] Cf. Askmark, *Ämbetet i den svenska kyrkan*, pp. 4-9, also Heubach, *Die Ordination zum Amt der Kirche*, pp. 115-117.

[35] Davies, *Spirit*, p. 176. Baptism and the Eucharist are *sacramenta evangelii*, "the two Gospel sacraments" (*ibid.*, pp. 84, 123, etc.).

men who were sent out with the means through which Christ was present among men, i.e. with baptism and the Gospel. When men received them and were baptised and heard the Gospel, the Church came into being. Still today the same process is at work and Christ is creating His Church with His word. Neither baptism nor the proclamation of the Gospel are privileges given to the bishop or minister. Children have long since been baptised even by women, and the same is true of the preaching of the Gospel. Reservations about women preaching have typically been expressed in regard to the preaching which is part of the Church's central act of worship, the Eucharist. But the Eucharist is not a doorway into the Church, it is rather a communion for those who have already entered the Church. Little by little, however, it was restricted exclusively to the local minister or priest after the original missionary task which had been carried out in the period of the early Church had come to an end.[36] The acts which are the ground of the Church and through which persons are received into the Church are not bound to the ministry even by tradition, though generally they are performed by the ministry. Christ Himself is at work in baptism and the Gospel creating His Church. *The primary source from which the Church comes into being is the free and open font of baptism.*

The significance of a statement such as this is increased by the mutual recognition of one another's baptismal acts which prevails among the major denominations. To assert that a person is baptised in the name of the Father, and of the Son, and of the Holy Ghost is to treat that person as having been baptised with Christ's own baptism.[37] We do not ask if that particular Church has the proper creeds or the true ministry in apostolic succession. We do not even ask if the sacrament

---

[36] Modern missionaries in Asia and Africa are in one respect more like the apostles of the early Church than our modern parish priests or ministers in the West. On the interpretation of 1 Pet. ii.9 we must, of course, begin with Ex. xix.5-6. On the other hand we have no reason to assume a "special priesthood" in the New Testament. No group in the early Church is designated ἱερεῖς as the Old Testament priesthood was. Riesenfeld's assertions about the democratisation of the functions of the ministry (*En bok om kyrkans ämbete*, pp. 68-69) have no real basis. Cf. in regard to the Reformers the illuminating discussion in Prenter, *Skabelse*, pp. 574-576.

[37] Cf. Lampe, *Seal*, pp. 242-243, 245.

has been celebrated by a minister or just an ordinary member of the Church, man or woman. What *has* happened is that this person has entered the Church through the door of baptism and received the gift of the Gospel. He is now in the Church. We therefore pass on immediately to "the acts which follow" —instruction in the faith, continued nurture in the word, confession, and the Eucharist. In doing all these things the Church is saying that *there exists in the world a single Church of Christ which is grounded on baptism, the first and never to be repeated sacrament.*[38] Precise definition is given to this basic view by the different denominations in a variety of language when at every baptism they proclaim unanimously the words of the Apostles' Creed: "I believe in *the* holy, catholic church."[39]

While admittedly these subsequent acts deepen the communion of the baptised with one another, in practice they also create divisions among different parts of the church catholic which is grounded on the one baptism. In particular the Eucharist has become an outward and visible sign of schism pointing to the divisions which exist among believers, whose baptism is at the same time acknowledged to be Christ's own baptism. On the ecumenical level it is reasonable in this situation to *start with baptism* and try to solve the complex problem of the unity of the Church from this starting-point. But on the local level where we have Churches situated in particular areas it is no less fruitful to take baptism as the starting-point. The early Christian Churches were designated by geographical names—Corinth, Philippi, Ephesus, Rome, etc. In places like Corinth and Galatia there were quite clearly very great divisions which we should nowadays call "divisions at the Lord's table" or "lack of intercommunion" (1 Cor. I.10-12, III. 3-5, IV.6, Gal. II. 11-13). And yet in spite of this Paul addresses the separate groups in these places in a way which clearly shows that he took it for granted that they were members of a single body and belonged to a single Church.[40] (The

---

[38] Cf. Torrance in *S.J.T.*, 1954, pp. 268-270.

[39] See also Torrance, *Royal Priesthood*, p. 105 on the Nicene Creed, baptism and the Eucharist.

[40] Cf. Nygren, *Christ and His Church*, pp. 98-99, 108-111, and also John Knox. *The Early Church and the Coming Great Church*, 1955, pp. 35-41.

existence of a great many different local Churches which lack any integral connexion in our modern city often seems to us quite artificial. The city is a unit whose means of communication break through the artificial boundaries of the Church. It would be a worthwhile task in our day to find out what are the real social groupings within the geographical unit of the city.) The concept of Christianity which is extending throughout the ecumenical movement is that the geographical division is primary (the Church in Sweden, the Church in South India, etc.) and that here discussions about local unions are of paramount importance.[41] But even on the local level in the narrower sense, e.g. in an industrial community where there are several competing places of worship, each belonging to a different denomination, it would be a recovery of the vitality of the early Church if the geographical aspect were again to come first. Christ has only one Church in one place, and all who take part in its worship regard themselves as members of it, even in their separation from one another.

This will have two or perhaps three things to say to us. In the first place, it increases our missionary responsibility for those who live in the same place but take no part in any worship at all. The mission of the Church does not take place in a vacuum, and mission, as the early Christian Church undertook it, involved the recognition of "limits" (see e.g. II Cor. x.13-16) when the Gospel was taken out to the ends of the earth (Acts 1.8).[42] In the second place, a local fellowship is always a fellowship of people who come together in their daily work to serve one another and whose coming together becomes a part of the communion of the Church. And the third thing, and in one way this is the common root of both world mission and daily service, is the unique relationship between Church and creation of which both of these activities are expressions: in its mission and diaconate the Church, which is the body of Christ, turns itself towards the whole of creation as servant.

[41] We should remember that the external order of the Church even in the New Testament was different in different places. This variety did not destroy its unity. Cf. von Campenhausen, *Kirchliches Amt*, pp. 326-332. We shall return to the question of large cities and territorial Churches in our last section below, when we shall deal with prayer and praise (worship).

[42] See also Rom. xv.19-24, I Thess. 1.4-8. Cf. Jacob Jervell, "Till spörsmålet om tradisjongrunnlaget for Apostlenes Gjerninger," in *N.t.t.*, 1960, pp. 160-175.

L

CHAPTER II

THE CHURCH AND CREATION

World Mission and the Diaconate

IN THE Gospels the work of Jesus has two aspects: He preaches the Gospel and He heals the sick (e.g. Mt. IV.23, Mk. 1.39). By exercising this twofold ministry He reveals that He is the promised Messiah (Lk. IV.17-21, and especially 18, 19, and also Mt. XI.5).[1] When later He sends out His disciples to carry out the work of redemption, those whom He commissioned, the twelve (Lk. IX.2) and even the seventy (Lk. X.9), are charged with the same task: they are to preach the Gospel and heal the sick. In His final commission after the resurrection we again find this combination of preaching and mighty works, e.g. in the concluding verses of the extant version of Mark's Gospel (Mk. XVI.15-18, 20). We also have the abundant evidence of Acts when the work of apostles is regularly described in terms of the same combination of word and deed (e.g. Acts VIII.4-8, XVI.17 f., and especially III.6-26). As Einar Billing has emphasised in his analysis of this twofold ministry, the two elements feed in to one another. The act of healing not only bestows physical health, but is also itself a *word*; it proclaims that the kingdom of God has come: "If it is by the Spirit of God that I cast out demons, then the kingdom of God has come upon you" (Mt. XII.28). And the word in turn, as we have frequently noted above, is not simply a verbal description of a condition which would still exist even without the explanation. On the contrary, the word of Jesus and of the apostles is an action through which something wholly new comes about. The word of forgiveness does away with guilt in the same effective manner

[1] For what follows see Billing, *De etiska tankarna*, pp. 298-309, Gustaf Wingren, "Eschatological Hope and Social Action," in *Lutheran World*, 1954, pp. 23-29, and Henrik Ivarsson, *Kyrkan och diakonin*, 1959, pp. 5-26. Throughout this section we shall examine preaching and "healing." Our concern is to hold word and work together, but at the same time to let the work or healing retain its own function side by side with the preached word.

as the word of command and healing does away with sickness.[2] Jesus is "mighty in deed and word" (Lk. xxiv.19). It should be stated at the outset that this double aspect of word and action which we have noted in the ministry of Jesus and the apostles is fundamental to the attitude which the Church today takes to its own ministry. The Church has an obligation to fulfil in regard to creation, and this obligation is divided into the two parts of word (mission) and action (diaconate). The specific biblical basis of the Church's mission is the proclamation of the Gospel to the nations which followed Christ's resurrection. It may be assumed that this would be fairly generally accepted. The specific biblical basis of the Church's diaconate or ministry of service is the healing of the sick which from the beginning was a regular part of both Jesus's own messianic activity and the mission of the apostles,[3] though this latter statement is not generally accepted.

The background against which both of these activities are carried out is one of conflict—a hostile power holds mankind in bondage. In our earlier discussion of the fall in the Old Testament we made reference to the double aspect of Adam's fall. Man is a slave to sin and does what is evil. But he is also in subjection to death and is haunted by the fear of losing his life. This double bondage is not just an idea which we find in a book, viz. the Bible. It is an experience common to all men apart altogether from what the Bible has to say. All men know what remorse means and are well aware of that peculiar human experience of bondage which is felt as fear of ill-health or of danger to life. In the Bible these two elementary experiences are interpreted in relation to God as loss of fellowship, in relation to the neighbour as the inability on man's part to do other than seek his own security, i.e. as a failure of love, and in relation to the world as a loss of the capacity to exercise dominion (cf. Rom. 1.18-32). If man's bondage consists in sin and death, then his redemption consists in forgiveness and life and therefore in the preached word, which removes guilt

---

[2] Cf. Billing, De etiska tankarna, pp. 304-308, also Försoningen, pp. 72-73, where he speaks of the dramatic character of the Gospel.

[3] See especially Ivarsson, Kyrkan, pp. 11, 13, 19. The feeding of the hungry, etc., belongs, of course, to the care of men's bodies. One can render such service in silence. But we cannot preach and remain silent at the same time.

from the conscience, and also in the life-giving activity of worship, which nurtures and heals the body.[4] In other words redemption is offered to God's creation through the Church's mission to the world and its diaconate or service of men. Redemption is thus the restoration or *recapitulatio* of creation.[5] That which is destroyed in Adam is restored in Christ (cf. Rom. v.15-19).

The distinction which Martin Luther made between spiritual and earthly government is expressed on the anthropological level as a distinction between "conscience" and "body." The word of the Gospel is to hold sway in the conscience and expel from it guilt and desperation, though the body has still to live in "the earth of works and of the cross." In Luther these distinctions, if we may use the phrase, are saturated with eschatology—the conscience was already "in heaven" through the Gospel, while the body, which had still to face death, was moving towards the life which the conscience had already attained.[6] What happened to the body followed close upon what had already come to pass in the conscience, and had a derivative value in relation to the Gospel which was present in the conscience. Sin was the root of death (Rom. v.12) and therefore the preaching of the Gospel was the ground of redemption. The victory of the Gospel in the conscience was followed by the emergence of life, gradually and with struggle, in the body, though the victory there would not be complete until the resurrection of the dead on the last day. The care of men's bodies had independent value, for the external part of creation was also of God, though from the standpoint of salvation this ministry of physical care and service of one's neighbour was of relatively minor significance. The *spiritual* use of the law, where the law drives a man to despair and forces him to turn to

---

[4] See also Mk. iii.14-15, Mt. x.7-8. The "serving of tables" by the deacons in Acts vi.1-6 is properly part of our discussion here. This service is parallel to the "ministry of the word," of which it was at first part. Sin is the source of death (Rom. v.12), the Gospel of the diaconate. And yet the dominion of death and the work of the diaconate are relatively independent in relation to the preaching of the Gospel, which is directed against sin.

[5] Cf. also Anton Fridrichsen, "Jesu kamp mot de urene ånder," in *S.t.k.*, 1929, pp. 304-314.

[6] E.g., W.A., xl. I. 213, 30-214,21 and 469, 23-27 (Larger Commentary on Galatians, 1535).

Christ, is hence designated its chief use, in comparison with which the civil use with its welter of daily occupations and the duties it involves is of minor significance.[7] "Serving tables" is defined also in the New Testament as a detached part of a greater original whole in which preaching and healing both were included from the beginning (Mk. iii.14 f. and parallels) but in which nevertheless preaching was the dominant factor, for it was the "ministry of the word" to which the apostles still felt they ought to devote themselves (Acts vi.2-4). Thus "mission" in earlier times had the predominance over "diaconate," to use the traditional terminology. In our present situation the reverse is rather the case. The Church's proclamation of the Gospel has often to be justified in America and Europe on the grounds that it has beneficial social consequences. Even more commonly, missionary work in Asia or Africa is defended on the grounds that it builds hospitals and provides doctors, etc. In both cases service, i.e. the care of men's bodies, is set above the preaching of the Gospel, i.e. the care of men's consciences.[8]

In such a situation it is easy to create the impression that the Church loses its real significance and purpose when, at home, welfare measures are increasingly adopted and economic aid to poorer nations becomes a concern to the better off inhabitants of America and Europe. This latter expression of concern is fairly recent, but it will certainly take precedence in the future, at the sacrifice to some extent of interest in world mission among the Churches in America and Europe. But when the Church and the Gospel appear to be found wanting in this regard and to be growing less important in the view of the ordinary man in the street, this is because the *Church itself* has a thoroughly secularised outlook, and hence inwardly accepts that the purpose for which it exists is to promote and bring about social and cultural advancement. But if the responsibility for these functions is assumed by others, e.g. by

---

[7] Cf. Runestam, *Den kristliga friheten hos Luther och Melanchthon*, p. 160. When we turn to examine the idea of recapitulation in the Church fathers we find here too that the victory over sin, Christ's victory in His temptations and on the cross, is the source of His victory over death on Easter Sunday. The resurrection flows from the victory on the cross.

[8] See here David Lindquist, *Varför diakoni?*, 1958, pp. 141-143.

national or international institutions, the Church has then no specific task to perform. We have previously seen, however, that to do what needs to be done in the world God the Creator has appointed and continues to uphold earthly government among all men, independently of the preaching of the Gospel.[9] The unrecognised demand which cries out through human hunger, thirst, and sickness, is sufficient to bring into operation throughout the earth a multitude of different occupations and activities. But Christ was not born to set this activity of law and good works into operation, nor was it for this that He died. The work of Christ is primarily the Gospel, and this Gospel which is proclaimed to all nations arises from His resurrection and is to be found only in the Church.[10] The Church may never abandon or curtail this objective, for there is nothing else which can take its place. The significance of the Gospel can be lightly dismissed only where the power of the law is no longer felt and where there is no sense of guilt, i.e. where no concern for the Gospel is felt. If man asks for forgiveness, only the Gospel, i.e. "mission," can offer a solution. But if it is a matter of food or clothing, there are many who can be of help. This has always been so. The problem is in no way a modern phenomenon. Many had fed the hungry and healed the sick before Christ and the early Church assumed this task for the good of men. The unique and supreme function of the Church is the preaching of the Gospel.[11] Here as elsewhere we lose our proportions when we lose sight of God's universal rule of law among men.

The sick, whom Jesus healed, were restored to health by His help only temporarily. The life which they regained was lived under the threat of death, and sooner or later was destroyed by death. But even though the gift which they received brought only a temporary cure, the gift was still given. That is to say,

[9] Cf. also Peter Brunner, in *Lutheran World*, 1958, pp. 246-247.

[10] Cf. Davies, *He Ascended*, pp. 169-171, on the ascension, also Koch, *Auferstehung*, pp. 240-241, on the connexion between Christ's resurrection body and the Church as the body of Christ.

[11] Luther's identification of *ecclesia* and *evangelium* as "spiritual government" in distinction from law, body, or "secular government," is to this extent justified. Cf. Törnvall, *Andligt och världsligt regemente hos Luther*, 1940, pp. 88-113. We shall return later in the present section to the weakness in this identification.

it is a mark of love that it gives, and some of its gifts are corruptible but others incorruptible. It is enough to know that the gift is good, and if it is, then it is worth sharing with our neighbour. The early Church preached the Gospel, but at the same time cared for the hungry and thirsty, and though this latter service had only a limited range, and could not do away with all the need in the world, it was still undertaken. The Church in this early period did not attempt to provide meals for all in need.[12] But the fact that other people do good does not absolve me from a similar responsibility, provided that my concern really is to do good and not just put a particular "Christian ethic" into effect. This would merely indicate an unhealthy desire to demonstrate the absence of any goodness outside the Church. Jesus's healing of the sick and the loving care shown by the early Church to those who suffered need are essentially of a kind, a relatively independent activity alongside the preaching of the Gospel and the Church's mission to the world.[13] When we turn from the New Testament and the early Church to the Lutheran Reformation, we discover that for the Reformers a man's calling in any station or work has sufficient justification in the need of his neighbour, and is also of some passing benefit to life on earth, or to the "body," as they expressed it. And all these secular or material vocations are included within the "earthly government," which is thus seen to be a large and distinctive form of diaconate in which all Christians live the life of baptism in their daily lives, bearing the cross for one another, and sharing with each other all the good things of creation—"food, clothing, house and home," in a word "daily bread."[14] Above and beside this diaconate, as in the early Church, there is the "spiritual government," which is the preaching of the Gospel, i.e. the mission of the Church, the proclaimed word, which is heard in the midst

[12] There is an original discussion of the earliest diaconate and the nature of the feeding in Bo Reicke, *Diakonie, Festfreude und Zelos*, 1951, pp. 25-27. Cf. also Nils Johansson, *Det urkristna nattvardsfirandet*, 1944, pp. 286-291.

[13] The Christian Church is responsible for these services to mankind, and this obligation to those who are outside the Church is implicit in the Church's fellowship with Christ. Cf. Paul S. Minear, "Gratitude and Mission in the Epistle to the Romans," in *Basileia*, 1959, pp. 42-48.

[14] See the connexion made by Luther between the first article and the fourth petition of the Lord's Prayer in his Shorter Catechism.

of the paganism of Antichrist, and which bestows the imperishable gift of the forgiveness of sins, life, and salvation.[15]

This brings us back to our discussion in the previous section where we dealt with baptism and the congregation. "Diaconate" refers to the daily service of all the baptised. It is the work of the members of the "body" in service of one another (1 Cor. XII. 5 ff.). There is a notable essay by Henrik Ivarsson on the meaning of the diaconate in which he closely identifies the diaconate with the fundamental responsibility which every man has for his fellow-man, a responsibility which is binding upon *every member of the Church*. Thus service cannot be replaced by *ad hoc* works of charity nor absorbed into a purely preaching or missionary diaconate, still less, of course, be concealed in an exclusively liturgical function. Deacons who evangelise, take part in liturgical acts, or engage in works of charity, are necessary, and there is enough for all of them to do. But the primary factor which gives rise to service is *baptism*. Our modern desire to have special dedication services whenever there is some particular work to be done in the Church is partially responsible for the disastrous harm which has been done to baptism. Every baptised Christian is a deacon, even though his service consists in the simplest of daily tasks for his fellow-man.[16] The Church must give heed to this expression of service, if it is not to lose what has been an essential aspect of its work among men from the very beginning. Jesus preached and healed the sick; so did the apostles. The Reformers also preached, but instead of healing they kept emphasising vocation, or quite simply a man's place of work, as the sphere in which baptism is to be carried into effect. In so doing they brought a great many forces into play whereby men might minister to one another. In a Lutheran parish in the seventeenth century it was impossible to distinguish between the civic community and the Church community. The leaders of the parish with their pastor in the midst were what we might call local government officials, but they were such on the basis of baptism, and even in the least spiritual of their activities were

---

[15] The folk churches of Europe represent world mission in that they bring the Word to the local congregations. Cf. Krook in *En bok om kyrkan*, pp. 251-255.

[16] See Ivarsson, *Kyrkan*, pp. 44-47, 53.

part of a community of prayer and worship. The separation between the civil and ecclesiastical communities which is taking place in Europe today cuts the Church off from the outside world, the very place in which the incarnation occurred, and from the mass of people who are slowly but surely becoming a purely political community—the State.[17] *In this situation the concept of vocation must be renewed as a matter of urgency.*[18] Only so can we maintain the balance between preaching and healing which existed at the beginning. Instead, however, we find ourselves with a theology which limits itself to the narrow concerns of preaching and the sacraments, turns its attention inward to the sanctuary, and leaves the outside world to group movements or "Moral Rearmament."

The situation of the Church in America clearly holds out new opportunities for doing something constructive in this area, and not simply on the practical level but also on the level of theory. In Europe we still have an original, medieval unity of Church and civic community, though this today is gradually being torn apart. To the extent that the Church in this situation may exhibit any concern for human life in its totality, such concern is expressed in a determination to maintain the façade of a national Church, even though the original unity which lies behind the façade is slowly disintegrating. Here the attempt to conserve is a failure. America, on the other hand, is a country, not yet fully developed and lacking a medieval history, in which groups of individuals are settling down and building. To the extent that there may exist in this situation any concern for human life in its totality, such concern is expressed in a determination to construct something in a relatively amorphous situation in which multitudes have no connexion with the Church, and all who are members of the Church are assigned different responsibilities.[19] Here the attempt to construct is a

[17] Cf. Lindquist, *Varför diakoni?*, p. 97. The performance of "works" turns us from the Church out to society.

[18] Einar Billing's works on vocation, the concept of the territorial Church, and the interpretation of external "history" were an attempt to adjust the balance against the interpretations which had been found from the first. The effort which he made needs to be made again, though we would be critical of his starting-point in Exodus.

[19] Cf. Ivarsson, *Kyrkan*, pp. 43-44, on "stewardship," an American theological concept which belongs to our period but has roots in the New Testament.

success. An external situation of this kind also affects the purely theoretical side of theology and particularly its choice of subject-matter and its field of inquiry. A theologian in Europe feels obliged by his whole environment to attempt the task of inter-preting and analysing something which belongs to the past. An American theologian feels a similar obligation to attempt the task of interpreting and analysing the present.[20]

It is quite evident that the world mission of the Church and its diaconate or ministry of service are sustained by two dis-tinct groups, viz. missionaries and deacons, to use the tradi-tional terminology. But these were not found in classical Lutheranism. In their stead the ministry of the Word was regarded in the national Churches of Europe as a local expres-sion of world mission, just as the diversity of daily work was regarded as a vast diaconate which was wholly concerned for men's physical needs. This grand concept could be maintained only on the basis of a twofold assumption. On the one hand the work of the minister had to be entirely subordinate to the Gospel, i.e. to the preached word. On the other hand the daily activities of each member of the Church from Monday to Saturday had to be placed entirely under God's universal rule of law, i.e. the first use of the law. *Both of these assumptions are overturned in pietism.* For pietism does not regard the Church as regulated by the Word or daily work as regulated by the law.[21] It regards the Church rather from the point of view of a quali-tative change—the operation of the Word in the heart forms a fellowship which is held together not by the word and sacra-ments but by spiritual experiences shared in common. It regards society in a similar way—man's daily life has not yet been permeated by the Spirit, and does not manifest the operation of God. Provision may indeed be made for the individual through temporal ordinances, but only when these have done all for the individual that they can do, does he go through the "crisis," and only after that are the true converts gathered into

[20] Cf. Wingren in *Lutheran World*, 1954, pp. 26, 18-19, 29. A good combination of past and present is to be found in Robert L. Calhoun's essays, "Work and Vocation in Christian History," and "Work as Christian Vocation Today," in the volume of essays, *Work and Vocation,* 1954, pp. 82-115, 159-185.

[21] Cf. Helge Brattgård, "Bibeln och människan," in *Magnus Friedrich Roos' teologi,* 1955, pp. 340-341.

the *ecclesiola* of those who have "spiritual" qualities. Karl Barth has pointed out that pietism was a forerunner of the widespread individualism and emphasis on personality which prevailed in the nineteenth century.[22] This was perhaps the last occasion when a popular cultural phenomenon arose in the Church and then spread to art, letters, and philosophy. In an earlier period it was always in the Church that the fine arts flowered, but in modern times popular culture comes first, with the Church following in its trail. Pietism may well be the last example of the Church giving birth to culture. The widespread preoccupation with human qualities which we find in art and literature throughout the nineteenth century is to some extent its product. *Even before any secularisation had appeared in society in general, pietism was nullifying the understanding which the Lutheran Reformers had of the Word as creative of the Church and their view of the law of God as the motivating force in men's daily work.*[23]

Concurrently with this development there arose a need for particular individuals who were prepared to assume responsibility for mission and lay service. It was quite logical that pietism should provide the ideal types for both. Institutions of lay service and missionary societies have had from the first specific ideals and requirements, generally unexpressed but nonetheless quite clearly defined, concerning the particular type of Christian conduct expected among their workers, requirements which are not as generally expected, for example, of a prospective parish minister. Modern agencies for mission or lay service are markedly pietistic. This means that the doctrine of the first use of the law has seldom any place in the picture which the prospective missionary or worker has of society. God has no direct dealings through the law with the society to which the "deacon" ministers or with the pagans to whom the "missionary" comes. His first contact with these areas comes by way of a conversion which is experienced within the Christian believer, and which precedes His activity in these areas. This whole way of thinking, at times quite complicated, involves an indirect denial of the first article of the Creed.

[22] See Karl Barth, *Die protestantische Theologie im 19 Jahrhundert*, 1947, pp. 102-103, etc.

[23] Cf. Brattgård, *Bibeln och människan*, pp. 304-310, 359-366.

It is unreasonable to expect that the enterprises which are conducted in the areas of mission or lay service could be disentangled from this theological distortion, when the theological experts are unwilling to extricate themselves, persist in focusing their attention on the second article of the Creed, and regard the related disappearance of the first use of the law as an advantage rather than a loss.[24]

The conversion to which we refer is not the day-by-day outworking of baptism, but a question of a light which dawns on the individual and produces a particular type of activity. The outworking of baptism in a conversion of daily death and resurrection is essential in whatever occupation we may be engaged, both at work and at home. The general affinity which pietism has with nineteenth century individualism and emphasis on personality helps us here to understand better its view of personal experience and quality. The missionary and the deacon (or deaconess) have religious tasks and require religious qualities. But they need their special qualities in the same way as an artist needs his own particular qualities before he can become an artist. And since all the emphasis is laid on the possession by separate individuals of qualities which produce a conviction that an exceptional way of life is the only real option, this strange passivity also is encountered among the bulk of ordinary people. Those who are endowed with particular qualities—in the world composers and poets, in the Church missionaries and lay workers—are regarded with a sentimentality akin to worship.[25] The only thing that the majority need do is to admire and support the minority. But all this is a piece of romanticism which impoverishes the work of the Church. The members of the Church cease to be *members*, each with his own responsibility, and become the supporters of the few and the audience, as it were, of the professional Christians. It is therefore appropriate to underline this primary

[24] See, e.g., Søe, *Kristelig etik*, pp. 203-206. On the other hand Søe frequently rejects the common pietistic estimate of the religious qualities of individual men. Cf. *ibid.*, pp. 12-13.

[25] In an earlier period this way of thinking was not found. Luther wrote hymns for use in worship in essentially the same way as he wrote lectures on books of the Bible for his students—the music was not the product of his own lyric bent. He wrote not as a gifted individual but as a member of the Church who set other members in motion, so that the whole "body" sang.

truth that *each member of the Church has a particular service.* Particular ministries of service and particular mission work are based on the diaconate and the missionary responsibility which belong to all.[26]

But whatever kind of theology our modern foreign mission and diaconate may have had in the past, both have a necessary function and there is a good basis for each. If there is anything in them to be criticised, the criticism may very well be expressed in an inner theological self-consciousness among those responsible for the mission or diaconate involved, but it is a self-consciousness of a positive and not a destructive kind. The awakened nationalism among the coloured peoples of Africa and Asia creates new difficulties almost every day which hinder the work of mission. At the same time the new welfare society, which has arisen where the classical national Churches formerly predominated, displays a grudging and uncooperative attitude towards the desire of the Christian Church to clothe the Gospel in an earthly garb through its own social and charitable work, which parallels the welfare activity of modern society. World mission and diaconate both come into play as opportunity affords in a situation of opposition, and in such a situation it is imperative that we define the theological basis of their task.[27] A Lutheran Church which has had its general theological position defined during the Reformation period, but which at the same time in its own Reformed confessions clearly puts the Bible above the Reformation as its rule of faith and life, has the opportunity of showing that the two activities, a special foreign mission in other parts of the world and a special diaconate at home, are both admittedly innovations in comparison with the sixteenth century, but as particular obligations they are still early Christian in character, and are tasks which Christ Himself entrusted to the Church.[28]

The weakness in Luther's approach lay in the sharp

---

[26] Cf. Lindquist, *Varför diakoni?*, pp. 62-64, and Ivarsson, *Kyrkan*, pp. 40-42, on the diaconate, and Minear in *Basileia*, 1959, p. 48, on mission.

[27] Cf. on this whole problem Hendrik Kraemer, "Mission im Wandel der Völkerwelt," in *Der Auftrag der Kirche in der modernen Welt*, 1959, pp. 291-307.

[28] The commission consists in the continually recurring unity of "preach" and "heal the sick" in Christ's commission to the apostles and His summons to evangelise. See Mk. III.14-15, Lk. IX.2, X.9, Mk. XVI.15-18.

distinction which he made between "conscience" and "body," or, to be more precise, in his correlation of this distinction with the fundamental distinction between Gospel and law.[29] Despite vigorous attempts Luther never succeeds in breaking through the walls which he himself had systematically erected.[30] The Gospel put an end to guilt in the conscience but brought about no healing in the body. The doctrine of recapitulation in the early Church dealt much more radically with the antithesis of life and death as the fundamental antithesis of human existence, and so could do justice to the passages in the synoptic Gospels which dealt with Jesus as *healer*.[31] For Luther the sickness mentioned in these passages was rather an expression of guilt, and consequently the healing act of Jesus was an expression of the "forgiveness of sins."[32] But this is to hold the Gospel apart from the body, and this meant that Lutheran theology had no essential place for a diaconate which originates directly in the Gospel and the spiritual government. At this point modern Lutheranism can and must learn from the early Church, and in the final resort from the New Testament and indeed the Bible as a whole, by acknowledging the particular diaconate which in modern times has sprung up in Churches throughout the world, often under the influence of pietism. The same thing is true of world mission in our day. The modern missionary who travels to the ends of the earth illustrates much more clearly than the static parish priest of sixteenth century Lutheranism ever could one obvious aspect of the New Testament Gospel, which is that it

[29] When Törnvall, *Andligt och världsligt regemente hos Luther*, pp. 177-178, tries to demonstrate the connexion between the Gospel and Luther's conception of *iustitia civilis*, it becomes only too clear that *the Gospel cannot be given concrete expression in what is done for men's physical needs* within this Lutheran framework. What is done for men in the world is done by the "law" or by secular government.

[30] Luther's contribution to the doctrine of recapitulation which was developed in the early Church is fully treated in David Löfgren, *Die Theologie der Schöpfung bei Luther*, 1960, especially pp. 163-165.

[31] Grundtvig is a unique example of a type of Lutheranism which really thinks in terms of a contrast between life and death, directly influenced, no doubt, by the writings of Irenaeus. See Harry Aronson, *Mänskligt och kristet*, 1960, pp. 14-16, and especially pp. 223-224, footnote 167, where we see a contrast between Grundtvig and Luther, and also pp. 241-244, 288-291, where the dangers inherent in Irenaeus's line of thought are evident.

[32] Cf. Ivarsson, *Predikans uppgift*, pp. 48-49, and especially 66-67.

extended to "all nations" (Mt. xxiv.14, xxviii.19, Lk. xxiv.47, Rom. xvi.25 f.) and to "the end of the earth" (Acts 1.8).[33]

We have repeatedly drawn attention above to the fact that the kerygma is addressed to the "nations," and have stressed that here we are dealing with a connexion between the Gospel and *creation*.[34] The Gospel is essentially something that restores and recapitulates. If we put the first article aside and begin with the second, we lose sight of a vital aspect of the Gospel. In order to point out the need to clear away some of the theological underbrush, we have intentionally included the present section in the chapter, "The Church and Creation." The election of a single nation, Israel, and the downfall of this one nation constitute the two parts, though the two are mutually contradictory, of a single divine action. And this single action involved not only Israel, but throughout had reference also to the "nations" and to the whole of mankind.[35] The history of Israel thus lies between the prehistory of Genesis, which is mankind's history, and the New Testament which, through the expanding world mission of the early Church day by day, is also mankind's history, or, more accurately, *becomes* mankind's history.[36] This outward movement to the whole of mankind and the extensive quest "to the end of the earth," which is characteristic of the Church's mission, are balanced in regard to the Church's diaconate by a similar love for the whole of man, and this love extends also to his body, and not least to the ills and needs of his body. God has created the whole of mankind and the whole of man. The Bible looks to the deliverance of creation, but its outlook is eschatological. The gathering of "all the nations" before the throne of Christ (Mt. xxv.32) will not occur until the last day. In the same way the "resurrection of the body" will take place on the last day, and until that time all care for men's physical needs is merely a patch on something that is falling apart. As long as there is

---

[33] Cf. also Cullmann, *Christ and Time*, pp. 160-169.

[34] Cf. Lindeskog, *Studien*, pp. 180-187, Gärtner, *Areopagus Speech*, pp. 229-241.

[35] See also A. Causse, *Israël et la vision de l'humanité*, 1924, pp. 52-58.

[36] In regard to prehistory and Deutero-Isaiah cf. Hartmut Schmökel, *Jahwe und die Fremdvölker*, 1934, pp. 109-114, and also pp. 67-68, 5-6. On the connexion between Pentecost, mission, and the Church, see *Die Heidenmission*, pp. 194-196.

any opposition and hostility to God, part of the original decree for creation is incomplete, and its fulfilment can be an object of hope without yet being visible to sight. The distinctive mark of mission and diaconate is that both are vehicles for the restoration of the original creation and to this extent they serve Christ and creation at the same time.[37] The relationship which the missionary or deacon has to God does not cut them off from creation but rather keeps them close to it, just as Christ in His incarnation was nearest to God when He gave Himself for the world. But mission and diaconate are also marked by the peculiar restriction of "not yet." Try as they may, neither the missionary nor the deacon in their service attain their ultimate goal, which will come about only in the resurrection of the dead.[38]

The tendency to regard the dominion which Christ has gained through His resurrection and ascension as applicable only to the Church is connected with the influence of High Church thinking and pietism which has left so profound a mark on modern theology. The theories of succession in High Church circles restrict Christ's rule to the Church alone, and in a similar way the predilection which we find in pietism for the quality communicated by conversion restricts Christ's dominion to the godly or to the true Church, and this quality is interpreted in essentially the same way as High Church thinking interprets the quality communicated by succession, i.e. as an endowment possessed by certain individuals. Neither of the two thinks seriously of Christ as the living Lord who rules without being subject to the limitations created by the presence or absence of particular qualities in particular individuals. Nor would the one say about its bishops or the other about its revivalists what the New Testament says about the apostles, if there were not some obscurity in regard to episcopal consecration or conversion. If it can be said that there is some obscurity in this particular epoch, this merely increases one's impression of the power of the new quality, given in consecration or in conversion. In contrast, the New Testament speaks to us with the assumption that Christ is alive and is Lord of all in His Church,

---

[37] Cf. Dahl in *Background*, pp. 440-442.
[38] Cf. Billing, *Försoningen*, pp. 100-101, 120-121.

including Peter, the "rock" of the Church.[39] The authority of
the Church is the Gospel, not the ministry or the spirit-filled
man. There is a further aspect of Christ's sovereign rule over
the Church and His Lordship as these are exercised through
the Word of the Gospel, which once brought the Church into
being and which must still be addressed to the Church as real
news if it is not to go astray. We have dealt with this earlier. In
the period of the early Church it was believed that in His
resurrection Christ became Lord of "all creation," and therefore that His dominion extends far further than the Church,
which is simply one part of His dominion.[40] This gives the
Church a place in Christ's own dealings with the whole of
creation (Col. i.13-29, Eph. i.10-23, Heb. i.1-3, ii.8, 1 Cor. xv.
24-28, Phil. ii.9-11, Eph. iii.10, and Heb. x.13). The Church
comes out to the whole of creation in a movement of love.[41]
And this outward movement, which is essentially incomplete
and presses toward an unseen goal, always to be met by a repeated "not yet," is the Church's mission and diaconate.
The former comes with the Gospel to the whole of mankind,
the latter with healing to the whole man. For Christ is Lord
of *all* men and of *all* creation.

This outward movement to creation is the redemptive
activity of the Gospel. To regard the channelling of the minis-
trations of the Church in particular ways as regulative in our
ecclesiology is to make early Christian usage and custom
normative simply because they are early Christian. This is
fundamentally a legalistic way of thinking; in essence it is
Judaism, though with the New Testament in the place of the
Torah, and it keeps the Church from being *regulated by the
gospel*. Though such a theology may cite at will from the New
Testament, it is still basically not just unrelated to the Gospel
but actively hostile towards it. Those who have been influenced
by this legalistic approach are quite unwilling to accept that
the Church is governed by the Gospel—to them such an

---

[39] Thus the Spirit is not canalised within the Church but is Lord of the Church,
"the Lord and Giver of Life." See Hendry, *Holy Spirit*, pp. 57-67.

[40] Cf. Richardson, *Introduction*, pp. 211-212.

[41] See also Fritz Blanke, "Unsere Verantwortlichkeit gegenüber der Schöpfung,"
in *Der Auftrag der Kirche in der modernen Welt*, 1959, pp. 193-198, where the author
emphasises man's responsibility in dealing with nature in a technological age.

M

assertion is both repugnant and inadequate. In contrast to this the New Testament and also the Reformation have the singular virtue of a passion for freedom and can discard even early Christian usage and custom when these have no saving worth and consequently were not appointed by Christ, for the only gifts which Christ has brought to men are salvation and the outward means of salvation. The institution of circumcision, for example, was accepted by Christ and the apostles, but was not appointed by Him, and therefore the Church was free to deal with it as it chose.[42] If we allow the New Testament to be a book of laws by which we determine when freedom is applicable and when it is not—it is applicable for instance in regard to circumcision, for this freedom is explicitly attested in Gal. v.2, but inapplicable in regard to the ministry of elders, for not one verse in the New Testament suggests that we can dispense with this—if we treat the New Testament in this way, then we are obviously changing it from Gospel into law. The only gifts which Christ has brought to men are the Gospel and salvation, but included in these is the healing of the sick or the diaconate, which is the physical aspect of the work of the Gospel. And as such, the redemptive acts of the Gospel are works of recapitulation and are a response to a need which exists in creation even before the Gospel comes.[43] It is true that those who feel this need are forced to make light of it and treat it as merely a superficial affliction which can be alleviated among other ways by raising material standards. To says here that the Church must give closer attention to this need and set it in a large eschatological perspective does not mean that material care is to be disregarded. If it did, the Church would be making itself more spiritual than its Lord was. Despite the vast scope of His ministry, He still found time to heal those who were physically sick one at a time.

As soon as we begin to discuss material concerns we are in an area in which God the Creator holds sway through the

---

[42] See Ramsey, *Ethics*, pp. 75-76.
[43] Cf. Fridrichsen in *S.t.k.*, 1929, pp. 304-305, 307-308. Theologically, this is the right place for an interpretation of "the groaning of creation" (Rom. VIII.19-22). See also Prenter, *Skabelse*, pp. 587-588.

universal law prior to and independently of the preaching of the Gospel. The word proclaimed in the Church's mission is wholly new in comparison with what is done in its ministry of service. This diaconate may produce new works as a result of the loving concern and inventiveness which have their source in the Gospel, but these are still *works*.[44] Like all human works which are done for the sake of the neighbour they have certain limitations: in temptation they give no answer to the accusations of the conscience and they do not make those whom they benefit righteous. Even the best and purest works in the world are mingled with other "old" works which even the Gentiles did before the Christian era. They were done by those who were under constraint and lacked the inner willingness to do them. Outwardly the "old" are as good as the "new." Jesus called on His disciples to follow His example in bearing the cross, but the only one who did so was a man "from the country," and even then he carried it because he was compelled to (Mk. xv.21). The exclusive position to which the Gospel lays claim in the realm of faith has no counterpart in regard to works. The Christian command to love can be called "a new commandment," but it can also be called "an old commandment," which was known and in force before Christ. It is not surprising, therefore, that the writers of the New Testament hold to existing moral standards in regard to outward conduct.[45] The natural law is not to be rejected by the Church but provides the setting in which "the new activity" unfolds.[46] This adherence to existing expressions of fellowship is in fact a direct expression of *love* and the openness to creation which characterises the Church from the centre of its fellowship with Christ outwards. It does not imply subordination to any law but rather an attitude of sovereignty and freedom in regard to

[44] There is a strong emphasis on the distinctive character of the diaconate in this respect in Paul Althaus, "Der theologische Ort der Diakonie," in *Z.S.T.*, 1954, p. 295. Cf. Lindquist, *Varför diakoni?*, pp. 149-155, Ivarsson, *Kyrkan*, pp. 51-58.

[45] Cf. Dahl in *Background*, pp. 439-440. See also Heinz-Dietrich Wendland, "Zur socialethischen Bedeutung der neutestamentlichen Haustafeln," in *Die Leibhaftigkeit des Wortes*, 1958, pp. 34-46.

[46] Cf. Gunnar Hillerdal, *Kyrka och socialetik*, 1960, pp. 52-54. Also to be noted in this connexion is Helmut Thielicke's theological ethics and especially his positive use of the concept of compromise, to which Hillerdal is indebted.

existing forms of life, which are at the one time affirmed and reformed.[47]

[47] See Ramsey, *Ethics*, pp. 349-350, Wendland in *Die Leibhaftigkeit*, pp. 45-46. A good example is Eivind Berggrav, *Staten og mennesket*, 1945, especially the references to "local elements" and "social groups" on pp. 139-147.

The New Activity

We now propose to elucidate further in the following section the questions which we have just raised. Since the aim of love is the good of the neighbour, if I have such an aim it means that I have ceased to be concerned with personal pleasure or advantage. It is precisely this forgetfulness that makes the new activity of the Christian life *new*. The reason for including the present section in the chapter which deals with "Church and Creation" is the central position given to the neighbour in Christian ethics, the central concern of which is "the other," or, as Luther puts it, *man*—not God and not oneself, but the one apart from us.[1]

We return here to the "unity in trinity" mentioned above. Both the pure creation itself and sin can be considered from the three standpoints of our relationship to God, our relationship to our neighbour, and our relationship to creation. In relation to God, purity consists in unbroken contact with the source of life, and sin, in a similar way, in a hardened attitude which is closed to the source of life. Purity is open to the source and can give to the neighbour and serve his needs, but sin has to grasp and compare and be consumed by envy. Purity is free and sovereign in regard to creation and exercises joyful dominion over it, but sin hankers in its greed and idolatry after wealth, honour, or a "high standard of living," begs for its happiness from these impotent things, and grovels before the creature.[2] But on the cross of Christ purity is attained by a single tempted man, who is obedient to God and gives up His life without bowing down to any idol. In the resurrection of Christ the victory which was attained on the cross is offered to the many who, receiving the Gospel, are gathered into the

[1] Cf. Ramsey, *Ethics*, pp. 12, 18-21, 60-61, 79-90, 153-190.
[2] See Eph. v.5, Col. III.5. Cf. Vajta, *Theologie des Gottesdienstes*, pp. 8-10.

Church from which the new activity comes out to men. The source of this new activity is communion with the Father, with Christ, or with the Spirit—the three are a single divine Being. God Himself is in the victory of Christ and is afterwards at work among men through the Spirit, and the Spirit is given in the Gospel which stems from the death of Christ and was proclaimed to the nations immediately after the completion of Christ's work. But if the source of the new activity is communion with God in faith, its object is the neighbour who is our fellow-being.[3] This explains the sovereign attitude towards creation which marks the new activity and its freedom from idolatry in dealing with the good creation. This freedom is the outgrowth of faith. Love, which comes from faith, is not God's first work in the world, but is the restoration of creation to its original purity and the revival of a true attitude to the things of creation which man has misused and drawn into his perversion. Christ is indeed more than Adam and the gift in Christ indeed "abounded for many" (Rom. v.15-21), and in the New Testament the command is accentuated and heightened, or "widened" as the Fathers preferred to put it.[4] But man in creation was created from the first ever to receive anew and to grow by receiving. The heightening of the command does not imply a new departure in the direction of Marcionism. In its very heightening the new activity is the restoration of creation. Christian love, therefore, deals with the old creation in the manner intended and designated by God from the beginning.

The new activity thus illustrates once again the "unity in trinity" of which we have frequently spoken above—it involves a receptive attitude towards God, a readiness to give to the neighbour, and lordship over the world of nature. There are good reasons, however, for dealing in the present section

[3] Cf. Anders Nygren, *Filosofisk och kristen etik*, 2nd ed., 1932, p. 306, and *Agape and Eros*, p. 96. This unity of faith and love is the lasting contribution made by Nygren in his theology but his work cannot by itself be made the basis of a theological ethic.

[4] Irenaeus develops this view with great clarity in his *Adversus haereses*. See, e.g., *A.h.*, IV. xxiv (Stieren's ed., IV xiii). The "widening" of the natural laws in Christ is dependent on the fact that all laws are fulfilled in Christ. This is how the sharpening is interpreted in the Sermon on the Mount (Mt. v.17-47).

particularly with the emphasis on the neighbour which characterises this new activity. There are good reasons also for
retaining the antagonistic perspective, and consequently for
keeping in view the factor of continuing sin and therefore of
the power of the law, fear, and constraint, which affect even
the Christian life. Until the end has come, these realities must
make us couch the significance of our earthly experience in
terms of eschatology and the interpretation given to death
by faith.[5]

It is illuminating in this connexion to recall Luther's doctrine
of the civil use of the law. In this the cardinal point is not that
all men know what it means to do good. Luther does indeed
speak of knowledge or of the law which is written in the heart.
But this writing on the heart is a form of God's coercion of all
men. The primary point is that God rules in the world through
the law, and the law is not some residual piety in man's inner
being, but is a divine function by which God sustains His
created world in spite of the fact that men are evil.[6] And here
the neighbour—this vast mass of our fellow-creatures—has a
part of great significance to play. The requirements, needs, and
desires of our fellow-men are the means by which the Creator
sees to it that many different kinds of service are carried out.
Self-interest forces men to serve others in order to be able to
live themselves. We may summarise the essential element
in the civil use of the law and the earthly government in the
statement that *the neighbour himself forces his demand upon us.*
He does so by the mere pressure which his needs and demands
create in our lives, even when we have no love for him. All this
has nothing to do with human goodness or wickedness. It is a
divine creative act which cuts across all ethical qualities and is
as elemental and imperative as the creative act brought about
through sexual instinct and the begetting of children. The cry
of the new born infant for food is a primary cell of the earthly
government, but the same cry comes in a more articulate
form from adults, the sick, the injured, the defrauded, and the

[5] Cf. Peter Brunner in *Lutheran World*, 1958, pp. 246-248.

[6] Rom. II.14-15, XIII.1-6, are applicable here, as also Gen. IX.1-7. See too Reidar
Hauge, *Gudsåpenbaring og troslydighet*, 1952, pp. 237-246, Ruben Josefson, *Bibelns
auktoritet*, 1953, pp. 178-193, C. H. Dodd, *New Testament Studies*, 1953, pp. 129-
142, and Günther Bornkamm, *Studien*, pp. 93-118.

dying. In such ways the Creator calls on us to serve with our hands: to have bodily existence on earth means to be subject to God's omnipotent law. The use of force by the police, the protection of those who defend us, farming, fishing, healing, and trade, are all products of human toil and bring our fellow-beings some gift which they need—defence, protection, food, health, clothing, or shoes.[7] To know the weariness caused by the hunger and thirst for help which comes to us from those among whom we are set is an inescapable part of the "cross of our vocation," and hence is "death."

The civil use of the law thus means that good is done in the world, even though the doer himself is not good.[8] The driving force within the earthly government is the *neighbour*, who may thus be the occasion for our good works, even though he himself is not good. Neither the person in need nor the one who does good possesses goodness as a personal quality. The word of Jesus is applicable here: "No one is good but God alone." Only the Creator is good, and therefore what He creates is good, even when it is transmitted through wicked instruments.[9] Even before the Gospel is preached and quite independently of fellowship within the Church, all who pursue their daily callings are bound up with their neighbours in a network of relationships in which the Creator has dealings with them, just as they themselves react against God in the simplest tasks of daily life and keep resisting Him within this relationship which was established at birth. The new activity is brought into operation by the proclamation of the Gospel which is "good news" by reason of the fact that it sets itself against the universal law which is embodied in human relationships. The Gospel does not come into a world which has known nothing of the operations of the true God, as Marcion suggested, but into a world which abounds in the works of God, a world where fear reigns and guilt dwells, and where, therefore, the wrath of God is in fact experienced as a concrete, palpable

---

[7] Cf. Franz Lau, *Luthers Lehre von den beiden Reichen*, 1952, pp. 49-53. On force see especially Werner Elert, *Das christliche Ethos*, 1949, pp. 536-537, and cf. also Ramsey, *Ethics*, pp. 166-184. See too Mt. VII.9-11.

[8] Cf. Løgstrup, *Den etiske fordring*, pp. 161-162.

[9] This is particularly striking in regard to sex life. Cf. Sundby, *Luthersk äktens-kapsuppfattning*, pp. 13-16, 22-32, etc.

and indeed inescapable reality. The Gospel is a new act on the part of the same God who has been active throughout the world in His work of creation apart from the Gospel.[10] If this worldly solidarity in which men are set from birth is disregarded we shall get the wrong idea about the new activity which faith and the Gospel bring about, for it will come to be viewed simply as an unrelated ethic derived from the Gospel. Characteristically enough, the term "attitude" is quite often used to describe it.[11]

Pietism, in which the first use of the law and the first article of the Creed played little part, formulated an interpretation of man as an isolated individual which was completely different from the view which we find in the period of the Lutheran Reformation. Hence, too, the admonitions of the New Testament became for pietism little more than a reflecting surface in which the individual examined himself to see whether he had the "attributes" which according to the Bible were necessary for him. The gradual transformation of the individual became the substance of the scheme of grace. For the Lutheran Reformers, on the other hand, the man who hears the biblical exhortations is caught up in the relationships of the earthly government: even though he is unconverted, and apart altogether from his faith or lack of it, God has already forced him to do things which prove to be of benefit to his neighbours. But when the Gospel comes to such a man in preaching, it is accompanied by the exhortations which arise from the Gospel, and the focus of these is not any Christian "attributes" but the *neighbour*.[12] That is to say, the person mainly involved in exhortation is someone other than the one who hears the Gospel—perhaps his son or daughter, wife, father, fellow-worker, subordinate, superior, etc. As Ivarsson has expressed it, the preaching of exhortation is an act which involves the neighbour of the one who hears it—preaching is a "service of

---

[10] Cf. Günther Bornkamm, *Das Ende des Gesetzes*, 2nd ed., 1958, pp. 24-33, an exegesis of Rom. 1.16-3, 26, a lengthy passage which clearly forms a single argument. See also Pierce, *Conscience*, pp. 85-86.

[11] Nygren's failure to speak positively of the government of the law and his definition of the Christian ethic as an agape-type of ethic are closely related. On the "love-type" see Nygren, *Filosofisk och kristen etik*, pp. 228-230.

[12] See in this regard Ivarsson, *Predikans uppgift*, pp. 264-268.

the neighbour," and apportions tasks to be done for the benefit of those among whom we who hear the Gospel live each day. Since the Gospel is creative of the Church and since it is always accompanied by exhortation—to works or to love—the Church as a whole may be thought of as an event which has consequences for the neighbour and the whole of creation. Thus the present section is properly included in the chapter which deals with the Church and creation.[13]

It is in Luther, of course, that we find this conception of the integral relationship between the new activity and the neighbour dealt with systematically and in greatest clarity. If we treat the Bible as a unity, with Genesis first and Revelation last, we shall also see how firmly the Lutheran conception is rooted in the scriptures. We think in particular of the striking similarity between the Reformers and the New Testament in their preaching of Christ as the example to the Christian of good works and in their interpretation of "imitation." Christ gave Himself for others and those who follow His example do likewise. Paradoxically, it is by paying heed to his *neighbour* that the disciple follows *Christ* (Mt. xx.26-28, Jn. xiii.14 f., 1 Pet. ii.18-23, Phil. ii.3-8, 1 Cor. x.31–xi.1, Rom. xv.1-7, Eph. v.25, ii Cor. viii.9-14, 1 Jn. ii.6, iii.16, Col. iii.13).[14] But even the broader framework, which Luther calls the civil use of the law and which has reference to God's dealings with all mankind, is solidly grounded in the prehistory of the Old Testament and the passages in the New Testament which speak of God's revelation in creation and of His judgment, law, and wrath against all nations.[15] This framework is also presupposed when the Gentiles to whom the Gospel comes in the missionary preaching of the New Testament are exhorted to "return" to the God from whom they turned away, and when in the same preaching "forgiveness of sins" is proclaimed to them.

---

[13] Cf. Welch, *Reality of the Church*, pp. 206-209.

[14] See also the parallels to Mt. xx.26-28 in Mk. x.41-45 and Lk. xxii.25-27. We have dealt with these passages in our discussion of preaching above. See further *Theologische Literaturzeitung*, 1950, pp. 385-392.

[15] It must be stressed that the passages which speak of God's revelation in *creation* and the revelation of wrath are not contradictory but speak of the same reality. Cf. the summing-up in Günther Bornkamm, *Das Ende des Gesetzes*, pp. 33-34, footnote 67.

Such preaching is incomprehensible apart from the broad framework of creation and the law. But the question of fidelity to the Bible, though it needs to be raised, is not of itself decisive. It is more important that our own moral situation provide the basis for the concept of the first use of the law. Any theory which suggests that the Bible is the only available source of knowledge about what good works we are required to do is contradicted by the realities of the ethical situation which confront us each day. All Christians have to do with the Gentiles who "have not the law," but "do by nature what the law requires," and when it comes to concerting efforts on our neighbour's behalf, they are in some way involved, even though theologically we may adhere to Barth's doctrine of *Evangelium und Gesetz*.[16] The ethical situations enountered each day of life are situations in which we have dealings with the Creator. In this instance we do not derive our assurance from books, not even from the book of books, but from life itself.

A further part of our ordinary experience is the element of "antagonism," or the conflict between good and evil. To say that God uses the law to compel men to do good works for their fellow-men throughout the world does not by any means imply uniformity of ethical response. Everywhere we can see men doing things of their own free will which hurt their neighbour and which we can say are more or less distantly akin to murder. Here we are confronted by the surd-like factor which could perhaps be designated the "obstructive" or "opposing" element, and which is very often actively at work even where the end result is a help to the neighbour (or a taking away of injury from the neighbour). The laws of a country and the penalties which they threaten have the effect of breaking down the opposition of those who refuse to serve their neighbour and of demanding service of those who have no love in their hearts and in whom no new creation has taken place.[17] This antagonistic interpretation is of importance for the proper understanding of the profound connexion between the new activity and

---

[16] Cf. Hauge, *Gudsåpenbaring*, pp. 245-246, on Rom. II.14-15.
[17] Cf. Walter Künneth, *Politik zwischen Dämon und Gott*, 1954, pp. 81-88, 156-157. See also Hillerdal, *Gehorsam gegen Gott und Menschen*, pp. 28-80, Sundby, *Luthersk äktenskapsuppfattning*, pp. 29-40.

all the natural good of the "old" creation. That is, it allows us to maintain the connexion between natural and Christian without having to detract from the goodness of the natural, and yet it becomes possible to assert without qualification the *newness* of the new activity which has its origin in the Gospel. The Gospel or the spiritual government breaks down the obstruction or opposition in a manner which is essentially different from the minatory, repressive and purely obstructive methods with which the civil law keeps evil within reasonable limits, and it does so by regenerating.

Though from one point of view the old commandment and the new are the same, for the same divine will is to be found in both, yet Christ's commandment is *new*.[18] He stands before us in the scriptures, expressing Himself in words which are unquestionably authentic, as one who forgives sin and sharpens the older demand at one and the same time. His offer of forgiveness and His accentuation of the old constitute a unity and are both connected with the fact that He *creates anew*. He is the creative Word incarnate which now in the death and resurrection of Christ breaks down opposition in an essentially new way and "destroys the works of the devil" (1 Jn. III.8): "The darkness is passing away and the true light is already shining" (1 Jn. II.8).[19] But it is not just the Old Testament law which is accentuated in the Sermon on the Mount. The same words about a heightening of the demand can also be used by Christ in relation to the kindness of the Gentiles or even common decency in which there is no "running over" (Mt. v.47). The overflowing love cannot break through unless much more of the obstruction has been removed. But even where the obstruction remains and all that can be achieved is a minimum of outward respectability, this limited measure is still of relative value, for it preserves and sustains life and makes life possible. To sacrifice our own welfare for ungrateful fellow-creatures and to protect children and family, and with

---

[18] Cf. Hillerdal, *Kyrka och socialetik*, pp. 33-39: the method is certainly suggested in the New Testament, but natural law is made the framework of the system.

[19] It is in precisely this context that the character of the "old" commandment and the "new" in the commandment to love is emphasised (1 Jn. II.7-11). On the relationship of "light" to creation on one side and the consummation on the other, cf. Richardson, *Introduction*, pp. 67-71.

them ourselves, from starvation, are two quite disparate acts, but they are both an expression of the Creator's care for His Creation and combine to form a relative unity when compared with the activity of the "enemy," which is murder.[20] To be kindly disposed towards father and mother in a static and patriarchal culture and to "hate" them in a time of martyrdom (Lk. xiv.26) are two responses which it is extremely difficult to reconcile, and yet both may be expressions of love.[21] Despite the fact that accentuation at this latter point leads to a rejection of the old solidarity, the new commandment with its demand to hate may have its origin in the same source from which the old commandment concerning respect for one's parents arose. The accentuation does not by any means run counter to the law in its earlier form.[22] When something comes to take the place of an idol, there is love even in the "hate" which casts the idol from its throne. Where no situation of martyrdom exists and no created being claims our worship we are to honour parents and superiors as formerly.

The connexion and the distinction between natural law and the commandment of Jesus is from one point of view a reflection of another connexion and another distinction. In His work of redemption Jesus restores man to the pure created state and therefore to the purity which was lost in Adam's fall. Even in his state of purity, however, Adam had still to face his temptation. The cross of Jesus, on the other hand, is actually the *last* temptation of the new Adam, the Redeemer, who is now free of temptation and death and helps those who are tempted "from the right hand" of the Majesty on high (Heb. i-v).[23] Redemption gives more than creation when it restores creation. We are dealing here with a connexion and distinction between natural and Christian, and both are reflected on the level of

[20] The devil is the "murderer" (Jn. viii.44). It is characteristic, therefore, that a negative attitude to the concept of natural law is often connected with a negative attitude to the antagonistic element in the writings of the New Testament and consequently to the conception of the devil, etc. Thus Karl Barth's negative attitude in both these respects is quite typical and goes right through his writings.

[21] Cf. Lindsay Dewar, *An Outline of New Testament Ethics*, 1949, pp. 90-91.

[22] On the question of commandment and law cf. also Paul Althaus, *Gebot und Gesetz*, 1952, pp 7-11, 14-21, 23-28.

[23] Men are still tempted in the Church, and it is possible for them to fall, though not for the Head of the Church. See 1 Cor. x.12-13.

law or commandment. Christ will give those who are His own complete freedom from temptation and death only in eternal life, but even now He brings them to eternal life through the Gospel and baptism. The commandment which follows the Gospel and baptism and which is heard in the exhortation of the New Testament (which in fact is baptismal exhortation) is simply the natural law with love for the neighbour as its centre, though since this law is grounded in the Gospel and baptism, the assumption now is that those who hear it and do what it commands are *on the way to the resurrection of the dead*.[24] But this same "evangelical" assumption means that we shall find *a willingness to suffer and die* in those who here and now obey this law. This is what is meant by the accentuation, newness, and heightening of the law. The Christian attitude is that of a natural love for the neighbour which is thoroughly "of this world" and conveyed in the rough forms of men's daily vocations, but it is filled with a new willingness to *suffer* for the good of the neighbour, and to do so with *joy*.[25] This is why the Christian Church was the elixir of life amid the disintegration of the ancient world, and the same vital power often recurs, especially during periods of martyrdom, in the continuing history of the Church. Among a number of indications that the Christian faith has lost its substance today, hardly anything is more terrifying than its loss of joy and its self-centred complaining when faced by persecution and reproach. Two things apparently unrelated but really belonging together, needed to be restored by Christianity—first, the concept of the creation of heaven and earth and the second, the resurrection of the dead. If these mean anything at all, it will at once be recognised that the Church is to be turned towards the world in its life and work.[26] To express this paradoxically,

[24] See Jervell in *N.t.t.*, 1960, pp. 231-256.

[25] In this respect it is correct to speak of the spontaneous and unmotivated character of agape. But we require to speak of it in its Biblical framework, which is also the framework of our day-to-day experience, and determined as such by the natural law. This framework has been destroyed in Nygren's philosophical writings, and his valuable studies of the Christian conception of love have therefore acquired a flavour of Marcionitism.

[26] Its *preaching* is also marked by this. Luther is typical in this regard. See Ivarsson's discussion of preaching which "rules the conscience" in *Predikans uppgift*, pp. 144-158.

when the Church is turned towards the world it is turned towards the resurrection of the dead.

This holds true also of the manner in which the Church preaches the "exhortation" which is based upon the Gospel. We must make a distinction between this and the first use of the law, for there is a clear distinction between the two despite their profound connexion and despite the fact that both are rooted in the will of the Creator and both aim at serving the neighbour. The preaching of exhortation is derived from the *Gospel* and consequently from an account about a gift which Christ has given.[27] It originates, therefore, in a word of forgiveness which has been appropriated, and is not received grudgingly or under constraint, but gratefully, freely, and with a will to serve. Even as exhortation it sets forth Christ, not now as a gift for the redemption of the hearer but as an "example" for our own good works. Since this epic, narrative character is at the heart of the preaching of the Gospel, exhortation is part and parcel of the Gospel, the free gift to men, even when it summons them to follow Jesus through the cross to life and to imitate what He did. The work of Jesus was His giving of Himself for many, and correspondingly the task of His followers is to look to the needs of others and choose to do what benefits *them*. It follows that the rules and regulations of discipleship will vary according to the situation, needs, and difficulties of the neighbour. Despite the variation, however, there is only a single commandment: "You shall love your neighbour as yourself." At times this will mean having to endure overbearing masters at work (I Pet. II.18-23), at times raising money for those in need (II Cor. VIII.9-14), at times making concessions to the conscience of the weak and the burdened (Rom. XV.1-7), and at times caring physically for the needs of others (Jn. XIII. 14 f.). In each of these instances the New Testament refers to the example of Jesus and in speaking of Him always makes the same point of His *giving of His life* (I Pet. II.21-24, II Cor.

---

[27] Cf. Heinrich Schlier, "Vom Wesen der apostolischen Ermahnung nach Römer 12.1-2," in *Christus des Gesetzes Ende*, 1940, p. 57, Axel Gyllenkrok, "Några synpunkter på lag och evangelium i Luthers teologi," in *Ny kyrklig tidskrift*, 1953, pp. 84-85. Even in its first use, of course, the law can be preached. Cf. Ivarsson, *Predikans uppgift*, pp. 158-163. There is too much emphasis laid on this point in Dietrich Bonhoeffer, *Ethics*, 1955, pp. 271-285.

VIII.9, Rom. XV.3, Jn. XIII.1 ff.).[28] When exhortation is thus rooted in the Gospel of Christ's death, it is pointless to attach it to the commandments which are to be found in the New Testament. It is quite evident that in this regard we can be faithful to the scripture only by looking to our neighbour and seeking ever new ways of service.

Exhortation is thus derived from the Gospel and to this extent is something different from the law which constrains those who are in bondage to it.[29] The new righteousness is given in the Gospel and will be revealed in the life eternal. In the present time and before death, however, it must be given visible expression, and in its exhortatory aspect preaching is this evocation of the latent righteousness. But at the same time it provides a new impetus and willingness to serve, and along with these an inventiveness and the recreation of an old activity which was in process before Christ came with the Gospel.[30] For the unrecognised demand in human life of itself forces from every living creature every day the acts of service which the neighbour requires. The first use of the law and the new activity which has its source in the Gospel both focus on the neighbour.[31] The fact that a free and imaginative willingness to serve seeks the best means of benefiting the neighbour by no means excludes the possibility that the patient endurance which is required in simple, commonplace tasks may prove to be a more powerful inducement to show love than any other conceivable activity. Since this willingness to serve is free, its responsibilities cannot be ordered from without. It makes its own choice, apart from the law, and is "master of all laws." But it would not be free if it could not also choose to stay quite simply in an ordinary earthly calling or job which was in existence long before the birth of Christ, e.g. as a mother, daughter, farm worker, or tradesman, and there render service as in an "open prison." None of these occupations is deliberately

---

[28] See further, Mt. xx.26-28, Phil. II.3-5, Eph. v.25. Several other passages could be mentioned.

[29] Cf. Joest, *Gesetz und Freiheit*, pp. 109-113, 150-155, and also Schlink in *Antwort*, 1956, pp. 327-331. Joest's terminology is at times debatable.

[30] Günther Bornkamm, *Das Ende des Gesetzes*, pp. 45-48.

[31] Cf. Josefson, *Bibelns auktoritet*, pp. 192-193, also Prenter, *Ordet*, pp. 45-47, 54-55, 58.

chosen for selfish gain. All derive their origin from the creation of life, and at bottom the Creator Himself is the subject in each of them. God does not abstract Himself from His old creation when He allows His creative word to become flesh in Christ and fashion the new humanity through baptism. The man who is baptised is formed in the image of Christ in death and resurrection and thus becomes *man* in accordance with the primal decree of the Creator. But this death and resurrection occur on the level of everyday existence and in the external forms which have been from the beginning. Yet freedom is to be found even in the midst of the old creation.[32] For freedom expresses itself in service and lies concealed within the ever-changing relationships which we have with the neighbour in these apparently unspiritual outward forms.[33]

There is a gross misconception today about the use of terms such as "death" and "cross" in connexion with vocation. We begin with an attitude to life which is based on individual "rights" and encourages the individual to claim a great many things which are not thought of as gifts or "daily bread" for which prayer or thanksgiving should be made to God. Such an attitude is particularly common in the modern welfare state, which has shown that it has the power to give to those in need what they lack and to take away from the "idle rich" what they do not need. This is the positive side of the doctrine of "rights." On the whole, however, the ideology in question has failed to give *joy* to those whose standard of living has been raised, and this failure has its roots in the heart of the system, which is the very concept of rights. Joy is an attitude of thankfulness: to tell men that they have nothing for which to give thanks is to rob them of their thankfulness. If now from the basis of this ideology we look at what Luther, for example, says about "death" and "resurrection" in daily work, it appears to us that his language is marked by unconcealed, reactionary brutality and inhumanity.[34] We need to take a different

---

[32] Cf. Løgstrup, *Den etiske fordring*, pp. 122-125.

[33] See especially Prenter's clear exposition in *Skabelse*, pp. 115-116.

[34] In his *Kontakt med kyrkan*, 1960, pp. 72-74, Karl-Manfred Olsson chooses instead to describe Luther's view without making any use at all of what Luther has to say concerning "cross" and "death" in vocation. This, of course, makes what Luther says more acceptable to our modern world, but it conceals an important aspect of the Reformer.

approach to his discussion of death in order to understand it. A professional man who amasses worldly goods and honours and sees no other purpose in life than getting and keeping wealth has generally a terrible inward emptiness and is haunted by a distressing fear which is at bottom a fear of death. Another man may lose his life in a group and in one way be lost from sight, but in another see fruit springing up from his own life in the lives of others. Such a man may give of himself, and yet strangely enough his life is not empty of meaning but actually filled with purpose. It is like a grain of wheat growing up. To all appearances he is perhaps a jolly creature whose laughter is infectious, but the point is that he *gives* and lives *in others*. And this altruistic attitude, which is born in faith and in and of itself, even under somewhat limited conditions, represents dominion over nature and invulnerability, means that man has accepted his existence, including death. *Such a man lives "in the cross."* The factor of death and the factor of spontaneous freedom are integrally related.

It is quite obvious that this is the kind of person needed by the modern welfare state which, in fact, needs a "diaconate."[35] Since it is based to so large an extent on the conception of the rights of the individual, the welfare state accomplishes its task when it deals with material standards at the same time as it creates a hunger for giving *freely* and a thirst for the kind of man that lives *in others*. The locus of the new activity is not parliament or legislative assemblies but the multitudinous relationships which exist beyond these in places where many acts of service remain undone, even after the legislative bodies have done all that can be done in the way of passing laws.[36] When, therefore, the Church turns towards creation in the

---

[35] Cf. Lindquist, *Varför diakoni?*, pp. 151-152, Ivarsson, *Kyrkan*, pp. 31-33, 53-58. The "new activity" which we have described here is simply the diaconate as it is to be found in the New Testament, a responsibility which is laid upon all members and is not just the specialist activity of a certain group. The place of service is the relationship to his neighbour which the member of the Church has, and which he shares with no other. In consequence each individual has a unique task to fulfil in the sphere of works.

[36] See in this connexion also Berggrav, *Staten*, pp. 75, 80-82. The main thesis advanced in this book in regard to small social groups and local centres for the development of "authority" has not yet received sufficient attention.

N

new activity with the service which it has to offer, it is primarily a Church of "laymen," to use the modern but improper term. The new activity is quite simply the daily outworking of baptism, which is the ground of the Church. (If we speak of the baptised as "laymen," we are looking at them not from the point of view of baptism but of ordination, as if this were the ground of the Church, i.e. we regard them from the standpoint of something that they lack.) As we have frequently emphasised above, baptism is a sacrament that is opened to daily life and the service of our neighbour, and it is worked out in daily death and resurrection.[37] In saying this we have defined the true theological position of "sifting" or "choosing" from among the demands which are made upon the Christian in the environment in which he is set. One would expect, especially where the so-called theology of orders has exercised some influence, that this "sifting" would be markedly political in its outline. To those who represent this theological view the natural law is embedded in certain "orders," in particular state and nation. They have failed to see that the law is operative in the constantly varying relationships of life.[38] In consequence the law became petrified and could be read off the political structure of society. Thus "sifting" became primarily a political thing. It implied, for example, a repudiation of racial discrimination and certain military actions, etc. It is, of course, quite true that a Christian believer must be critical of political forms which exist in the society in which he is set.[39] But this criticism is simply one aspect of a "sifting" which is undertaken every day on an individual level in the relationship which every living being has with his neighbour. The civil use of the law has effect primarily in our relatively obscure relationship to our neighbour, and similarly the exhortation which arises from the preaching of the Gospel points towards the same relationship. We choose among the many demands made upon us by our neighbour every day without making any great issue about it

[37] Cf. Lerfeldt, *Den kristnes kamp*, pp. 178-185.

[38] It is typical of Løgstrup, on the other hand, that he begins with the relationship to the neighbour itself and not with order, e.g. *Den etiske fordring*, pp. 17-28.

[39] Cf. Sundby, *Luthersk äktenskapsuppfattning*, p. 269, footnote 52.

or bringing it to the attention of those whose business in society it is to pass legislation.

The danger of subservience to princes and rulers which is an undoubted accompaniment of traditional Lutheranism is not the only one in this connexion. An even greater danger today is *that we shall cut ourselves off from personal relationship to our neighbour*. In a peculiar way certain radical forms in politics come to usurp the function of *love*—we will vote, for example, for a political programme which offers people certain benefits, but at the same time make personal relationships a private sector of life. We may vote, for example, for a scheme which is prompted by love and still evade the united demand of both law and exhortation that we shall do what is of benefit to the particular neighbour whom we have. And this danger increases when we begin to put together commandments which we find in the New Testament, but which we have wrested out of their context (the proclamation of the Gospel), and make them subsections of a law which governs the Christian life.[40] But to detach these commandments from the Gospel is to detach them also from the supreme rule of love for neighbour. They become as rigid as the "regulations" laid down by the state, and are almost always negative—they forbid divorce, the marriage of divorced persons, abortion, and so on. Behind this veil of obedience to the Bible we can live our lives in complete privacy, cut off from and undisturbed by our neighbour's need. The entire attitude, in fact, runs counter to the universal natural law and the exhortation of the New Testament.

There may be some justification for speaking about the political "*leitourgia*" of the Christian,[41] but our political activity as Christians is part of the much wider framework of the responses which we make each day in dealing with our neighbour. The earthly government can force us to act on behalf of our neighbour, and we sift and choose from among the

---

[40] When Riesenfeld in *S.t.k.*, 1958, pp. 255, 260, speaks of "the new Torah" in the early Christian Church, the connexion between the Gospel (i.e. missionary preaching) and this "law" is lost. The commandments have no essential relationship to the gift of the Gospel.

[41] On the meaning of this expression of Barth, see Hillerdal, *Teologisk etik*, pp. 180-185. In his work, *Kyrka och socialetik*, pp. 86, 100-101, Hillerdal employs the same term for his own purpose.

demands which it lays upon us when, turning our eyes to Christ who is set before us in the preaching of the Gospel, we remain where we are in our allotted place among neighbours whom we cannot satisfy without causing conflict. We must make a choice. In principle we make the same kind of choice in politics. Democracy gives us a sphere of authority which the members of the early Church did not have, i.e. it multiplies the relationships which we have to our neighbours and gives us many more neighbours than we should otherwise have had.[42] But this does not alter the nature of our sifting and choosing. The real decisions are made primarily in our daily occupation, not in the legislature. But those whose basic view of the part which the Gospel plays in discriminating among existing patterns of conduct leads them to connect it with Luther's doctrine of vocation (and not just his doctrine of the ruler), must recall that Luther was dealing with occupations and activities in which quite simply *no choice was possible*. When there was something which could not be reformed, there was no other course but to reject it (e.g. the occupation of the moneylender or the monastic life).[43] If we were to apply the same critical test to modern society we should be compelled to put a question mark against more than one way of earning a livelihood, not least within the amusement industry. In a dictatorship there are many occupations which are not open. Yet the essential thing is not finally affected by these eliminations or rejections, but *is rather the acknowledgment of the vast number of occupations and callings*. The new activity is faithful to the old creation and renders its service in the natural relationships of life in which men come in contact with each other every day.

[42] From the point of view of rights democracy represents an increase of benefits for the individual. From the point of view of the Christian faith it represents in particular an increase of relationships to a neighbour. The former idea has helped to produce the democratic pattern. The Bible has produced neither monarchy nor democracy. But Christian faith can participate in both and give meaning to both.

[43] W.A. x. 1. 317, 21-24 (Sermons, 1522). It has been a weakness in later Lutheranism that it has accepted Luther's criticism of different vocations in the sixteenth century without scrutinising the occupations of its own day. The underlying assumption was therefore that demonic activity last flourished in the sixteenth century.

It is now time to attempt to summarise what can be said about the *newness* of the new activity. In the first place, this *newness* consists in an accentuation or heightening of the demand—we could even call it an eagerness to accept the demand. The demand shifts from the act to the inward desire or inclination, which give place to the outward act. Accentuation of this kind is worked out with great consistency in the Sermon on the Mount. The will to evil which resists God's will and at times in the New Testament is designated "the old man" is dealt a harder blow by the heightening than by the old and more external demand. When the commandment is thus accentuated, it is a deeper part of my inner being which is judged.[44]

In the second place, men are addressed in the accentuated command of the New Testament from the side of the *Gospel*. Since the Gospel is an account of a series of events among which the crucifixion of Christ occupies a central place, and since an appeal to "imitate" Christ's way springs directly from this account, the appeal presupposes that those who hear it are on the way to death, but it is a death which is a foretaste of resurrection and therefore of freedom and joy.[45] The factor of death in the obligation to service which is laid upon us means that the believer is open to the life which is lived under the law and which is the lot of all men. The factor of freedom means that the believer looks at his situation here on earth from the standpoint of "heaven," for he is already in heaven through faith. He is free in the midst of bondage, and does not merely toil to fulfil set obligations but formulates the service which he renders to his neighbour in sovereign freedom. He does so because of the joy which always runs through a duty which has been forced upon him and which he changes into an "open prison." We may mention here what we have just said about the accentuation of the commandment in the Sermon

[44] Cf. Billing, *De etiska tankarna*, pp. 74-75, 122. By taking his point of departure in the Old Testament Billing sees that this judgment on the innermost part of man's existence is specifically biblical. In Greek ethics a crisis *within* the spiritual part of man is inconceivable, for the spiritual is distinct from the physical.

[45] Cf. Edouard Schweizer, *Erniedrigung und Erhöhung bei Jesus und seinen Nachfolgern*, 1955, pp. 141-150.

on the Mount. The radical commandment of Jesus is one side of His own radical type of conduct and therefore one aspect of His crucifixion.[46] The man who in obedience gives up his own life for others is imitating Christ, and hence doing something new, in spite of the fact that his imitation takes place in the old forms of life.

In the third place, this new activity is a direct consequence of participation in baptism and the Eucharist. The sacraments are divine events which place men in a kingdom other than the earthly kingdom, and at the same time they are filled with the humanity of Jesus. Baptism brings the baptised into union with Christ's death and in so doing points to a life which is lived for the good of others. The Eucharist means the risen Lord is continually coming to fulfil in men the work of the once and for all baptism with which they were baptised. But when Christ comes, He brings "the night when He was betrayed" with Him—the night when more than at any other time His humanity was emptied, and when through this very emptying His victory was won (Phil. II.5-11).[47] What we have just stated about the sharpening of the commandment in the Sermon on the Mount and about the assumption, explicit in the Gospel summons to imitate Christ, that those who hear the Gospel will be willing to suffer on behalf of others, can be wholly subsumed in this third category. Since the Gospel and the sacraments are the marks of the Church and at the same time are also the source from which the new activity originates, the present section is clearly part of the larger context of Church and creation. The new activity is new and yet it is true to the old creation, for it is there that our neighbour lives, and works are to be done, and water, bread, and wine are to be found. The sacraments imply an absolute proximity to the earth, and yet without lessening this close connexion they remain heavenly realities.

[46] This connexion between the radical demand on the one hand and the death of Jesus on the other, as we have seen earlier, is missing in Gogarten and Løgstrup. The preaching of the Gospel has therefore in their view no critical function to fulfil in relation to moral norms.

[47] See the whole of the discussion on the humanity of Jesus and the cross. Cf. Cullmann, *Christology*, pp. 174-181, etc.

The Resurrection of the Dead

The Church in its work among men moves forward to a point where the structure of the old creation breaks down. We have discussed eschatology several times in different sections above, and have particularly emphasised its future aspect. There is a tendency in modern theology, however, to concentrate entirely on a present, "realised" eschatology. Considering the frequent references which we have made to the problem of eschatology so far, it should not be necessary in a book which deals with the Gospel and the Church to deal also with the resurrection of the dead. But this is actually involved in our discussion of the relation of the Church to *creation*, if we adhere to our definition of the content of the new activity. The Church in its work among men moves towards a goal, and only when we keep this goal in view do we see clearly the profound connexion between the Church on the one hand and creation on the other.[1] From this narrowly defined viewpoint we now turn to discuss death and resurrection as a separate subject.

There is no harm in looking back once more at the two preceding sections. We saw in the first that world mission and diaconate are parallel expressions of the uncompleted movement of the Church into all the world. The Church's mission extends to the whole of humanity, its diaconate to the whole man. When "all nations" have heard the Gospel, then the end will come (Mt. xxiv.14), and they will all be gathered before the throne of Christ (Mt. xxv.32). World mission thus culminates in the resurrection of the dead. It is much the same in the case of the healing and life-giving work of the diaconate for men's physical well-being. The Church's ministry of service operates in the face of constant opposition, for hunger is not eradicated by serving tables and disease is not terminated by practising medicine. If we try to indicate when the diaconate will meet with complete, final success, we come again to the same conclusion. Only in the resurrection of the dead will men be whole.[2] In the immediately preceding section our discussion of the "new activity" led us again to creation, since the neighbour

[1] Cf. also Emil Brunner, *Das Ewige als Zukunft und Gegenwart*, 1953, pp. 205-228.
[2] Cf. Cullmann, *Christ and Time*, pp. 157-164 (on mission) and the same author's *Immortality*, pp. 21-45 (on the resurrection of the body).

is central in this new activity. The object of our works is not God or our personal betterment but the "other"—a finite, mortal creature whom we come to serve in love. In this preceding section we found that there is a profound connexion between the daily service of our neighbour, our sharing in Christ's own death (which is "imitated" in an apparently unspiritual form of daily service), and our participation in the sacraments as the external means of Christ's presence. Service is both worldly and heavenly in character at the same time; it implies a willingness to endure suffering and gives us even now a foretaste of the resurrection of the dead. This, however, is the point which requires further definition and which we are now to make our main topic. Death holds sway in the world whether or not the Gospel is preached and the sacraments administered. But when redemption is seen to be the transmutation of death, its scope is vastly extended: God is involved in every part of man's existence when He causes life to emerge from his death. Nothing now lies beyond His sphere of activity. And this scope of redemption in the life of the individual is at bottom the scope of the incarnation itself. When salvation was given to men, it was wrought out on the level of the manger, the wilderness, and the cross. Life comes to us under the guise of death, and the life which Christ gives us from baptism onwards is the resurrection of the dead.[3]

Our statement that human existence is filled with death and that death thus confronts us at every point should be taken in conjunction with our earlier assertion that human existence is filled with *law*. Wherever men turn they are confronted by the law of God. They cannot escape the demands to serve others which they meet on every hand. We enter into a relationship to God by being born and making the unalterable journey towards death which takes us further and further from birth. The process is forced upon us whether we want it or not. It

---

[3] Karl Rahner, *Theologie des Todes*, pp. 66-70, draws a straight line from the death of Christ through our death to baptism and the Eucharist (see also pp. 61-66, 76-77). As a Roman Catholic Rahner naturally introduces extreme unction at this point (pp. 70-71). He also regards the death of the martyr from the point of view of free will. It then becomes "die Tat," a witness like the baptismal act in Baptist Churches (see pp. 87-91). Despite the confessional line of thought there is much to be learned from this book. See also Gleason, in *Thought*, 1957, pp. 58-60.

begins at birth, but we were not asked if we wanted to become involved in it, and by the time it began it was too late to do anything about it. But to be forced to become part of the process with its predetermined starting-point and its inevitable end, and to have no freedom of choice, is a sign of the bondage and constraint in which we are set. In the meantime, however, men attempt in particular ways to rise above the circumstances in which they are set and which are determined by factors beyond their control. And yet it is in these that we hear demands made upon us. All of our actions are therefore interventions in the lives of others who have their being on the line which extends from their own individual birth to their own individual death. Their bondage is expressed to us, when our response is needed, as a request for our care or help.[4] Any doctrine of God which disregards this existence under the law and merely speaks of His attributes has really nothing to say to us. But the Gospel *has* something to say, because it is not this kind of doctrine and consequently does not merely analyse but speaks rather of the One who lived out His life on the same line which stretched from the stable at Bethlehem to the Cross at Calvary. Consisting as it does of certain propositions, the Gospel may be misinterpreted and regarded as a doctrine, but it is more difficult to misunderstand the sacraments. Baptism and the Eucharist are both thoroughly epic and narrative in character, but they also involve action. In baptism we are brought into death and raised to life. The starting-point and the halting-point on the "line" have suddenly been reversed. For the baptised person, death has been left behind (Rom. vi.3 f.) and he has no need to fear death in the future, for the future will bring life and not death.[5] The Eucharist similarly proclaims a betrayal and crucified Christ who triumphs in His death—the more He "falls into the earth" and dies like a grain of wheat, the more fruit He bears and the more He lives.

It must be borne in mind by all who preach the Gospel that

[4] Cf. Gleason again, *ibid.*, pp. 41-43, in reference to existential philosophy on the Continent and also to Heidegger.

[5] Cf. the whole context in Rom. vi.3-11 and also Eph. iv.22-24, where the reference to Gen. i.26-27 is obvious, and Col. ii.12-13. The whole of the Epistle to the Ephesians deals with baptism. See in this connexion N. A. Dahl, "Efesier-brevet," in *S.t.k.*, 1945, pp. 85-103. Cf. Richardson, *Introduction*, pp. 341.

the Gospel and the sacraments recount or "portray." Few
scholars in the history of dogmatics have plunged into the
mystery of the preached word with such persistence or individuality as Luther. In pondering on this mystery he constantly
returns to the significance of the symbolic language of preaching
—metaphor is the only adequate form of expression.[6] Abstract
language which defines and extracts doctrines from the Gospel
sets itself above the incarnation and so becomes a vehicle for a
theology of glory. Luther's attack on abstract language was not
based on aesthetic grounds, though we can detect in his attack
upon it the aversion of the born artist towards the literalistic
meaning, but quite certainly the "sophists" too ("these asses,"
he calls them) are also lacking in knowledge. The real heart of
the matter, however, is as always the concern which is to be
found in the Lutheran Reformation for *the Gospel in contrast
to the law*. The Gospel is addressed to the man who is imprisoned
in law and guilt, and we do not get to this man if we treat the
simple description of Christ which we find in the Gospel and
the simple, visual actions of the sacraments as too unsophisti-
cated to go with the "proper" language about God. Quite the
reverse: the "proper" language about God *always* speaks
of a human life, for it sets forth Christ as the one who alone has
lived out His life on the line between birth and death without
failure or defeat. He is the only one who has found the life that
Adam was created to find, and therefore also the only one who
has revealed the nature of the Creator and who, living now in
eternity, has power to declare the truth about God.[7] The im-
prisonment which we endure between birth and death is an
expression of our bondage under the law. The Gospel, which
always has regard to those who are in bondage to the law and is
addressed to them, speaks of a human life which was lived on
this self-same line but broke out of it through His resurrection
on the third day.[8] The whole effect of the Gospel consists in the

[6] See among others E. T. Pedersen, *Luther som skriftfortolker*, pp. 409-412. The
treatment of Luther gains in interest here by being included in a discussion of
modern forms of demythologising.

[7] In regard to the metaphorical language, cf. Bring, *Dualismen*, pp. 103-132,
where Luther's attachment to an old tradition of frequently grotesque metaphors
is described in detail.

[8] It follows from Karl Barth's opposition to natural law that he is also opposed
to any description of death conveying God's law and judgment. For him

resurrection of the dead which is even now offered to men in baptism.

If we regard death as a purely biological phenomenon, we have essentially the same conception of it whether it strikes men or animals. It is probably here that we see the decisive difference between this view and the Bible. The writers of the Bible were naturally acquainted with the same phenomena as we are—men and beasts die, and they die, moreover, it seems, in almost the same way. But the Biblical writers did not have the modern, purely biological view of man, nor did they regard him as a species of animal. When death strikes man it is something different, for man was appointed to rule over all creation, and he carries this destiny within himself, even when he fails to realise it. Death, therefore, impairs something quite different when it strikes men—it impairs a decree of the Creator and thereby gets a despotic character which otherwise it does not have. When modern theology adopts a biological view of death, this relatively uncritical approach is one indication among many that it lacks a theological *anthropology*, and assumes that it can operate with dogmatic propositions in a vacuum (anthropologically speaking) without inevitably destroying the meaning of its language. But it does: redemption becomes something different and loses its character of restoration, and the Gospel in consequence turns into something different. Even the theology which today stands closest to Heidegger's existentialism, Rudolf Bultmann's demythologising interpretation of the New Testament, has a tendency to treat death biologically and strip it of its tyrannical character and the unnatural connotation which *thanatos* always has in the biblical

---

the law is given in the Gospel or in Christ. Christ's death is a "Gericht Gottes," but our death is only a "Zeichen." See *Church Dogmatics*, VOL. III, PT. II, 1960, pp. 593-605, and especially pp. 605-606: "The centre of this (New Testament) insight is God's *judgment* (Gericht) accomplished in the crucifixion of Jesus Christ. No other man stands at this centre, and therefore no other *really* stands under the judgment of God. Other men, Christians consciously and the rest unconsciously, find themselves on the *periphery* around this centre, and therefore—for we must now take up this concept—under the *sign* (Zeichen) of this judgment" (the italics are Barth's). All this follows logically from Barth's sequence of "Gospel and Law." If we begin by denying natural law, we shall, of course, come to this view of death. The deprecatory reference to Heidegger and Sartre as "preachers of the law" (p. 605) is also typical of Barth.

writings.[9] In the philosophy of Heidegger the death of the individual is regarded rather as a key to real existence—when I am confronted by the death which is personal to me, I am freed from the universal "man" and become truly myself. But such an interpretation of death renders the Gospel unnecessary, for it means that man has already attained his real self in this interior individualisation. Resurrection then comes to mean the obliteration of true existence.[10] The tremendous concentration on the true self or the individual in Bultmann indicates that his interpretation of the law is largely confined to the spiritual or theological use of the law, while he appears to regard the civil use as unimportant. These different aspects of demythologising appear to be diametrically opposed, but systematically they are in fact closely connected.

In Bultmann all that comes before and all that follows the present is eliminated, at least to the extent that it may claim to have any independent importance in comparison with the kerygma which is preached in the present. The resurrection of Christ on the third day is simply the present offer of life which the believer receives in preaching. We may by all means speak of Christ's resurrection, Bultmann holds, if we are referring to the proclamation of the Gospel in the immediate present. We may also quite readily speak of the resurrection of the dead on the last day, only by this Bultmann means the future which those who now hear the Gospel receive through faith in the Gospel, which is addressed here and now to the tempted individual conscience.[11] To the extent that Bultmann gives a place to the law in his system, he never speaks of the civil use of the law which is an expression of the Creator's own government of His created world, a government which He exercises by means of human labour, occupations, and earthly government. For this use indicates that the *world*

---

[9] Bultmann describes Paul's view of death in his article on demythologising in *Kerygma and Myth*, p. 17, but at the same time regards this view as unacceptable today (*ibid.*, p. 5). He starts with the assumption that Paul's interpretation is meaningless.

[10] See Martin Heidegger, *Being and Time*, 1962, pp. 304-311. Cf. Benkt-Erik Benktson, *Den naturliga teologiens problem hos Karl Barth*, 1948, p. 74, footnote 124.

[11] In Bultmann, *Kerygma and Myth*, pp. 202, there is a direct connexion with Luther.

itself is significant to God and ends any idea that everything in the world centres on me and my individual existence. In Luther the law is a factor through which God primarily governs and rules *all things*. Some things need to be done in life and others forbidden. The object to which the law is addressed is the body and its aim man's outward works. A secondary factor is the appearance of the law in the conscience, which brings us to the spiritual use of the law. A judgment is now made in the conscience and the lie of self-righteousness is put to death.[12] This is the "principal use" of the law, for by means of it a man is conveyed from earth to heaven through death and towards resurrection, and is fashioned after the image of Christ in accordance with the Creator's will and the baptism which he has undergone. We cannot, however, reduce Luther's doctrine of the law merely to a doctrine about the spiritual use of the law. To do so is always a sign that (unlike Luther) we are operating within a purely individualistic framework,[13] in which both past and future get absorbed by the present and hence by the kerygma which is operative in the present. The resurrection of Christ on the third day, the civil use of the law, and the resurrection of the dead on the last day have this in common, that they are events which affect *all* men. God's dealings with me personally in temptation and faith can never be anything but an expression of His dealings with all men. When His dealings with me become identical with His dealings with all, I have obtained a place in the centre of things which does not properly belong to me.

It is thus a matter of considerable importance to us not to give a purely biological interpretation to death, if we are going to have any understanding at all of the meaning of *creation*. There have been times, for example, when the first article of the Creed has been lost, but when the attempt was made to rehabilitate it, the doctrine of creation came to be interpreted in a vitalistic sense. God is then identified with life or certain vital forces, and the result is almost always a superficially

[12] See W.A. xl. 1. 479,17-486,16 (Larger Commentary on Galatians, 1535). Cf. Gustaf Ljungren, *Synd och skuld i Luthers teologi*, 1928, pp. 308-310.

[13] Bultmann's reference to the world as "profane" (*Kerygma and Myth*, p. 211) also points in a direction quite contrary to that of the civil use, even though he quotes Luther to defend his argument.

optimistic religion of enlightenment. But that which gives depth and breadth to the belief in creation is permanent contact with the account of the fall and its neglected "hidden" side, according to which *everything*, even the destructive factors in human existence, is construed and apprehended and indeed accepted as an inevitable concomitant of our relationship to *God*.[14] It is just as important, however, that this introduction of the "cross" as part of the relationship to God to which faith assents (which means that *sub contraria specie* it is life-giving and filled with joy) is not understood to imply a narrow distinction which restricts death to the present and transfers the resurrection to the eschatological future. *The resurrection of the dead is already taking place, for God cannot be other than Creator*.[15] This statement can also be expressed Christologically in the following way: the divinity of Christ secured its victory over sin and the curse by coming down and being itself tempted in the humanity of Christ, *and now Christ brings men to victory and life by putting them in the way of the cross*. The *communicatio idiomatum* has direct consequences in Christology for our interpretation of the life of faith of all believers. The humanity and divinity of Christ can no more be separated than the cross and death of the Christian can be set apart from his victory and joy, for they interpenetrate one another. We need hardly add that what we have just said can be directly expressed in terms of our doctrine of the sacraments and ecclesiology. The significance of baptism, which is the ground of all ecclesiology, is that it gives to all who are baptised the life of Christ's resurrection, and it is worked out in dying daily to the old nature on the level of daily life. The Eucharist signifies fellowship with the betrayed Redeemer on the night of His death, and at the same time praise, thanksgiving, and a foretaste of the heavenly banquet.[16]

This means that the present is penetrated with a death and a

---

[14] Cf. also von Rad, *Genesis*, pp. 96-99. It is strange that Cullmann can describe the relation between life and the body in the future with such clarity, when he never describes the relation between death (i.e. the law, or wrath) and the body in the present.

[15] The positive contribution of Torgny Bohlin's *Den korsfäste Skaparen*, 1952, e.g., pp. 320-382, is its emphasis on this point.

[16] Cf. Aulén, *Eucharist and Sacrifice*, pp. 136-138, 206-207.

resurrection which are a continuing reality. The destructive and the constructive events are counterbalanced, for they are a single whole, since anthropology and Christology share a common structure. If we hold that man is identical with the Adam of whom we read in the prehistory narrative, and that baptism brings him into the massive "conversion" of the whole of his former way of life, it becomes impossible to believe that he can attain life except through death. If real life is a total conversion of actual life, then this actual life can be formed and built up only by being destroyed.[17] And this conversion of Adam's way of living (i.e. of my way of living) is not something which is to come about primarily in some event which is taking place in my life now, but has already taken place in the tempted humanity of Jesus. When Jesus on the cross had destroyed the old, Adamic element, the multitude expected Him to come down there and then from the cross without dying, and stop the onset of death, but their expectation was a Satanic temptation (Mt. xxvii.42 f.). Christ's victory, which struck at the root of Adam's way of life, was attained through His acceptance of the cross; He refused to cling to divinity, but chose rather to be emptied. In the crucifixion itself the "conversion" has already taken place. Christ's death, even as such, already abounds in the true life which Adam lost. And this conversion by Christ of the pattern of my existence (i.e. the pattern of Adam's existence) is not something that belongs to the past, but is a present experience here and now through the Gospel and the sacraments, which are the ground of the Church.[18] Christ dwells in the outward means of grace by which the Church is built up, but at the same time these can be seen to be means of grace only as they extend to those who hear them and partake of them. Baptism, as the Gospel proclamation of the image of Christ, and the repeated distribution of the Eucharistic elements, give us a new life which is at one time the life of Christ and our own true life, but they do so in a form which always judges our old self and puts it to death.[19] Death and resurrection take place in the present.

[17] Cf. Brunner, *Das Ewige*, pp. 121-124. [18] Robinson, *The Body*, pp. 47-48.
[19] See Hahn, *Mitsterben*, pp. 124-145. See also Ernst Percy, *Der Leib Christi*, 1942, pp. 43-46.

This is particularly applicable to the Eucharist, since the Eucharist is a meal and consequently by nature is a recurring and constantly repeated act in which the same gift is given to the same persons at short intervals. God gives the communicant something new through the presence of Christ in the Eucharist, but this same God surrounds him on every side in his daily life which is filled with death and law. But this death is now swallowed up by the life of the resurrection, thanks to Christ who comes to men over and over again and gives Himself to them; and the law now has limits put to its accusations when men, in confessing their sin, repudiate the old self which the law judges, but also when they receive Christ, the new and pure Adam, in the communion. The unity of confession of sin and thanksgiving in the communion represents a unity of death and resurrection from two aspects. In the first place, in confession the communicant puts off the old man: the coming of Christ and the praise offered by the new man expel the old.[20] Those who share in the communion with us put away other expressions of the will to evil, but all of these represent a single whole, that of the corrupted life of fallen Adam. The communion, however, gives rise to new individual expressions of service, and these also constitute a single whole in the body of Christ. In the second place, Christ Himself is present in the Eucharist with His death and resurrection. This is the dominant aspect of the sacrament and the source from which individual confession and regeneration arise.[21]   The Church is the body of Christ, all of whose members have different responsibilities to fulfil in their individual relationships of daily life, but they are all sustained by the same blood which they receive in the Eucharist. The same God is at work in daily life and in worship. We do not come to experience a new reality in the sanctuary, but find rather the same God whom we have met in every part of our lives. But we experience Him now in a different way and everything now takes on a different aspect—what once seemed

[20] Cf Prenter, *Skabelse*, pp 539-542.

[21] The second use of the law culminates in the proclamation of the image of Christ in the Gospel, and the image is also proclaimed in the words spoken at the Eucharist in the Words of Institution which speak of the last night and Christ's self-giving. Cf. the fuller treatment of the purpose of the law in Wingren, *Creation and Law*, pp. 181-182, 193-195.

to be death now is seen to be life.[22] Every worshipper has at one time or another noted the strange paradox that worship is at its purest when the need is the greatest. The explanation of this paradox is that the gift in worship is and continues to be *the resurrection of the dead*.[23] In worship we encounter the Creator who creates *ex nihilo*.[24]

The life of the resurrection, according to the unanimous biblical witness, is a life of common praise and continuing worship. The Revelation of John in particular, the last book of the New Testament, is almost monotonously explicit in witnessing to this truth—in the resurrection continuously new songs of praise will be lifted up (e.g. Rev. v.8-14, vii.9-16, xix.1-8, etc.).[25] In both fellowship and praise there is a repudiation of the Adam-like tendency to clutch at eternal life as a prize to be grasped (cf. Phil. ii.6). Eternal life belongs to the future if it is *unbroken* eternal life we are thinking of, eternal life where there is no longer any struggle against temptation but rest from struggle. It is, however, important not to contemplate this future from a present which is dominated by the old nature and therefore by Adam's desire to grasp and keep. The idea that eternal life can be enjoyed while others lack it is a perversion. It would imply a total contradiction in terms to speak of an eternal life possessed by the old Adam, who must *die*.[26] Eternal life is praise, but praise does not keep to itself, for in virtue of what it already is eternal life has been set free from the desire to keep, and offers praise and glory to another. But eternal life is now also common praise, a song in which our own voice blends with others, in company with whom we remain

[22] Cf. Koch, *Auferstehung*, pp. 330-338.

[23] Irenaeus applies this to the Eucharist in the frequently quoted passage, *A.h.* iv. ii (Stier iv. ii. 2-3). The creator fills the whole earth with a life which is achieved through death. The grain of corn falls into the ground and dies in order to rise up in new wheat, indeed in the bread which is brought to our lips in the Eucharist and feeds our bodies. The elements of the Eucharist, the bread from the ear of wheat and the wine from the vine, grow up out of the earth and give nourishment to our bodies, which will one day be cast into the earth in hope of the resurrection. The units of creation and worship have often been preserved at those times in the history of the Church where Irenaeus's doctrine of recapitulation has been studied. Cf. Aronson, *Mänskligt och kristet*, pp. 148-151.

[24] Cf. Löfgren, *Theologie der Schöpfung*, pp. 21-37, and especially pp. 272-308.

[25] The metaphor of the feast points in the same direction. See Richardson, *Introduction*, pp. 372-376.   [26] Cf Prenter, *Skabelse*, pp. 618-619.

O

a united whole.[27] In this respect "hell" is to be defined as the total absence of praise, which is the same thing as being totally shut off from others in a desire to possess which cannot be quenched, since no part of creation fills the vacuum or evokes praise. There is no longing for heaven in hell, for heaven is praise, and it is the refusal to praise which is the essence of condemnation. "Hell" exists in the present here on earth and is not reserved for the future. Nor is eternal life confined to the future. Common praise is lifted up here in the present in worship which allows us to share even now in eternal life. The life of worship is the resurrection of the dead.

To say that the life of salvation flows out of death thus does not imply any automatic salvation from death. All men must die. There is, however, an existence apart from life while death continues, the reality which we have just referred to as "hell." If death is to become life, it must be death to the old, acquisitive nature.[28] But at the last judgment those who have "saved" their lives will be called into judgment. Christ Himself accordingly tells us that no man can pass judgment either on himself or on his neighbour (Rom. xiv.4, 10-13).[29] A life may be given away to others and to all appearance conceal what is given. It belongs to the nature of giving that it cannot be isolated from the group. When it becomes an attribute or quality in a person, isolated and taken by itself, giving ceases to be what it is and becomes its opposite, keeping. At the heart of the unity of work and worship which was to be found in the old national Churches of Europe we find a common sharing of tasks under-taken for mutual benefit. This sharing implied that in one sense men had deferred passing judgment on those around them and chosen instead to give to them without picking or choosing or favouring particular groups; and this giving was concealed in the forms of ordinary daily work and set within the total framework of the administration of the means of grace in the parish church, and therefore of Christ's own giving to "the

---

[27] Cf. also Paul S. Minear, *Horizons of Christian Community*, 1959, pp. 26-36 and the same author's essay in *Basileia*, 1959, p. 47.

[28] Cf. Peter Brunner in *Leitourgia*, VOL. I, 1954, pp. 250-254.

[29] It is impossible for man himself to give the answer, as Mt. xxv.31-46 indicates. He can judge neither his own case nor his neighbour's *coram Deo*. See Paul S. Minear, *Christian Hope and the Second Coming*, 1954, pp. 102-105, for a discussion of the passage.

many." When we lose this kind of communion in our own day, the Christian Church is in spiritual peril.[30] Within a generation or two it can completely abandon its classical relationship to baptism and the Gospel, make rule and law the basis of the Church, and sit in judgment rather than act as servant; in its judgment, moreover, it will be concerned with superficial qualifications and in the end combine this with a sectarian doctrine of the Eucharist in which the main problem has to do with who may and who may not celebrate the sacrament. While this deviation persists, national and state Churches may continue to survive, obstinately defended by those who attach hardly any importance to the sacraments and do not feel any need to live by them, since they wholly disregard the judgment of God in the present and His final, future judgment. Where these two aberrations exist, both ominous, the cure for both is to realise afresh the connexion between worship on the one hand and the resurrection of the dead on the other. In doing this, in other words, we reassert *the connexion between the Church and creation* in both areas.

If we think of baptism and the Gospel as a "starting-point" and not as the daily refuge of all who are members of the Church, and if our concept of the Church is determined by reference to a closed fellowship gathered around the Eucharist and an absolutised Church order which is regulated by the ministry, the Church ceases to be open towards all mankind. Here the "true" Church is defined in terms of demarcation lines. But to define the Church in this way by bounds and limits is to bring eschatology into the present, for to be within the Church is to have already reached the final goal.[31] To be a member of the Church is to be saved. Against this, however, we must emphatically insist that the command to evangelise and Pentecost and therefore the conclusion of the Gospel narrative

---

[30] Cf. Billing, *Den svenska folkkyrkan*, pp. 62-65. Billing's whole concept of a folk church is a bold attempt to avoid this danger. The ideas of calling and of the territorial church, centred on the worship of the local, parish church, are therefore central. If we lose interest in these basic realities, we also operate with a new concept of folk church.

[31] Cf. the original idea of "the time of the Church" in Torrance, *Royal Priesthood*, pp. 43-62, a chapter which, in spite of its obscurity, has a great deal to say about the Church and the idea of succession.

and the early part of the Acts indicate *a movement which will not come to an end until all nations rise in the resurrection of the dead.* Everything that the Church does, even expulsion from the congregation by which a member ceases to be within the Church (1 Cor. v.5), aims at bringing the salvation of Christ to men. In its mission, therefore, the Church moves out to all nations (Mt. xxiv.14), and when it has attained its final goal, Christ Himself will separate, judge, and divide (Mt. xxv.32). Then the enterprise, which the Church has been appointed to proclaim, will have extended to *the whole of creation.* When this openness, which was so evident in the interpretation of the Church in early Christianity, and this attitude to mission are lost, it is partly at least because the belief in creation is in some way deficient and there is a failure to understand that the God who is known in worship and prayer is the Creator of all the world. He is at work in all the world in the whole of human life at the same time as He is at work in little groups assembled for prayer, and sends His Church with the Gospel out among those who are under the law.[32]

If on the other hand infant baptism and the Gospel develop into a folk Church which does not judge or discriminate, the inner communion which unites the baptised in the Church is lost. Consequently the belief in creation is detached from the Christ event to which the Gospels bear witness, the event of death and resurrection. Both baptism and the Gospel make this event central and hold it out to all in order that they may die and rise again each day, until they experience the final death in expectation of the final resurrection.[33] The communion which continually draws the baptised together again is the

---

[32] The Gospel is addressed to those who are under the law, and this point of reference, which we have emphasised earlier, is related to the central place occupied by death and resurrection in the Gospel. The Gospel is resurrection brought to bear on a situation where death holds sway. The second use of the law is based on the first use, on the demands made in the world around us. Cf. Ivarsson, *Predikans uppgift*, p. 74.

[33] The future aspect of eschatology has been emphasised by Cullmann in particular and before him by Folke Holmström, e.g. in *Det eskatologiska motivet*, 1933, pp. 353-407. It is quite clear that Holmström has directly influenced Cullmann with his relative freedom from Barth. See *Christ and Time*, p. 63, footnote 5, and the review article in *Revue d'histoire et de philosophie religieuses*, 1938, pp. 347-355, especially pp. 352-354.

communion of worship, of which the repeated Eucharist and repeated preaching are part. It is a communion which holds out the same gift to all who partake and it safeguards the individuality of each, since death and resurrection are both present realities in our daily living. The daily life of each member of the Church is constantly nourished by the sacraments. In opposition to those who would derive the folk Church from the first article alone we must insist that the connexion between Church and creation cannot be clearly defined unless we connect this doctrine of daily vocation and work with that of the sacraments and worship, i.e. with our doctrine of *death and resurrection as present realities.*[34] Only so shall we be able to show the significance of baptism and the Gospel. The factor of judgment and death cannot at this point be put aside.

The work of the Church among men thus moves towards a point where the structure of the old creation is broken.[35] The closed, sectarian type of Church which tends to bring the eschatological future down into the present time of the Church and to abandon the movement out to the ends of the earth, and the open, unrestricted folk Church, which tends quite consciously to reject any mention of judgment or death, are both in danger of losing eschatology altogether. The solution will not be found by discussing the question of affiliation or the meaning of Church membership, etc. The main problem is different. We need to examine the significance of the sacraments. This will mean at the same time discussing the resurrection of the dead, the event which includes the past (Christ's completed work), the present (the life of the Church in the present time), and the future (the last times).[36] In our present

---

[34] K.-M. Olsson's failure to speak of "death" is connected with the fact that in his concept of the Church the sacraments and worship have no essential significance (see *Kontakt med kyrkan*, pp. 100-121).

[35] Cf. Cullmann, *Immortality*, pp. 44-46. The emphasis on the resurrection of the *body* is not to be understood in such a way that the framework of the old creation is retained (see 1 Cor. xv.24-28, 35-57). If, for instance, we oppose cremation on theological grounds, we must raise the question whether we are really operating with a biblical view of "body."

[36] Grass is critical of the "cosmically" oriented eschatology in *Dank an Paul Althaus*, pp. 67-78. He also seeks to avoid the purely existential interpretation. The individualism to which he resorts could be avoided by adopting another concept of Christology and doctrine of the sacraments.

context, in which our interest has been focused particularly on the relationship between Gospel and Church, it is necessary after this general discussion of Church and creation to keep the individual well in view. By doing so we shall relate his participation in the Church and its worship to his daily work and service of his neighbour.

CHAPTER III

MAN IN THE CHURCH

The Last Judgment and our Baptism

THERE are some aspects of the New Testament doctrine of baptism which are almost neglected in modern theology. To be baptised means to have undergone in baptism not only death but also judgment.[1] This connexion between death and judgment in baptism need not surprise us since the two are so integrally related elsewhere in scripture.[2] Baptism is the act of faith and conversion which follows from the hearing of the preached word. The words of the Gospel of John are relevant at this point: "He who hears my word and believes Him who sent me has eternal life; he does not come into judgment, but has passed from death to life" (Jn. v.24). Death and judgment have *passed away*.[3]

Here as elsewhere, of course, the background is the prehistory of the Old Testament. In a situation which has been determined by Adam the life that is lived according to the flesh means death. Unless there is a change of direction the only end to this road is death. But to "put to death the deeds of the body" is *life* (Rom. viii.13). The work of Christ is to change the direction set by Adam, and it culminates in His death and resurrection (see 1 Cor. xv.21 f. where Adam is referred to by name and cf. Rom. v.12, and vi.4, which refers explicitly to baptism and speaks of the "life" which has been raised from death in baptism as its final consequence). All who have been baptised are affected by this change which Christ has wrought

---

[1] See C. F. D. Moule, "The Judgment Theme in the Sacraments," in *Background*, pp. 464-481. Cf. Richardson, *Introduction*, p. 341.

[2] Cf. Stauffer, *Theology*, p. 150-152.

[3] Cf. C. H. Dodd, *Fourth Gospel*, pp. 148, 413.

in the direction which Adam, that is to say which man, has chosen to take, for baptism in fact means death and resurrection.[1] To undergo baptism means to reject the old life and be given a new life. In order to attain life, therefore, we must put to death the "deeds of the body," and it was primarily for this that Christ suffered on the cross. It is required of us now only that we should be "in Christ." And we are brought into Christ through baptism. Baptism can be administered only once. Once we have passed this gateway no re-entry is ever again possible. Those who have been baptised can never become as though they had never been baptised or pass through this door a second or third time. The cross is the essential part in the restoration of all creation to its primal purity, and every baptism once and for all brings those who are baptised into the sphere of restoration) The Church, made up as it is of ordinary men and women and grounded in baptism, is thus in its total life a living proof that the work of restoration is even now being carried on in the midst of a humanity which is still moving in the direction set by Adam, i.e. which is still dominated by the selfish desire to get, to have, and to hold.[4]

This is a particularly clear exposition of the reversal by Christ of the direction set by Adam in Phil. ii.6-11. There was (and is) a way opposed to Christ, an unwillingness to empty oneself and take the form of a servant, a refusal to humble oneself and become obedient to God. This is the way of counting equality with God a thing to be grasped. But Christ refused this way and willingly accepted the cross. Hence He is now "highly exhalted" and reigns as Lord. God condemned Adam, who got the opposite of what he was looking for, death rather than life. But He raised Christ from the death which He had voluntarily undergone, so that at every point, the line of Christ was a reversal of the perverted line of Adam. As a result there is now life in place of death, and life moreover which is not grasped in selfishness but given by God. This is Christ's unique position among men: He is the source from whom new life is continually given to the many (Rom. v.15-21). To be baptised means to be accorded a place in this gracious activity of His. Baptism is therefore an obvious starting-point for ethical

[4] Moule in *Background*, pp. 466-467.

instruction.[5] For this reason too the content of such instruction is love for others or, to express it in different terms, the imitation of Christ. The two things, however, are one and the same. Concern for the well-being of others coincides by an inner necessity with the imitation of Christ (Phil. II.3, 4 gives expression to the injunctions which are inspired by the image of Christ in vv. 5-8).[6] Baptism points beyond itself to the relationships into which it brings the baptised. It is the reverse of the acquisitive attitude which clings for dear life to what is created. The admonitions addressed to the baptised bid them break away from this restless acquisitiveness which has its source in the fear of death and the craving for life, and change their attitude both in regard to their neighbour and to death. In Christ death has become life and our neighbour part of the humanity for which He suffered death, and which His body, the Church, now prays for and cares for (see the whole context of Col. 1.14-29, where the reconciliation of "all things, whether on earth or in heaven" and of "every man" is regarded as the culmination of the death of Christ. This reconciliation is achieved on the apostle's side through personal suffering and voluntarily chosen death).[7]

We are now dealing, however, with the other side of death. Death is not only past and done with, it is also a destructive reality which has still to be faced by the baptised. To regard it from this different aspect is illuminating. Baptism at the one time points forward to a death that is still to come and points outward to the neighbour, i.e. to service which is still to be done for the benefit of the neighbour. This means that judgment is not just past and done with but in a sense is still to come, and that this future judgment is a judgment upon

[5] In Jervell, *Imago Dei*, pp. 206-208, Phil. II.6-8 is thus directly connected with the exhortation in Phil. II.1-5 (see especially p. 208). The whole passage has to do with baptism.

[6] Cf. also Ernst Käsemann, "Kritische Analyse von Phil. II.5-11," in *Z.T.K.*, 1950, where the whole passage is interpreted from the point of view of the contrast between Adam and Christ (pp. 343-344), but where the point of the exhortation becomes "freedom from the world" in the usual Bultmannian fashion (pp. 354-359).

[7] On the connexion between Col. 1.15-17 and the creation narrative in Gen. 1 see Dahl in *Background*, p. 434, and also Jervell, *Imago Dei*, pp. 198-201, 218-226. On the concept of mission implied here cf. Richardson, *Introduction*, p. 254, Robinson, *The Body*, pp. 71-72.

men's works. It is certainly confusing that the New Testament and Paul in particular can speak at the one time of a justification apart from works which has already taken place, and also of a judgment upon works which is still to come.[8] But at this point we are trying to look at the problem from the point of view of the relation between baptism and the last judgment. Baptism is a total judgment which has already taken place, but which is followed by other "judgments" of a different kind throughout the life of the baptised. In the same way baptism is also a total death which has already taken place, and which is followed by a daily putting to death of the old nature. It is our thesis that these subsequent forms of judgment and death are in the first place interconnected, since death is judgment, and in the second place are connected with the unrepeated act of the baptism, the inner meaning of which is unfolded in these subsequent acts. It is also our thesis that we enter into these acts in worship, particularly in the Eucharist, and that in spite of their destructive aspect they give life, for through them Christ's own life is offered to the baptised *sub contraria specie*. The last judgment, therefore, may also from one point of view coincide with the victory of life and righteousness over death and sin, and thus be regarded by faith as salvation, the final revelation of the redemption sealed in baptism.[9] But it is possible to acknowledge the last judgment in this way only when we submit to judgment here and now, i.e. when we confess our sin and repudiate any righteousness of our own. "Justification by faith alone" is a living and daily reality when the individual lives by his baptism until the final judgment. In the present chapter it will be our task to examine our subject as it were from below, from the point of view, that is, of an individual member of the Church. A brief glance at baptism and judgment will therefore be appropriate at this point.

There has been considerable discussion in modern theology about the relation between realised and futurist eschatology.

---

[8] Cf. Eidem, *Kristna livet*, VOL. I, pp. 78-85, Joest, *Gesetz und Freiheit*, pp. 155-169.
[9] This is included in the well-known conclusion to Luther's *De servo arbitrio*. See Bring, *Dualismen*, pp. 341-356, and also Aulén, *Faith of the Christian Church*, pp. 138-140.

Bultmann has been the staunchest advocate in our day of the former, while Cullmann is unsurpassed in the vigour of his insistence on the futurist aspect of eschatology and its radical distinction from all realised eschatology.[10] In Sweden, oddly enough, the problem has aroused hardly any interest, while in Norway and Denmark the debate has centred rather on the doctrines of hell and eternal life respectively.[11] In regard to our present discussion the real problem does not concern present and future in general, for baptism in a particular way affects all that we have to say. At the beginning of Col. III Paul speaks of a death which has already taken place, and it is clear that his reference is to baptism (the terms which dominate the whole passage are death and life, putting certain things away and putting others on, the old nature and the new, and so on). The important thing to note is Paul's translation *from* the death which has already taken place ("You have died, and your life is hid with Christ in God," Col. III.3) *to* his trenchant appeal: "Put to death what is earthly in you" (Col. III.5). The things to be put away are anger, malice, etc., i.e. conduct and attitudes which are all too obvious facts of human life (Col. III.5-7). The things to be put on are forbearance, forgiveness of one another, etc., again behaviour which directly affects our neighbour or can benefit our neighbour (Col. III.12 ff.).[12] We should note that Paul relates the death which has already occurred to Christ's coming appearance in glory, a glory in which those who believe in Him, i.e. who have "died" with Him, will share (Col. III.4). We should also note how he similarly relates what is to be put to death, i.e. the "old" nature which should really be dead but which still exists in spite of baptism, to the wrath which is to come (Col. III.6, cf.

[10] See Bultmann in *Kerygma and Myth*, pp. 35-43, Cullmann, *Christ and Time*, pp. 139-143, 237-242 (Bultmann's programme of demythologising, as well as his commentary on John, had already been published by 1941; five years later Cullmann was attacking both these writings). The debate has generally been of little interest outside Europe. It is in Europe that the decisive positions were formed.

[11] In Sweden the fullest treatment of the relationship between present and future from the standpoints which have been adopted on the Continent is found in Torgny Bohlin's doctoral thesis, *Den korsfäste Skaparen*, pp. 117-138, 193-273, 307-415.

[12] Cf. Dahl in *Background*, p. 436.

III.25).[13] The wrath which is coming will fall on what at present is subject to the onset of death, if it endures that long.[14]

If that is the relationship between present and future we cannot use purely cognitive terms to describe it. There has been a common tendency, particularly in the theology influenced by Barth, to make a distinction between present and future, but to make this distinction entirely a matter of *insight*. The reality which will be revealed in eternity is the same as that which is disclosed in the incarnation, except that now (in eternity) it is wholly perceived and understood, whereas before, to faith alone, it was not. The line which extends from present to future will therefore afford no new victories, for the victory has already been won. All that we can gain in the future can be defined simply as an increase in our understanding of what has already been received.[15] This emphasis on understanding can of course be justified on biblical grounds, and for early Christianity certainly the new thing to be given in the future is "sight" (I Cor. XIII.12, II Cor. v.7, I Jn. III.2). But there are also many passages in the Bible which speak of the performance here, in the intervening time, of works which are, as it were, reflex actions prompted by the mighty act of the cross and the resurrection. If it were only a matter of cognition, it would be natural to define the meaning of Christ's redemption in a doctrinal statement and leave it for the future to reveal the full meaning of such a dogma. But on the line between present and future there is baptism. Those who are baptised are put to death and raised to life, and this double action is a present reality and will be a continuing experience day by day until the future finally becomes the present. If baptism is not this, it has lost its meaning and when the final judgment comes the old nature will remain what it was. It

---

[13] Cf. Richardson, *Introduction*, pp. 78-79.

[14] Cf. Pierce, *Conscience*, pp. 66-74, where it is argued that the power which restrains evil is wrath, even though it may be in the form of authority (Rom. XIII.4), and it is even now at work, helping to free men from the wrath to come (see also pp. 85-86). Ordinary secular power is one aspect in the present time of the "last judgment," but only one aspect.

[15] Cf. Torgny Bohlin, *Den korsfäste Skaparen*, pp. 404-406. Cf. Karl Barth, *Church Dogmatics*, VOL. III, PT. III, 1961, pp. 363-367, where the emphasis on clarity is equally one-sided.

has not been destroyed and it has not been judged. Even so, a man may still be saved, "but only as through fire" (1 Cor. III.15). The necessity of purification cannot be avoided.[16]

It is in this context that C. A. Pierce discusses the Pauline doctrine of conscience (e.g. in Rom. II.14 f., XIII.4 f., and in this connexion Rom. I. 18 ff., and 1 Cor. IV.4 f., and elsewhere). Conscience relates to a man's actions and judges them as evil. The judgment of conscience is a prelude to the last judgment. It is present in every individual, and if we choose can be heard and obeyed.[17] To listen to the voice of conscience and obey it is to submit each day to the judgment which is to come. To fail to listen means that the judgment has still to be faced. Another precursor of the final judgment is the judgment passed in courts of law on criminals; a third, strange though it may be, is bodily illness or infirmity (1 Cor. XI.29-32); and a fourth, Church discipline (1 Cor. V.5).[18] When a man is "in Christ," everything can promote his salvation. Baptism simply continues to unfold its inexhaustible content, viz. life through death, in everything that happens to him. Nothing is profane any longer, and nothing is purely biological any longer. The hidden meaning of the incarnation interpenetrates the whole of the created order and brings into being springs of life which are just below the surface for any who dig to find them, i.e. wherever there is faith, or repentance, or conversion. This willingness to acknowledge one's guilt and to reconsider one's way of life, and in reconsidering it to believe, in spite of all appearances and the buffetings of life, means to be ready to submit to death and judgment, but at the same time it also means a daily resurrection from the dead. This is what Luther had in mind when he spoke of our "being clothed each in his baptism."[19] For the Church member who tries to live in this fashion the Gospel is not a first stage, marked by conversion, after which he is to

---

[16] Cf. Moule in *Background*, pp. 479-481.

[17] See Pierce, *Conscience*, pp. 66-68, 85-86, 111.

[18] Also to be included here is the strange idea that we "give place to wrath" when we refrain from avenging a wrong (Rom. XII.9). See also Rom. XIV.10-12, 1 Pet. II.23.

[19] On the term see the last sentences in the fourth section of Luther's Larger Catechism. The old nature dies and the new rises daily in the man who is "clad in his baptism."

submit to certain commandments and be governed by these rather than by the Gospel. On the contrary, the Gospel is his daily sustenance. He lives only by justification by faith. This is the way by which he comes to experience the commandments of God, and His control of life, and His judgment.[20]

The passages in the New Testament which speak of a final judgment of men's works, as throughout the Bible, are not spoken in a vacuum. They do not refer to a circumstance entirely unrelated to its context. On the contrary, the judgment of which they speak is a reality experienced by those who hear what they say, if this message touches and stirs the conscience. Mt. xxv.31-46 describes a future division among the nations. But no two persons hearing this passage will apply it to the same daily realities. Christ the Judge reveals in His judgment the relationship which every man is to have to his neighbour, though he may not perceive it, and as long as this particular passage is read until the end of time, each of the countless multitudes who hear it will interpret it in a different way. Only the individual knows in his conscience what needs to be done in his own circle, and only he sees where judgment is passed upon him.[21] This is the moment of his conversion as it is the moment of the Gospel. Those whose consciences have been aroused by the word which speaks of "the least of these," Christ's brethren, cannot but number themselves among the "cursed" who are on Christ's left hand. An age of marked pietism concerns itself with the question of how and by what psychological process the wicked who are on Christ's left can be brought to love their neighbours and come to be numbered by reason of their merits among those on the right. The supposition is that such an impulse lies within man himself. But the biblical testimony is that it is Christ who gives this impetus, and that in the incarnation it is to the accursed that

[20] In regard to the positive role played by the conscience and the sense of guilt see Heinz Häfner, *Schulderleben und Gewissen*, 1956, pp. 133-135. The author is a depth psychologist influenced by existentialist philosophy.

[21] Cf. Minear, *Christian Hope*, pp. 102-105. The same thing is true of all passages which speak of judgment according to works (e.g. Mt. xvi.27, Jn. v.29, Rom. ii.6, ii Cor. v.10). Cf. Eidem, *Kristna livet*, VOL. I, pp. 78-80, where several passages are cited, Joest, *Gesetz und Freiheit*, pp. 155-195, who gives an acute analysis of the whole problem, and finally Paul Feine, *Theologie des Neuen Testaments*, 6th ed., 1934, p. 391, on Heb. iv.12-13.

He comes—to the out and out sinners whom He has already judged and who have assented to His judgment. The impulse to love is not in man but in the Judge Himself.[22] The baptised examine their actions "in Christ" and all that they do is continually brought under ever new judgment. What is worth keeping is sifted out, the rest is rejected.

The word of judgment which the New Testament speaks judges those who hear it. The references to Sodom (Mt. xi.24), Tyre and Sidon (Mt. xi.22), the men of Nineveh and the Queen of the South (Mt. xii.41 f.) are not objective statements concerning the moral conditions of these Gentile nations. They are a cutting word which reveals the situation of the Jews in the time of Jesus. As soon as they are spoken the judgment comes upon those who hear them. God has had dealings with Nineveh and the South and has found response among them. Now He is dealing with men through Christ—in whom He has revealed far more of His innermost being. And now, therefore, He is looking for the response of a change of heart. But if there is no disposition on the part of those who hear Christ to accept His judgment, they will be judged with greater severity than the men of Nineveh and the others. The vantage ground to which Christ refers in the words, "Something greater than Jonah is here" (Mt. xii.41) is the accomplishment of the mighty works which Sodom, Tyre, Sidon, Nineveh, and the South had never seen but which had now taken place in Capernaum and the neighbouring regions, the chief among them being the final, revolutionary event of the sign of Jonah, the death and resurrection on the third day (Mt. xi.20-24, xii.39 f.). As we have seen earlier, the "something greater" which is now present and the accentuation of the moral requirement which it makes are to be seen supremely in the death of Jesus at Calvary.[23] The natural law of love for one's neighbour has not been replaced by something entirely different or by a Christian commandment which has a new and hitherto unknown point of reference. Rather, the natural law is *accentuated* through the

---

[22] See especially Joest, *Gesetz und Freiheit*, pp. 179-180. If we speak of the content of a biblical passage without *at the same time* speaking of those to whom it is addressed, we lack the very means of dealing with the problem of judgment.

[23] This is the key point in the section dealing with the new activity, above.

preaching of the Gospel and *heightened* to the point of requiring the death of those who hear it, i.e. that they shall come to the likeness of Christ and be formed after His image, putting to death the old nature of fallen Adam and bringing into being the new nature of the primal creation, which is the image of God in Christ. This is the culmination of baptism—the restoration of uncorrupted humanity.[24]

But the factors which bring about the accentuation and heightening of the natural law also enable us to choose and distinguish among the multitude of demands which are laid upon us by those among whom we are set. If we do not expect that our imitation of Christ will mean suffering, we shall have no easy escape from the demands made upon us, and shall cease to be able to say no to some and thus to distinguish between them. But if we are aware that suffering is to be our lot, we can then stand firm in face of the appeals made to us which spring from selfishness, hunger for power, or injured pride. The conscience bound to the Word of God is to judge what love for our neighbour really demands of us. It is prepared to deal with external problems when the time is ripe, and it is confirmed rather than weakened in its attitude when these difficult situations arise. It was not coincidental that Luther evolved the doctrine that man's daily work is marked by the cross and at the same time prided himself on being the most obstinate creature in the world. On the other hand, however, it is strange that his teachings about bearing the cross should have been interpreted in a later age to mean submission to the authorities, and in practice nothing more.[25] It may be that we can find an explanation of this in the characteristic Lutheran stress on the neighbour. The sphere in which a distinction is made between the demands made upon us by our fellow-men is not primarily parliament, government, or other legislative organ, but the

---

[24] But even the man "in Christ" is a tempted man, who is still able to fall (cf. 1 Cor. x.1-13). The restoration which excludes any possibility of fall belongs wholly to the future, and also implies a heightening in comparison with Adam in his unfallen state, for in Adam's case the fall was still a possibility. This freedom is something unique to eternal life. Cf. Wingren, *Creation and Law*, pp. 35-36, 100-101, and also the biblical references. See also Richardson, *Introduction*, pp. 245-247.

[25] Cf. Lau, *Luthers Lehre*, p. 88.

relationship which the Christian has to his neighbour, that is to say in a relatively personal relationship which will vary in each case. Political matters are a special instance of this basic norm and a democratic society broadens the *mise en scène* by giving us more neighbours, but it is still the same reality with which we are dealing. Those who approach Lutheran teaching from the side of Roman Catholicism or the Calvinist tradition tend to prejudge the whole issue and make political attitudes primary, i.e. they seek to point out common social practices which affect all Christians alike. And this, it is maintained, is where Luther's teaching is so weak and his answers so inadequate.[26] In the highly political involvement in which Churches today find themselves we may well ask whether in fact it may not be good for us to adopt a little more of this "inadequacy" of the early Church. Greater self-control could express a more profound moral earnestness. The actions for which we are held responsible in the last judgment are the things that we have done in relation to our neighbour, and though concealed at present, they will be revealed after death.[27]

It cannot thus be the task of Christian ethics to formulate decrees which are to take the place of the freedom to pick and choose from among the demands of our neighbour. There is, however, no question here of any subjective or personal morality. The total picture is made up on the one hand of the earthly government and the civil use of the law, and on the other of the spiritual government, worship, and the sacraments. We have now come to a point in our discussion when it is possible for us to coordinate the elements which theology often allows to remain disconnected, viz. the first article, baptism and the Eucharist, the two uses of the law, and the Church. Life and liturgy are inseparably related, and it is now time to define the points of connexion between them. When

[26] See, however, the chapter, "Der Neubau der Sittlichkeit," in Karl Holl, *Gesammelte Aufsätze zur Kirchengeschichte*, VOL. I, 6th ed., 1932, pp. 155-287.

[27] As long as death remains, works remain. All that we do up to the end we do under the law. Cf. Häfner, *Schulderleben*, pp. 178-179, who, in spite of his completely different starting-points, is highly instructive in his view of guilt. Existentialist philosophy reveals a striking affinity to the theological doctrine of *law*. Strangely enough, this particular philosophy has been used as a means rather of harmonising Gospel (kerygma) and philosophy. Here if anywhere there should be a gulf between the two!

P

we do so we are at once confronted by the whole question of "baptism and the last judgment."

Human life, even apart from the Gospel and the sacraments, is implicated in a nexus of demands and destined to end in death. The civil use of the law has its origin in the universal need for life and food. The Creator continues to create through human toil, which takes from creation and passes on to others what it has found there. The first article of the Creed flows into the first article of the law.[28] Christ was born into this world, put under the law even in the purely external sense, and crucified by earthly authorities who had been given their power from God (Acts iv.27 f., Jn. xix.11). His death is the baptism which reverses the direction taken by our humanity, and one by one men are pulled into this movement of conversion through baptism and the Gospel. None can be governed by the law without also being tormented by the law. The realisation of guilt is independent of the Church, for guilt exists apart from the Gospel.[29] Even apart from Christ the conscience represents an anticipation of the last judgment in the awareness which all men have of the suffering of their fellow-men. To hear the cry of human need—"I was sick . . . I was in prison. . . .—and to see the look on men's faces in their anguish is to experience the law in its spiritual use and to be aware of the judgment. But the condemnation of the law comes to its height only when the Gospel proclaims the likeness of Christ. The one who gave up His life on the cross and made no demands on men solicits in the burdened conscience a positive awareness of guilt which no preaching of the law could draw forth.[30] In this totality of guilt the individual sees himself as he really is, with the "old" nature of the fallen Adam upon him. But it is possible to see himself in this way only from some point outside Adam, that is to say only when he is in the Gospel. The

---

[28] Criticism of the doctrine of the *usus civilis*, therefore, also affects the first article. A clear example of this is Søe, *Kristelig etik*, pp. 203-206.

[29] See Ivarsson, *Predikans uppgift*, pp. 71-75.

[30] If we assent to the first use of the law, we shall not find any difficulty in Jn. xvi.9, as Søe seems to, *Kristelig etik*, pp. 206-207, footnote 5. We must, of course, be critical of the argument that we become aware of guilt in the main only after the Gospel, e.g. Søe, *ibid.*, pp. 21-22, or the same author's *Religionsfilosofi*, 1955, pp. 78-96.

new man who is Christ is risen when the second use of the law comes to its fulfilment. The double work of baptism, which is to put to death the old nature and raise up the new, has already started in the baptised. In order that this operation, once begun, may not cease, the table of communion is ever anew spread before us. In the Words of Institution Christ is again set forth before our eyes "on the night when He was betrayed." Sin and self-condemnation are at the heart of the sacrament, and therefore confession and absolution are also part of it. All who communicate are to expel the old Adam from their hearts. But it is for precisely this reason that the note of thanksgiving is to sound here in our worship.[31] Christ is risen, and even now offers eternal life in the midst of the old creation through ordinary bread and wine.

The condemnation of the old life which we experience in Eucharistic worship is the same judgment as that which we experience in baptism. There the old nature was put away and the new began. But since all through life the old keeps coming back, Christ's coming over and over again in the Eucharist denotes His continued condemnation of the old. This judgment is declared in the confession of sin which the communicant makes, thereby endorsing the judgment, and is cancelled and blotted out by the word of forgiveness which is the declaration of his acquittal. This aspect of the Lord's Supper does not detract from the "Eucharistic" emphasis or introduce a gloomy note into an occasion of rejoicing. It affords rather the very ground of such rejoicing, and is the other side of the coin, as it were, which is set against the unnatural "old" which has now been renounced. Hence also there is an identity between the Eucharist as an eschatological meal, which is marked by an eager expectation of the resurrection of the dead, and the Eucharist in which judgment is passed upon the old and which is marked by eucharistic rejoicing in the presence of Christ.[32] The effect of baptism extends to the whole of human life and comes to its fulfilment only in the resurrection of the

---

[31] In Davies, *Spirit*, p. 203, footnote 154, confession of sin and Eucharist are contrasted with one another in an unrealistic way.

[32] Cf. Moule, *Sacrifice*, pp. 30-43, and also the same author's essay in *Background*, pp. 466-468.

dead. The Eucharist in its repeated form makes it possible for those who have been baptised to die again to the old and rise again to the new. The repudiation of the old Adam and the acceptance of Christ are both involved in this transaction, which also points forward into the future. All of this takes place in the period which precedes death, and faith cannot accept and transform the partial death which precedes final death only to treat physical death at the end as a purely biological phenomenon. Faith, which endures the blows of life and accepts them as a judgment which yet holds grace within itself, remains faith even when confronted by physical death. Indeed, this is all it can be when faced with this last grim reality; that is to say, it awaits a kindgom in which even death itself has become the means of life.[33] For those "on the way" to the judgment there is, of course, no means of determining in advance what their future blessedness or struggles will mean for them. Definite knowledge will come later, day by day, but in face of approaching death faith consistently remains open, receptive, and forward looking.[34] By being thus open it keeps the final judgment in view and therefore life and salvation in view.

We could also express this otherwise by saying that faith keeps Christ in view, for we can never speak of Christ apart from the cross and the resurrection. The life and salvation which He offers are different from any other life or salvation. To remove the element of judgment from salvation means to offer salvation to the old Adam. But this is to make salvation an attainment which sets a man apart from other men. And any such idea means that like Adam he is again seeking something for himself where he should re-think (*metanoein*) about himself and become converted. But to keep Christ in view is to look to one who took the opposite course from Adam and who

---

[33] When Rev. xx.10-14 speaks of "the second death," it is referring to a will opposed to God which has refused to submit to judgment and death. Luther has wrestled with this whole problem more seriously than most, especially in his *De servo arbitrio*.

[34] It is to this extent correct to say that the new thing which the future will bring is sight or clear understanding. But this new clarity is based on the fact that new judgment and new death *have taken place*. The cognitive aspect cannot be isolated as in Torgny Bohlin, *Den korsfäste Skaparen*, pp. 404-406.

offered forgiveness from the cross and now holds out this same forgiveness to men through the Gospel. Those who hold themselves thus open to Christ are saved when they are judged, and for them salvation consists in this worship of the Son and their praise of His mighty acts. To live the life of divine praise as it is constituted by the two basic acts of baptism and the Eucharist is to live by the righteousness of faith. Day by day the Church receives its life from the Gospel when its members live by the sacraments or by the Spirit—the two things are one and the same.[35]

This fellowship with Christ, however, continues to be a fellowship with Him only as it remains a communion between those who are baptised and other men. To hold that fellowship with Christ is an experience to be enjoyed in isolation from others is to turn it into an attainment to be grasped, which means to be excluded from it. Much of the discussion about the eventual salvation of the unbaptised is based on the false assumption that the necessity of being baptised is a qualification for membership in some coterie of the saved. But baptism is primarily Christ's own baptism, the general baptism at Calvary, in which the whole of mankind was involved and from which the Church, concerned as always to move out of itself to the world of men with its gifts and its offer, came into being. To have part in this greater baptism means personally to confess and praise Christ within His Church and to be willing to receive baptism and bring it to others. It does not mean to assume an attitude of judgment in regard to those who have not been baptised.[36] Why these should be in such a state and remain outside the Church is a problem to which we can generally give no answer. There are certain situations when in spiritual counselling we can say to a particular individual that he should be baptised according to the rites of the Christian

---

[35] The connexion made by Davies, *Spirit*, pp. 84-164, between baptism, Eucharist and the *Gospel* is therefore of great systematic importance.

[36] Infant baptism may well be grounded in a firm assurance about the nature of baptism as a divine act, and is therefore scarcely a suitable basis for an argument in which the fact of having been baptised is transformed into a quality found in a certain group. Cf. Karl Brinkel, *Die Lehre Luthers von der fides infantium bei der Kindertaufe*, 1958, pp. 87-88, and also Löfgren, *Theologie der Schöpfung*, pp. 191-193.

Church. Then, however, this spiritual counsel is itself part of
Christ's own approach to those who lack understanding.
It is not a judgment about the superiority of the baptised in
relation to the unbaptised.[37] What the ministers of the Church
say and do, even in ordinary conversation, is a *vehicle of the
Gospel*, and in the last resort cannot be anything else, even when
they are speaking sternly. Anything that is said in human
dealings by way of warning, reprimand, or rebuke, can act as a
preparation for God's judgments, but it can never be identical
with the last judgment, even when excommunication is involved (I Cor. v.5). We may express this paradoxically by
saying that the Church is in the best position to avoid com-
mitting the worst sins of destroying faith and abandoning the
Gospel when it is made up of congregations which are set in a
particular locality, and which have contact with the world
through the lives of their members. As we have just observed,
worship and the sacraments are inseparably connected with
what God does in the world.[38]

It is a real question if an excessive preoccupation with personal salvation may not underlie the anxiety felt by a good
number of people concerning the state of their kinfolk in the
last judgment. We do of course have a real concern for our
neighbour in this situation and a desire for his well-being. But
the judgment involved in their anxiety extends to more than
those who hear it. For those who live by the righteousness of
faith without works it is a more natural question to ask why,
if any are rejected in the judgment, they themselves should
be spared. To ask such soul-searching questions means that we
have seen where the judgment really points and accepted the
verdict of the one who speaks the word of judgment (note the
transition from the question in Lk. XIII.23 f. to the answer given
by Christ). To live under the judgment of Christ is to live in
communion with one another. The old, fallen nature obtrudes in a
thousand different forms through the temptations which come
upon every member of the Church, but it is driven back in the

[37] See also Prenter, *Skabelse*, pp. 512-514.

[38] There has been a thorough discussion of the connexion between baptism
and Gen. 1 on the basis of patristic evidence. See, e.g., N. A. Dahl, "La terre
où coulent le lait et le miel," in *Aux sources de la tradition chrétienne*, 1950, pp. 62-70,
and also Jean Daniélou, *Bible et liturgie*, 1951, pp. 100-102.

daily judgment which fellowship with Christ involves. These unseen victories for the new life, attained in each individual's conscience, also involve for the members of Christ's body the common service of their fellows in daily life and work. To be "in the body" means at the one time to have fellowship with Christ and to have fellowship with one's fellow-men.[39] The factor that unites different individuals in a congregation is that they all *receive* from Christ. Those who are in the Church are not simply vehicles for the transmission of the Gospel to the outsiders, but themselves stand under the judgment of the conscience and understand that the Gospel has something to say to *them*.[40] Their common praise, offered in worship by many but "with one voice" (Rom. xv.6), is grounded on what they themselves have received.[41]

[39] See Robinson, *The Body*, pp. 46-58, and Moule in *Background*, p. 473.
[40] Cf. Karl Barth, *Christengemeinde und Bürgergemeinde*, 1946, pp. 8-10.
[41] The unity of the members consists in praise. Cf. Minear in *Basileia*, 1949, p. 47.

Freedom and the Law

In worship the many are brought together into a unity. What is done in worship has a unifying not a divisive effect. There is a bond that exists between those who have assembled for worship, a common focus and purpose, and a common sharing of the same gifts. They are the recipients of the Gospel and of freedom, and respond by pouring forth their praise. This freedom and worship is the heart of Sunday, the day of Resurrection.[1]

The implications of all this begin to become clearer for the individual worshipper on Monday morning. Then he has his own business to turn to, and for the time being it is something different from the matters which occupy the other members of the Church. The body which engaged in divine service on Sunday is now scattered and occupied here and there with the business which concerns each of its members. But these individual Christians are still the *Church* in their own places of work. Those of whom we speak in this chapter as "in the

[1] The distinctive character of Sunday appears most clearly in the early Church when, by celebrating this day, the weekly Easter, the congregation breaks out of its worldly surroundings. Cf. Wingren, *Living Word*, pp. 192-193.

Church" are at the same time no less "in the world." The
implications of baptism are worked out in the world outside
the boundaries of the Church, and it is there that the significance of worship is to be shown. The freedom which came to
be consciously understood as freedom in the offering of worship
in divine service must prove that it is indeed freedom in the
nexus of daily restrictions and difficulties that exist outside the
Church. If it cannot do this, it is a sham.

Here we shall be mainly concerned with freedom and the
law. In our discussion we shall keep in mind the individual,
and shall have regard on the one hand to worship and the sacraments and on the other to daily work and human relationships. In this way we shall see from yet another aspect that the
sacraments are the source of a real communion.

To begin with we must reiterate that those who are occupied
in the business of earning a living in the world outside really
are the Church. By this we mean that there is a tendency to
make the Church in practice identical with the ministry.
When the Reformers in the sixteenth century evolved their
teaching about marriage, their interest was centred in the
contrast with daily life which marriage involved, for it was here
that the purpose of baptism was fulfilled for man and wife.
Thus it was in the home of the people and in places remote
from the Church that the inner life of the Church was lived out.
But when we speak in the Church today of marriage the centre
of our interest has shifted quite radically to the ritual act,
i.e. to the ceremony which the minister performs for the couple
and which is over in a matter of minutes.[2] The change is a
significant one, and we become exclusively concerned with the
narrow liturgical act performed in Church as we gradually
lose the capacity to fashion daily life in faith. The strange
thing is that this concentration on the liturgical acts of the
Church (a concentration not restricted to high churchmen
either) comes to evacuate of meaning the fundamental liturgical
act, viz. baptism. For baptism loses its significance when it
ceases to apply to the whole of the Christian life from birth
to death. This shift in emphasis from baptism and therefore
from daily life to the Church involves also a reinterpretation

---

[2] See Sundby, *Luthersk äktenskapsuppfattning*, pp. 263-264.

of what it means to be "in the Church." Instinctively we think that the "Church" means those who to some extent or another are involved in full-time Church work, or at least are somehow connected with the Church and do not engage in weekday activities outside the Church.[3]

The fact of this dichotomy, where the Church is set on one side and the world of daily living on the other, makes it very difficult to bring the two together except in a quite superficial way. Any mere patching up of the dichotomy will produce a kind of neutral zone which has nothing to do with either the administration of the sacraments or daily life. The latent contact which the congregation has with worship on the one hand and daily work on the other will then be disregarded, and attention focused instead on the leading figures of Church or state. Among present day labour organisations, for instance, the Church looks with an eager eye at the institutionalised successors of earlier popular movements, in particular perhaps at the trade union movement with its immense centralised authority, though it is a few generations late in doing so. This movement had an insignificant beginning and was pushed forward little by little in out of the way places, often at great cost to individual workers who dedicated their lives to this cause and did not always succeed politically in the movement as a reward. It is quite obvious that the time has come for Christian ethics to examine the role of such protective groups in the lives of individual workers.[4] The significance, however, of such an analysis for the Church should not be exaggerated. But merely to patch up the split is to tinker with a superficial solution, for down in the daily life of the local congregations where the Gospel is preached and the sacraments administered, and where we are dealing with such things as home and earning a living, the divisive forces will continue to operate unless we change our attitude to worship and the sacraments. And when

---

[3] In consequence a book like Berggrav's *Staten*, which addresses concrete questions to modern society, may well be regarded by some as an untheological work and be disregarded by churchmen whose interest lies rather in the sacraments, ministry, and worship of the Church. The assumption is that sacraments and society represent different spheres.

[4] This is over-emphasised by K.-M. Olsson in his *Kontakt med kyrkan*, pp. 91-93.

we come to this point in the life of the local Church we find that it is the individual Christian who is the bridge of which we are speaking. Any radical cure is a painful process which cannot come about if the individual refuses to uncover his own individual problems. In one way everything depends on the relatively isolated "layman," who comes to church to worship and then goes back to his worldly vocation. He carries the burden alone. Should he stumble, he will get no help in any theoretical solution of the problem, be it theological or pastoral.[5] *It is individual men and women in their place of daily work who are the Church*. The problem of freedom and the law comes to a head in the realities of their daily existence. Now as always this actual existence abounds in problems and perplexities. There is certainly no need today to fight, for example, for the rights of trade unions. This has already been accomplished. But there is another task. Coming out of worship today the worshipper may instead turn his thoughts to the decline of family life, the problems of teenagers in his neighbourhood, or the intrusion of the means of mass communication wherever he turns. A television set has more influence today than any protective group could have—and very often the influence it wields lies beyond the control of those who are affected by it.[6] But it is clear that no two individuals have the same difficulties to face. Each has a different moral responsibility which arises from the unique relationship which he has to his neighbour and his unique situation in life. The strength of the view of the Christian life which prevailed in an earlier age was its awareness that "every man has his own burden to bear," and that the pattern of the Christian life varied for the individual as he looked for opportunities to bear the burdens which he saw oppressing those about him. The area, therefore, in which he was active

[5] Since the practical activity of members of the Church is here of central significance, we have something to learn from the attempts which succeed in giving ordinary Church members a *responsibility* in modern society and which at the same time make *worship* a source of power for these persons. We are not to despise American denominations in this respect. It is no accident that American writers very often keep the whole of their society in mind and try to illustrate their theme by taking Christian freedom as their point of orientation. See Ramsey, *Ethics*, pp. 46-48, 343-345, etc. Cf. Hillerdal, *Kyrka och socialetik*, pp. 108-110.

[6] Cf. James M. Gustafson, "Kontakt med kyrkan," in *Svensk kyrkotidning*, 1960, pp. 167-168.

was not parliament or the legislature but his home and place of work, each with its network of relationships and each differing with the individual. The emergence of democracy means increased possibilities for all of improving conditions of others, i.e. of serving their neighbour, by the simple means of casting a ballot. Christian love seizes these new opportunities gladly. But it is a real temptation from the standpoint of the law of love to suppose that we can transfer our service of our neighbour to the machinery of democracy.[7] Indeed, the greatest single lack of the modern welfare state is the need for personal relationships at the basic level of the places where people eat, work, sleep, or play. Improved conditions simply make us more painfully aware of this need. To express the matter differently and in more pointed terms, the more society reckons in terms of collective groups, the stronger becomes its need to find individuals who will pay heed to particular local needs and responsibilities. Such individuals have no wide influence, but to the extent that they are active they are like water springing up in the desert. This is how the Christian Church in an earlier age worked for the well-being and reformation of society.[8] Democracy has not in this instance created the need for a different form. Quite the reverse: where democracy and the welfare state have emerged, the need for the earlier form is all the more obvious.

In one sense this earlier form is marked by a strong Christocentric character. It derives from the Gospel which is set forth in worship, the Eucharist, and the "forgiveness of sins," to use the traditional terminology as we find it in Billing.[9] But it does so within a framework of fundamental importance. Its ethic is not derived from the Gospel, and any such Marcionite construction is fruitless and will gradually destroy the Gospel. The forgiveness of sins which is offered in worship presupposes a situation outside worship in which guilt continues to mount up again and again in the experience of daily living. It

[7] See here the striking discussion in Berggrav, *Staten*, e.g., pp. 139-156, about the place of groups over against the concentration of power at the head of the state. His book is prophetic and may suffer accordingly by proving more and more right in proportion as it is disregarded.

[8] Lau, *Luthers Lehre*, pp. 55-59.

[9] Cf. Billing, *Vår kallelse*, pp. 7-12, 20-23, 27-60.

presupposes, in short, a rule of law or "earthly government."[10]
Preaching in public worship and Christian education may also,
of course, underscore this demand for good works (in the
outward sense), and thereby serve the cause of social justice.
But if the word which the Church addresses to society does not
communicate the Gospel, it does not even convey that which
makes the Church the Church.[11] However the preaching of the
Gospel may accentuate the demand for good works, as long as it
merely accentuates this demand without making its accomplish-
ments possible, it still remains a word that belongs to "this
present age." The most it has to offer is judgment. And
judgment is a reality which is already experienced in the fact
of human life itself, when we hear the voice of the unrecognised
demand which arises out of all human need, and then pass on
without having brought help to those who asked for it.[12] When
the worshipper leaves the sanctuary, it is into such a world
as this that he goes, a world which in a peculiar way has already
been given its form by the God of creation and the law.[13]
He does not come into the vacuum where he can construct
an ethic based on the Gospel, taking his faith in Christ as a
starting-point, but into a world which has already been given
its form by God and where he already has many burdens to
carry.[14] He comes to worship because he already carries these
burdens. But when he goes out from worship, he does not then
for the first time assume the responsibilities which burden him,
but rather carries them in a new way, thereby proving master
of his old predicament with a new verve, choosing here and
there among the multitudinous demands made upon him and
transmuting them. But in the final issue he does assume them,
and does not get rid of them. He is still "under the law" until
he dies. But the strange thing about it is that he can remain
"subject" to the law while being free from the law.

[10] Cf. Hauge, *Gudsåpenbaring*, pp. 245-246, Dodd, *New Testament Studies*, pp. 138-140.

[11] Cf. Ivarsson, *Predikans uppgift*, pp. 158-163, on "preaching in the service of the secular government."

[12] Cf. Günther Bornkamm, *Studien*, pp. 115-118.

[13] Cf. K. E. Løgstrup, *Den erkendelseteoretiske konflikt*, 1942, pp. 89-104, where he discusses the idea of creation in a particularly interesting way.

[14] Cf. on the other hand Søe, *Kristelig etik*, pp. 203-206, where the doctrine of the *usus civilis* is criticised.

We have come far enough now to see that in describing the function played by the Gospel in any particular human situation we must be quite precise in our terminology and speak of "the critical aim of preaching," "discrimination," "selection," and so on.[15] All these terms presuppose an already existing form (*gestalt*) in society, and cumulatively the use of such terms implies that the first article and the first use of the law are antecedent realities. They are no less clearly implied in the expression, "forgiveness of sins," or even in the word "Gospel" as a designation of a word addressed to the Gentiles in the missionary preaching of the Church, than they are in the summon to conversion, i.e. to a return to the Creator, which characterises such preaching. The underlying concept in every instance is that human life belongs to the Creator.[16] In reading Luther we are struck by the fact that he does not develop any scheme of social conduct from his doctrine of justification by faith, but discusses this immediately after his doctrine of vocation, i.e. in the context of daily life. His doctrine is thus marked both by a fixed element and by flexibility. Daily life is accepted for what it is with all its obligations and duties, but in the midst stands a man who has been made free by the Gospel and who has an inward desire to serve his neighbour. Such a man is free *both* in his criticism of all law, or in framing a new series of commandments for himself, *and* when he sees that he must suffer without being able to make any change in the situation in which he is set.[17] Superficially at least the alternatives of making a change in one's outward circumstances and of simply accepting an existing situation would appear quite incongruous. In appearance one represents an achievement, the other a failure of achievement. But this is to look at things solely from the standpoint of the old, acquisitive Adam. The new man, who is Christ, looks at things with the eyes of the Spirit and in each case finds the common denominator of

---

[15] See in this connexion Lau, *Luthers Lehre*, pp. 88-89, who lays much emphasis on the fact that Luther's political preaching is critical, negative, and consequently discriminatory, not constructive, from the point of view of the Gospel. But this is a strength, surely, not a weakness.

[16] Cf. Gärtner, *Areopagus Speech*, pp. 229-241.

[17] Cf. Holl, *Gesammelte Aufsätze zur Kirchengeschichte*, VOL. I, pp. 223-224. The Spirit works in freedom.

service. The rearrangement of outward circumstances and the acceptance of existing conditions alike do service to our neighbour. A free choice is involved in each instance, and when it is made every other reality which we experience is transformed.[18] Only this can explain the contrasts which the early Church encountered and accepted: "As dying, and behold we live . . . as sorrowful, yet always rejoicing . . . as having nothing, and yet possessing everything" (II Cor. VI.9 f.).

This is nothing less than the death and resurrection of Christ now manifesting its power in the midst of the congregation, which in its turn is open towards all mankind. The capacity to live in such a way is given by the sacraments of baptism and the Eucharist. Worship and life are interwoven, and man is free even in the world of the law.[19]

But the "old Adam," who still thinks that anything he loses to his neighbour is gone for good and that what he keeps for himself is his alone, is not only to be found outside the Church. Even those who are baptised are still marked by the old egocentricity. God's disciplining of the human race though the earthly law does not cease at the moment of entrance into the Church, i.e. with baptism, as if those who had been baptised were no longer in need of such control. The laws of society also regulate the conduct of those who are Christian and do good for their neighbour. If there were no such laws, this would not mean that we should find Christians willingly assuming the responsibility for serving the needs of their neighbours, at least not universally, but rather withdrawing and tending to keep to themselves. We idealise the Christian life when we shut our eyes to the fact that some of the good we do—and by "good" we mean that benefits our neighbours— is forced upon us, and when we fail to see that the Christian too is set under earthly government. A realistic definition of the Christian life will make it plain that God has two spheres of action. When we leave the workaday world to worship we are coming from God but also going to God. We never withdraw from the relationship to God, but on all sides come into contact

---

[18] See also Elert, *Christliche Ethos*, pp. 310-313.

[19] Cf. Herbert Olsson, *Luthers socialetik*, VOL. I, pp. 134-145, on the relationship between anthropology and Christology.

with the work of His "right hand" or His "left."[20] This fact is of great significance for our concept of the Church. We can state precisely what are the specific responsibilities of the Church—baptism, the Gospel, and the Eucharist. But we must also insist that independently of these God is also active in the earthly government and in daily work, apart, that is to say, from the Church. If, however, we take this division of function between what we have spoken of as the work of God's right hand and the work of His left hand and debase it into a sociological division between those who are in the world and those who are in the Church, then we alter the very structure of the division,[21] and lose the connexion between creation and the Church.

The distinctive act of the Church is baptism, but when a person is baptised God uses the same disciplinary methods in dealing with him as prevailed before he was baptised. The consequences of baptism are worked out in the place where we make our living and in the performance of the tasks which we share with our fellow-workers who have not been baptised. If at this point we introduce the question of Church affiliation, or insist on a clear line of demarcation for the Church, or argue about what constitutes membership within it *without at the same time explaining the meaning of creation and the first use of the law*, we play havoc with the concept of the Church.[22] We cease to be able to conceive of the Church as subordinate to the Gospel and are forced to think of it in terms of particular qualities. If, however, we adhere to the doctrine of the two kingdoms, the divine activity in the Gospel and in baptism affects every aspect of our life within the Church—and the Church is clearly distinct from the earthly government. Baptism is the distinctive act of the Church, but the operation of baptism cannot take place

[20] Cf. Künneth, *Politik*, pp. 82-84.

[21] See Johannes Heckel, *Lex charitatis*, 1953, pp. 32-43. If we begin by discussing government we can quite easily go on to make a place for distinctions between men and thus do justice to these statements of Luther.

[22] Those who are critical of the national Churches of Europe from the standpoint of the American free Churches must remember this. The outward status of these old European Churches implies a view of creation and the law which is still to some extent maintained even when denominational theology has destroyed it. If the outward system of the folk church is destroyed, it may be the last stronghold which falls.

in the world as it exists at present. It can take place only where those acts which are constitutive of the Church are being carried out, i.e. where Christ comes to men in the means of grace. The law, which is involved in the outworking of baptism, was of course already in effect in the world before the preaching of the Gospel. But the Gospel is the antithesis of the law and abolishes it. The death which is brought into play in the actual administration of baptism is not something hitherto unexperienced or a more spiritual death, but is the same, immemorial enemy which has afflicted the human race from the first. But the resurrection which is offered to men in the sacraments of the Church is the opposite of death and abolishes it.[23] All through, the line of demarcation which sets the Church apart is clear.

If in criticism of any such definitive line it is then argued that the Christian's vocation has become merely law, death, and the cross, and has lost its character of joy, we have this answer to offer. The element of obligation in the Christian's calling is indeed an expression of these things, but, as we have explicitly stated, it is such *to the "old" man*. The "new" man, as we have also stated, who looks at his daily life with the eyes of the Spirit, is entirely *free and sovereign*, even when in bondage or when facing sufferings.[24] We cannot evade this bipolarity without producing an unrealistic and artificial picture of the Church and the Christian life. Only when death has done what it has to do, i.e. when we come after the last judgment to the eternal life of heaven, shall we be free.[25] In the meantime, however, our baptism spurs us on towards this goal; life goes on as

---

[23] See also Barth, *Evangelium und Gesetz*, pp. 29-30, where law and Gospel are paralleled by death and life (cf. pp. 11-13 where, however, the cognitive terms determine the exposition). Of interest here is H. J. Iwand, *Um den rechten Glauben*, 1959, pp. 100-109 (a reprint of the article, "Jenseits von Gesetz und Evangelium," in *Theologische Blätter*, 1935).

[24] An example of this objection is K.-M. Olsson, *Kontakt med kyrkan*, pp. 80-82. A similar objection was made sixteen years earlier in Gustaf Wingren, "Om Einar Billings teologi," in *S.t.k.*, 1944, pp. 278-281. We must also remember that Billing did not intend to reproduce Luther in his view of call; see *Vår kallelse*, p. 21, and also Billing's doctoral thesis, *Luthers lära om staten*, VOL. I, 1900, pp. 87-88, 187-188 Cf. *Nordisk teologi*, 1955, pp. 288-291.

[25] Eternal life is a heightening of Adam's dominion at the beginning of creation. At present, however, restoration is taking place. Cf. W.A. XLII.48, 19-35 (Commentary on Genesis, 1535-1545).

it did, and we alternate between worship and work, caught up in the last mighty transformation of which we have a foretaste in every Eucharist.

We can, of course, pursue the analysis still further. To speak, as we have just done, of the "old" and the "new" man may suggest some kind of psychological division or dichotomy within man himself, whose task it then becomes to hold together his other two constituent parts. But as we have frequently emphasised earlier, the "old" man can be seen to be old only in the act of forgiveness, and *forgiveness is the resurrection of Christ* offered and extended to us in the Gospel.[26] The old nature is, of course, a reality to us before it is forgiven in us, for we have already experienced it in temptation. But the whole point in temptation is that the old is not "old" unless it is such in relation to some "new." It is "old" when we try to make it old by treating it as "temptation," and by bringing such forces to play against it as will prove to be our "new" being in the event of our victory. The humanity of Christ, as we have shown, was seen in the fact that He endured temptation.[27] The two related elements of temptation and forgiveness which dominated our discussion of Christology earlier were seen to comprise respectively His humanity and His divinity, and to culminate respectively in the cross and the resurrection. On the other hand, however, they also provide a key to our understanding of the two anthropological concepts of "old" and "new." The new man comes to birth in baptism and in the Gospel of the forgiveness of sins. Again we are confronted by the same clear line of distinction between the Church and the world. But it is a distinction in function, for only the Church has been given the task of addressing the word of the Gospel to the world. Here again, however, it is wrong to reduce, this distinction into a sociological division between the tempted i.e. those who belong to the world, and the forgiven, i.e. those who belong to the Church. Temptation is something that affects every human being, and more than any Christ felt its burden. To the end of time the Church will face temptation, and only then will its trial finally pass. As both "old" and "new,"

[26] Cf. Bosch, *Heidenmission*, pp. 60-64.
[27] Cf. Cullmann, *Christology*, pp. 93-97, etc.

Q

man is a single psychological whole: he is tempted in his human
nature and receives forgiveness of sins from the Gospel. Psycho-
logically we can quite readily comprehend such a man and his
inner unity which underlies the struggle between the old and
the new within him.[28]

We are also aware of the characteristic alterations between
new creation and that which is forced upon us, i.e. the tension
between freedom and law which is our particular concern in
the present section.[29] If any freely accepted responsibility, which
we assumed, had universal support, there would be no such
thing as temptation. To be tempted means to look upon our
neighbour with the eyes of the old man. Every Christian knows
from experience what it means to be able to turn to good
account the necessity of accepting a particular situation in
which he becomes involved to the fullest of his capacity, even
though he can do no more than proffer help to those who need
it, while the outward circumstances remain the same. The
sovereign control by which he formerly moulded and refashioned outward circumstances now as it were turns inwards
and holds his own inner self in check. This, to be sure, is a
painful process, but at the same time he is lifted above his pain
to the source in heaven from which his mastery over his
environment originates. In this lies his invulnerability, and it is
a much more profound freedom than that which he experiences in putting things to right in the world. This is at least
the beginning of man's free dominion over external creation
and his degrading need to "have and hold," whatever the
price. The cross and death can underlie even the posture
of absolute power.[30] The point at which the Christian
chooses among the conflicting demands made upon him
may be seen most clearly at an apparently low level, i.e.
at the point where he has suffered personal loss and where
for this very reason he can look at everything from the position

---

[28] Cf. in this regard also Axel Gyllenkrok, *Rechtfertigung und Heiligung*, 1952,
pp. 88-89, where, however, a somewhat different attitude is taken.

[29] On the relationship between freedom and constraint as the most difficult
point of Luther's ethic see Billing, *Luthers lära om staten*, VOL. I, pp. 193-194. Cf.
Gustaf Wingren, *The Christian's Calling*, p. xii.

[30] Cf. Lerfeldt, *Den kristnes kamp*, p. 115, but especially Löfgren, *Theologie der
Schöpfung*, pp. 246-248.

of a deeper obedience and of a heightened and accentuated demand.

Such an interpretation of sovereignty exercised in suffering is a logical consequence on the level of Christian ethics of the primary Christological affirmation that the victory of Christ was secured on the cross, i.e. in the midst of His sufferings. All that we have to say here about freedom and law in the life of the Christian is a consequence of the great Christological affirmations about the cross and the resurrection which we have discussed earlier in the chapters, "Christ under the Law," and "Christ and the Renewal of Creation." *But we cannot change the order.* We cannot begin with the Christian life and then look at the cross and victory of Christ as an example of this life. For everything turns on the fact that Christ *alone* has surmounted the most dreadful of all temptations on the cross, and that He *alone* has risen on the third day. Only then did baptism and the Gospel come to men. For this reason too all that we have to say at this point about freedom and law in the life of the Christian is based on *the Gospel and the sacraments.* Freedom is rooted and grounded in service and whenever we try to define what freedom means in daily life we are brought back to this, i.e. to service.[31] The law, it is true, is rooted in human life and its pressures are felt in human life, but the uneasiness created by this universal law comes to a head only when the Gospel is preached and the table of the Eucharist spread, i.e. in divine service. This can provide the basis for a Christian ethic which will deal with the whole outward creation and the routine business of daily living, but which is still centred on the imitation of Christ and the movement through death and resurrection.[32] The centre of the Lutheran concept of vocation is baptism, and its doctrine of government is throughout an expression of a fundamentally sacramental view of life.[33]

In discussing the relationship between freedom and the law we have focused our attention on the individual who leaves

[31] Baptism is thus seen to be the central ethical concept. Cf. Jervell, *Imago Dei*, pp. 231-233.

[32] Cf. *Theologische Literarurzeitung*, 1950, p. 392.

[33] Cf. Wendland in *Die Leibhaftigkeit*, 1958, pp. 42-44, on the commandments of the New Testament.

the worshipping community and returns to his daily work.
We have stated that it was characteristic of the earlier Lutheran
interpretation of the relationship between the Gospel and the
society in which it is set to keep this connexion with one's daily
occupation well in view. There was no parliament, no right to
vote, and no democratic rule. Today, however, we have something entirely different in mind when we speak of Christian
social ethics, for the concern which we have for our neighbour
is conveyed principally through casting a ballot or by democratic enactments on behalf of our fellow-men. In this modern
setting the earlier interpretation of which we have been
speaking may easily be regarded as an archaistic attitude which
hankers for the past and seeks to revert to the social patterns
of a bygone age. There is little question that the doctrine of
vocation has frequently been given this conservative cast.[34]
We hear ploughing exalted, for example, as a God-given task
among those who have never so much as put their hand to a
plough. Many other examples could be quoted of a similar
pietistic withdrawal from the occupations of daily life. But
such withdrawal, where it exists, is a rejection of daily life
itself, and makes it impossible to maintain the earlier interpretation to which we have referred. For a characteristic mark
of this earlier interpretation was its close contact with the ever-
changing technical skills which developed in the places where
men worked. In this respect the period of Reformation is
typical. It did not look back nostalgically to the "godly
traditions of the fathers," which it regarded merely as super-
stitions, but seized the new technical achievements of its
day, printing included, and used them all while still brand
new in a pioneering achievement which brought great gains
to the movement for reform. The predisposition to idealise
the sixteenth century which we see in at least certain parts of
the so called "Luther-renaissance" has made the sixteenth
rather than the twentieth century the locus in which the law
had its full concrete embodiment, and has excluded our
own age, with all its own particularity, from any relationship

[34] See Edvard Rodhe, "Undersåte och medborgare," in *S.t.k.* 1944, pp. 257-270.

to God.[35] But the universal law which compels all men to serve their neighbour is operative in the actual world we know, which means that it effects change and is itself affected by change in the outward expression of its demands. Indeed it must change in externals in order to remain inwardly constant and really hold men to their jobs. Otherwise "love" becomes a fanciful day-dream that has nothing to do with reality.[36] In other words it ceases to be love, for love acts and does not just dream.

Thus since by works we are to understand the activity of many different individuals in many different places, which in the last resort rules out the possibility of objective evaluation, there is a limit to any theological discussion of freedom and law. The law is given an individual expression in the relationship which each of us has to his neighbour. In this concealed world demands are made upon us and accepted or rejected in a decision of the conscience which persistently maintains its individuality in the choosing and refuses to be reduced to any formula. We may abandon the theological discussion of the question without any qualms, for there is no question that the matter is a live issue for every individual.[37] The sceptics who have doubts about freedom, i.e. who question whether the conscience can be heard in the hidden worlds known to each individual, like to point out the absence of ethical results, and use this to bring up their constant argument that stricter regulations on the part of the Church are needed. It should, however, be called to mind that the New Testament does not speak of good works as wholly revealed to us but rather as still to be revealed in a final judgment which will extend to all. We also find that

[35] In a democracy the nominal "authorities" are in fact subordinate to the will of the people who thus declare their will "from below up" in general elections and are obeyed in changes of government. This is important in our discussion of civil rebellion. If a governing group assumes dictatorial powers against the law of the land, the use of force by the people may in fact be the punishment by the superior group of an inferior law-breaker (i.e. the dictator), i.e. a justifiable police action. In Künneth, *Politik*, pp. 257-261, the discussion of this point is too brief.

[36] In regard to the change, cf. Løgstrup, *Den etiske fordring*, pp. 77-121, where this problem is fully discussed.

[37] The New Testament view of conscience also points in the same direction. Cf. Pierce, *Conscience*, pp. 66-68. It should, perhaps, be added that in the next section, as here, we shall attempt to relate our theological discussion to a quite practical concern. Then, however, it will be the conduct of worship, not of our daily activities, which will concern us.

when we try to reflect on the meaning of human goodness, we are often confronted by those who at a cursory glance appear to have been unsuccessful in life and whom we would reckon to have few ethical achievements to their credit. If we are to be duly in awe that the admonitions of conscience in regard to our own achievements are a prelude to the last judgment, we may also dare to hope that the comforting recollections of what others have done for us are also a prelude to the judgment, and that at least we may be "the least of these His brethren," and therefore the objects of other people's kindness. Perhaps this is the profoundest Gospel in the narratives of judgment.[38] The decisive factor, however, in our present discussion is the concept of community which is implied in this kind of expectation of a coming judgment. It is part of a true koinonia to take as well as to give and to recognise that we ourselves are recipients of the good that others may do for us. To think of ourselves as the subjects of agape-love and always the givers, and of others as the objects of our love and always the recipients, is to make agape an ethically destructive concept, and the love which we have for our neighbour will be filled with contempt for men. In the earlier interpretation of the relationship between the Gospel and society, with its peculiar regard for the Christian's calling in the world, the Church was seen to be in existence wherever men lived or worked. To be set among those who had been baptised was to be set among the "saints." The traditional territorial or parochial Church in Europe is an expression of this basic understanding. The parish is constituted on the principle that all who live and work in the same neighbourhood belong to it. It embraces hundreds of individuals, each with his own means of livelihood. But this is where sanctification takes place and baptism is fulfilled.[39]

Obviously such an interpretation presupposes that God is at work in the world and also presupposes the earthly government

---

[38] Cf. Minear, *Christian Hope*, p. 104. A connexion could be made between Mt. xxv.31-46 and the strange variant of the subject in Lk. x.36-37. Goodness suddenly flows in a different and unexpected direction. No longer do I do good to any but receive it at another's hands. In this, the presence of Christ Himself as the Giver is hidden from view.

[39] Cf. Billing, *Herdabref*, pp. 60-69, for a description of the territorial Church.

and the universal constraint of the law. This still, however, leaves plenty of room for freedom, simply because it is individuals who are involved, each of whom has respect for the integrity of the little world of his fellows and takes pleasure in the variety of ways in which they differ from each other. A group made up of those whose common religious viewpoint draws them together knows far less about freedom if its members think they can identify the saved by particular distinguishing marks. To do this is to remove sanctification from the sphere of daily work, give it a stereotyped form, and equate it with a particular pattern of religious conduct. If on the other hand sanctification is bound up with our relationship to our neighbour, it is in this relationship, which is different for every individual, that we have our immediate, personal fellowship with Christ. This does not eliminate the fellowship which we have with our fellow-men on the horizontal level, but on the contrary comes to full expression within it, though always after we have sized up each situation and never by rote.[40] Freedom is therefore involved at every moment. When love sets to work in the guise of earthly government or daily calling, to outward appearance it may seem as though the law constricted freedom. This may indeed be the case if, for example, we forget about our neighbour and take some stereotype of Christianity, e.g. Lutheranism or Calvinism, as the pattern to be transmitted from generation to generation, while social relationships, and in particular our conduct towards our neighbour, are modified. But where the neighbour is made central, there is always an opportunity for freedom to exert itself, and a critical attitude to all laws, a mobility of action, and a new creation, come into play and can make even the "slaves of all" into kings of the earth. To repeat what we have said above, our modern welfare society badly needs the kind of man who has a deep loyalty to his calling, and the need is growing rather than diminishing.[41] He is the cement which binds together conflicting interest

[40] To be "a member of the body" means in the New Testament sense to have access both to Christ as head of the Church and to our fellow-members. In this way each member can be respected for his unique contribution and receive "honour" (1 Cor. xii.22-26), simply because he is different from the rest. Cf. Odeberg in En bok om kyrkan, pp. 71-73, and also Robinson, The Body, pp. 8-10.

[41] Cf. here also Berggrav, Staten, pp. 150-153, 177.

groups and keeps society from falling apart. Democracy has by no means created the need for a new form in this regard. If anything, the danger is rather that the use of the vote will come to transform the idea of personal, simple service, and transfer the warmth of this service from the periphery, where unrelated individuals, work, live, sleep, and eat together, to the political processes where all social services are bundled together. Our modern society urgently needs the earlier form,[42] which, of course, to remain true to itself, must express itself in terms of our own society. It must be expressed in terms of modern life. Otherwise to revert to the forms of a bygone age is a pretence and an escape from the daily life in which we are set.

The Church is at work wherever its members are engaged in their various callings, each living the life of *baptism* in his own occupation. But these separate individuals are also bound together in a unity through being members of the same body and being vivified by the same blood which flows through each of them. The function of the Lord's day is to refashion this unity and give substance to the life of baptism in "the acts which follow," notably in the preaching of the Gospel and the administration of the Lord's Supper.[43] Since those who are caught up in the business of daily life are set within the sphere of the law and the earthly government, the gift of the Gospel which they receive when they come to worship always comes to them as something new.[44] The assembling of the separate members to form a united worshipping community gives all who take part an experience of inward communion with one another which is unknown to the majority of men, but is the mark of the Christian congregation. But the community which finds its centre in the *Gospel* can never shut itself off from the world or turn itself against the waiting world of men for which it is responsible.[45] The centre of the fellowship is the gift which Christ gave to all the nations, and when this gift is enjoyed, the doors of the Church are open for others to enter and share it too.

[42] We look in vain for an emphasis on this basic point in K.-M. Olsson, *Kontakt med kyrkan*, but Olsson prefers to base his discussion on the modern collective groups which are to be found in the Church, e.g. pp. 96-98, 118-120.

[43] Cf. Cullmann, *Early Christian Worship*, pp. 76-77, Davies, *Spirit*, p. 124.

[44] Cf. Joest, *Gesetz und Freiheit*, pp. 180-195.   [45] Cf. Prenter, *Skabelse*, p. 587.

Prayer and Praise

Our last section is devoted to worship. But here too we shall be looking at worship in its relationship to the whole of man's life, for under the law this life too is a form of prayer, though it is idolatrous worship. Man begs and pleads for life wherever he can find it, even if he must look to the wrong source. Christian worship takes place in this setting in which worship is offered to the creature rather than the Creator.[1]

In this respect the Christian Church is distinct from the world around it. Something is done within the Church which is not done outside it. It enjoys a particular kind of communion which is to be found only among those who belong to it, and which comes to an end only when the Church comes to an end. True, the line which separates the Church from the world is not barred, and its whole *raison d'être* is to extend the communion which it experiences to include those too who live outside its open doors. But this openness to the world does not alter the fact that the Church is distinctive because unique events take place within it which do not occur outside. Among these we include not only what God does through the means of grace, but also what men do towards God and thus offer to God, i.e. human good deeds. Included in this category are prayer "in the name of Jesus" (Mt. XVIII.19 f., Jn. XIV.13 f., XVI.24 ff.) and also praise.[2] For the Gentiles do not praise the name of God or honour Him as God or give thanks to Him (Rom. 1.21),[3] but instead exchange the glory of God for the creature and worship and serve this creature rather than the Creator (Rom. 1.23 ff.).[4] This kind of perverted prayer in which worship is offered to the transient creature can never be prayer in the name of Jesus, and such worship of "images" can never be praise to the Creator. In the world of fallen men these true acts of prayer and praise have disappeared. But in the Church

[1] See Vajta, *Theologie des Gottesdienstes*, p. 7, and also Gärtner, *Areopagus Speech*, pp. 203-228.

[2] On prayer in the name of Jesus see Prenter, *Ordet*, pp. 120-126. Cf. Dodd, *Fourth Gospel*, pp. 195-196.

[3] On the meaning of this see Günther Bornkamm, *Das Ende des Gesetzes*, pp. 22-23.

[4] Cf. Jervell, *Imago Dei*, pp. 321-322.

they are seen at their height, one more indication that the
Church is humanity whole and restored.

This wholeness is expressed in man's return to what nature
itself already does. Here as elsewhere we see that heaven,
earth, and nature are purer than man is. Creation apart from
man is filled with praise for its Creator far more than the
Church. Day to day pours forth speech and night to night
declares that all is the work of God (Ps. XIX.3). The heavens and
the firmament (Ps. XIX.1), the coastlands and the deserts, all
offer Him praise (cf. Ps. LXXXIX.6, Isa. XLII.10 ff.).[5] The fact
that the ground is cursed (Gen. III.17) and creation groans
(Rom. VIII.22) does not limit the praise which nature offers,
and still the song of praise ascends to God from creation. For
the ground did not transgress and was not cut off from God
by its sin. The curse was put upon the ground on account of
Adam. It is a burden laid upon it. The "groaning" of creation
is therefore its eager longing for the revealing of the "sons of
God" (Rom. VIII.19 ff.). It is an accompaniment on the part
of creation, an accompaniment which waits for the voice of
man and follows it. Though it is man who is the problem,
it is clear from the very heart of things that it is also man who
is lord of creation and appointed to have dominion over it.
The whole of creation is in harmony with the Church and awaits
the fulfilment of God's purpose for men which is there being
achieved.[6] When the divine, creative Word became flesh
in Christ it took upon itself the outward covering of the living
being which had suffered most impairment, and so was made
man. But the rest of creation, which bore the burden put upon
it by its fallen lord, man, awaits the "last Adam," who will
restore it as the "life-giving spirit" (1 Cor. XV.45). The new work
of creation which Christ is bringing about in the Church now
follows. Thus the prayer of the Church blends with the groaning which already comes from the whole creation in a flood
which will come to its peak only in "the redemption of our

---

[5] See also Ps. CXLV.10, Is. VI.3, Job XXVI.14. Cf. Gerhard von Rad, *Old
Testament Theology*, Vol. I, pp. 361-364. It is clear that the praise of nature is
related to the direct connexion between God the Creator and all these outward
phenomena. They are "the works of His hands." In regard to praise in the Psalter
in general see Westermann, *Das Loben Gottes in den Psalmen*, pp. 7-9.

[6] Cf. Richardson, *Introduction*, p. 219.

bodies" (Rom. VIII.23). When this goal is attained in the
resurrection of the dead, the whole of creation—sun and moon
and everything there is—will share in the final outward
triumph.[7] When man is restored to wholeness no more will
any part of creation be misused, but everything will again be
"good," as in the day when creation began (Gen. 1.4, 10, 12,
18, 21, 25, 31).[8]

Thus even in the perverted form of his idolatry man reaches
out beyond his bondage. This search for a way out of his im-
prisonment can be seen in the simplest expressions of human
life. In the Gospels those who cry out to be healed are voicing
a prayer of need, even in this simple, primitive form, and when
Jesus hears their plea, again and again he regards it as "faith"
(cf. Mk. v.36, x.46-52, xi.22 ff., Mt. viii.5-13, ix.28 f., xv.21-28,
Lk. v.17-20, viii.22-25).[9] But these passages which speak of
Jesus as healer not only reveal what He did in response to
cries for help but frequently end noting the worship offered
by the persons healed to God and to their Healer (e.g. Lk.
v.25, vii.16, xiii.13, xvii.15, xviii.43). The healing Christ
undertakes God's new work of restoration among those who are
sick. The worship which He inspires is the praise of creation
to a Creator who is also Saviour, and this praise offered by
those who are healed continues throughout the early Church,
the worship of which was markedly Eucharistic and doxological.[10] Over and over again the Church is exhorted in the
New Testament Epistles to give thanks and to praise and
glorify God, individually and corporately (e.g. Col. iii.17,
Eph. v.19 f., Phil. iv.4 ff.). If prayer and "groaning" are an
indication that the Church has still an end to attain (and this is
particularly clear in Rom. viii.23-26), worship on the other
hand is a sign of how close to its goal the Church has come,
for the life to come is a life of praise (cf. Rev. iv.9 ff.). When the
sound of glad praise is heard in common worship, it is a sign

---

[7] See Cullmann, *Christ and Time*, pp. 141-142. On the last Adam as the restorer
cf. also Cullmann, *Christology*, pp. 169-181. On Mk. 1.13 cf. Schulze in *Z.NT.W.*,
1955, pp. 282-283.

[8] See here Löfgren, *Theologie der Schöpfung*, pp. 46-48.

[9] In regard to Luther's exposition of these or similar passages, cf. Ivarsson,
Predikans uppgift, pp. 48-49.

[10] See Lk. xxiv.53, Acts ii.46, etc.

that the life eternal has broken into the present time.[11] In themselves prayer and praise are an expression of what is transitory in the Church, for the Church is passing from the old to the new and from bondage to freedom. This transitoriness affects also the life of the individual within the Church, for to live by the Gospel and the sacraments is to be always ready to move on.

We must, of course, avoid making the absolute distinction between prayer and praise which theology tends to make. To say that prayer implies a need for which we pray and praise an answer to prayer for which we return thanks is to systematise need and its satisfaction in a manner quite alien to the Bible. For in the Bible the mighty works of God are glorified for what they are in themselves and not because they minister to our particular needs or satisfy them.[12] And prayer, from one aspect, is our opening of ourselves to God so that what God is going to do even "apart from our prayer," may be done "also in us" and come into play in our own lives, as Luther variously expresses it in his *Little Catechism*.[13] In prayer and praise man remains open to God, and by being open is ready to put to death the old and bring to life the new in his own daily existence, and ready also always to move on. This brings us back to the connexion to which we have frequently referred between death and resurrection on the one hand and bondage and freedom on the other. In the last analysis the connexion between these two rests on the *communicatio idiomatum*, i.e. the peculiar relationship between divine and human in Christ. Here we see a further danger in making too sharp a distinction between prayer and praise. Prayer is no more an indication of need than praise is an indication that the need has been

[11] Peter Brunner in *Leitourgia*, VOL. I, 1954, pp. 261-263, makes this a key point in Christian worship. Good reasons can be adduced for this. Cf. Minear, *Horizons*, pp. 29-31.

[12] We must keep in mind that the two oldest Creeds, the Apostles' and the Nicene, are hymns of praise for what God has done. Both, therefore, have a part to play in worship in connexion with the two sacraments, the Apostles' Creed with baptism and the Nicene with the Eucharist. Cf. Prenter, *Skabelse*, pp. 135-136, 138-140. On the doxological character of dogmatic affirmations cf. also Edmund Schlink, "Die Struktur der dogmatischen Aussage als oekumenisches Problem," in *Kerygma und Dogma*, 1957, pp. 252-256, which deals also with prayer.

[13] See especially Luther's explanations of the first four petitions in the third section of his discussion of the Lord's Prayer.

satisfied. The victory has been won for all mankind in the crucifixion. According to Mk. xiv.23 the thanksgiving spoken over the cup (εὐχαριστήσας) was uttered at a meal in which the betrayer himself took part (see xiv.17-20). Just before the passion began the hymn of praise was sung (xiv.26). And this commingling of abundance and need passes over into the early Church, as the Acts and Epistles clearly show, and becomes part of its martyrdom and giving of thanks (cf. 1 Pet. iv.16).[14] One of the few passages in the new Testament in which a particular act of worship is described is Acts xvi.25, where Paul and Silas are in prison in Philippi, their feet fastened in the stocks. In their praying and singing of hymns to God "about midnight" Paul and Silas represent the Church which has come among men and which exists for men. The reference to the others in prison with them is not without significance: "And the prisoners were listening to them."

There is thus among men a suffering Church, which is filled with praise to God and is thereby crowned with victory. The unity of death and resurrection does not imply a static identity between the two which would find the victory of the martyr in his actual acceptance of suffering. There is a movement "from down below" which has to take place if victory is to pierce the darkness, a lifting up by man of praise and prayer. It is a movement which is wholly dependent on God and derives the victory from Him.[15] We can think here at once of the many passages in the New Testament which speak of persistent and importunate prayer (e.g. Lk. xi.5-13 and parallels). Supplicatory prayer of this kind involves the same attitude on the part of man as worship does in a situation of distress. In either case there is what seems to be an obduracy and a refusal to be drawn into a particular situation without resistance, but deep down this obduracy is actually faith, a faith which responds to the constantly new creative activity of God and has the key to the abundance which He offers. To speak only of God and what He does without at the same time speaking in quite explicit terms of human behaviour and attitudes, i.e. of faith, prayer,

---

[14] Cf. Minear in *Basileia*, 1959, pp. 47-48.

[15] See also Prenter, *Ordet*, pp. 119-121. The use of the name Abba (Rom. viii.15, Gal. iv.6) is significant here (cf. Mk. xiv.36).

patience and praise, is to reinforce a docetic interpretation.[16] The prevalence of this docetism can also be seen among those who have fine theories of the *deus absconditus*. The moment things go a little wrong for them, however, there are long and gloomy faces. Yet how odd! No theories about the divine activity can ever weather the storm unless they are combined with equally explicit doctrines of human behaviour and attitudes in situations of need and stress, which are also, *inter alia*, doctrines about worship, and so about confession of sin, prayer, thanksgiving, and praise.[17] Any theocentric theology which takes no interest in liturgical acts will soon cease to be theocentric. It will similarly fail if at the level of liturgical expression it speaks only of the acts and activity of God in worship, i.e. if it holds only to "the divine nature." But it is important to leave room also for "human nature," and to have regard to the movement "from below" of *man's appeal to God*.[18] This is a necessary phase if the sufferings of the Church are to be crowned with victory, and is a part of the movement from death to life and from tribulation to new birth.

The appeal on man's side is also of course a work of God. This aspect of prayer may come to have particular significance in the doctrine of the Spirit and of the third article which we so much need in our theology. All unconsciously we have been drawn into a monophysitism or—to be more precise—a docetism in reaction to the liberal predilection for the human element alone. Consequently human weakness has been excluded from the divine operation. But according to Paul the Spirit is at work in man, who does not know what to pray for (Rom. viii.26). The presence of the Spirit "in our weakness," where He is at work "with sighs too deep for words," is to be identified with the wonder of Christ's own presence in the "weakness" brought about by the "messenger of Satan"

[16] Cf. Vajta, *Theologie des Gottesdienstes*, pp. 223-224, 259-262.

[17] Worship cannot in its turn be isolated from the purely personal daily problems of the individual in his relation to his neighbour. If, e.g., we give the communion a Eucharistic character by rejecting confession with its self-examination and judgment of the old from the sacrament of Holy Communion, this means that we are interpreting the sacrament as an escape. There is a liturgical joy which is merely a piece of escapism. Cf. Aulén, *Eucharist and Sacrifice*, pp. 108-109, 192-207.

[18] See in this connexion Hendry, *Holy Spirit*, pp. 51-52.

which we have previously discussed—in both instances Paul uses the same term, ἀσθένεια (Rom. vIII.26, II Cor. xII.9). The power which is "made perfect in weakness" is the power of the resurrection. Since the Gospel and the sacraments give the resurrection of the dead, their proper sphere is death, the point where the "weakness" is found.[19] When worship is the place of the recreative activity of God and consequently of the sacraments, this also means that worship is the place of human prayer and praise. In one way this movement "from below" to God on man's part appears to be something quite distinct from what God does in worship, and we get the impression that we are adding a human element to the divine in worship. But this is so only if the divine element has been emptied of its human nature, i.e. if a docetic or monophysitic interpretation of the presence of God has dominated our theological system. In actuality the movement "from below" is but one aspect of the presence of *God*. The prayer which gropes and fumbles for words which it cannot find is a fitting vehicle for the Spirit. And deep down beneath all this we see the operation of the cross of Calvary, which for all time to come released life-giving forces into a world of death to take effect where they had never been able to work before.[20] When Christ cried: "My God, my God, why hast thou forsaken me?", His agony was real. But it was in His very passion that He was Messiah and fulfilled the prophecy (Ps. xxII.2).[21] He is present in worship in the same way as He was present among His disciples—He is in the midst of those who are caught in the clutches of death and tribulation, but who have life in front of them.

Dogmatic speculation has its limits, however, and beyond these limits we cannot go. We speak about the activity of God in worship and of Christ's coming to us in the means of grace,

[19] Cf. Richardson, *Introduction*, p. 254.

[20] See also Hahn, *Mitsterben*, p. 159.

[21] The attitude of docetism is perhaps seen most clearly in the way in which its representatives at times make use of the messianic quotations in the New Testament. It is obvious that Christ's cry on the cross is taken from Ps. xxII.2. When, however, it is concluded from this that the quotation on Jesus's lips witnesses against a *real* anguish at being forsaken by God, we are operating with a doctrine which holds that divine nature is fundamentally irreconcilable with the human.

but something else requires to be said. It is men who are the recipients of what God does and who appropriate the means of grace, and therefore we must begin to speak of the human act in worship, i.e. of prayer and praise. Here again, however, something more will need to be said (and in our modern monophysitic situation this is an essential addition), if the discussion about man's part in worship comes to be merely an appendage to the theocentric argument which has preceded it concerning God's part. If it does, there is a real danger of synergism, and the work of salvation will be correspondingly apportioned in worship between human effort and divine. If then to what we have already said we add this third proposition: "Even in prayer it is God who is at work and not we ourselves," we are again lending support to a monophysitic or docetic view and constricting the human aspect.[22] For a true Christology or theory of worship, which is free from any monophysitic or docetic tendencies, ought to be able to deal freely with man's part in worship—prayer, confession, and praise—without in any way, even for a moment, jeopardising the divine action. The New Testament can speak without reservation about Christ's temptations, His struggle in Gethsemane, and His agony in having to take the "cup." Indeed, Adam's ruinous course is checked in this very humiliation, and in this very distress salvation secured for mankind for all eternity.[23] The statement which we have just made: "Even in prayer it is God who is at work and not we ourselves," is theologically in error in one respect. It presents us with a false antithesis and suggests that the two natures are to be regarded *a priori* as mutually exclusive. It would, of course, be difficult to define all this in a way which would avoid the dangers to which we have referred. What we need is a new awareness of *time* and of the *event* which takes place. The relationship between divine and human cannot be expressed in doctrinal statements which disregard time. We

---

[22] This is the danger in Richardson's definition, *Introduction*, p. 283, on the subjective act of faith: "It is, however, not something that we do. . . ." When a theologian sets himself against the liberals he seems to be forced into a monophysitic view of the Christian life.

[23] Here the testimony of the Epistle to the Hebrews is of special importance. Cf. Cullmann, *Christology*, pp. 95-97. See also Davies, *He Ascended*, p. 179, and cf. also Hendry, *Incarnation*, pp. 123-127.

must begin with the fact that dogmatic speculation has limits. *Then* comes worship, then comes the event itself—the sacraments are administered and the communicants make their individual confessions and petitions.[24] Systematic theology, if it is to be biblical, would do well to regard itself as a commentary on what is done in worship.[25]

Now that we have established the fundamental importance of time and event, we can see that there is a certain justification in the tendency mentioned earlier to make an absolute distinction between prayer and praise. Man lives in temptation and he lives by forgiveness. He dies daily and he is raised to life daily. He cries out in his distress and he gives thanks for his deliverance. In each case the two things are quite distinct from one another, and point to a particular reality—man's pilgrimage continues, and he takes new steps, one by one. The time appointed for his pilgrimage is the old, familiar period between the present and the time of death. It is a period which even apart from baptism and the Gospel is filled with judgment and law, and as he lives and moves through it man is confronted wherever he turns by duties which need to be done. The pilgrimage on which he sets forth in baptism is a new one, but it leads in the same direction. Its newness lies in the fact that all that was old, i.e. any part of human life that was lived apart from Christ, is conclusively *old* since "the new has come" (II Cor. v.17).[26] Everything takes on a different colour in this new light. Before when there was death there was no new birth. Death still exists, but now it is the gateway to something new and different. This means not merely that we have to do with a new reality, viz. "life," but also that the old reality of death has been transformed. We can express this paradoxically by saying that the old abounds in victory and life by the very fact that it is *death*, i.e. something which disappears and

---

[24] Cf. Schlink in *Kerygma and Dogma*, pp. 270-271. We should note that in our discussion of freedom and the law in the previous section we prescribed a similar limit to theological discussion. On the other side of the line is the working day of the individual.

[25] Cf. Wingren, *Theology in Conflict*, pp. 158-159. Preaching is simply *one* form of worship among many.

[26] But this new creation does not mean a break in the relationship with the old but a restoration and positive relationship to what God has created. See Dahl in *Background*, pp. 422-423, also Robinson, *The Body*, pp. 82-83.

R

comes to end, so opening up an ever new future. In this regard the act of praise and prayer from man's side, from "down below," is one of profound consequence. Taking his stand in the promise of the Gospel and baptism concerning his life, the man of faith lays hold of God in every situation and does not let Him go. This cleaving to God allows him to wrest the hidden blessing from every moment of his life. Even though it may be a moment of darkness and loss it slowly becomes a moment of life and light. It is a step in his pilgrimage and is therefore part of the final outcome. Everything is related to the goal of eternal life.[27] The function of worship in the life of the individual is to give and continue giving the whole content of baptism to all who are baptised. The act which more powerfully than any other fulfils this function is the Eucharistic meal, repeated as it is over and over again.[28]

For in the Eucharist the whole action of baptism takes place again, not in the form of incorporation into the body, which was once and for all, but in the form of the bestowal of life, which is constantly repeated. To no other liturgical act in His ministry did Christ attach such importance as to the Eucharist. The Words of Institution set Him forth in His risen power in such a way that each can hear Him speak: "This is my body . . . this is my blood." The communicants come to the Table to receive the bread and wine individually, and every other part of the service reflects this individual emphasis. Christ has the individual characteristics of the "new" man which the communicant has looked for in vain in himself. He won His victory on the night when He was betrayed. But this dominion and victory were not for Him "a thing to be grasped"—on the contrary, the Words of Institution show us a man who has been betrayed, who has suffered degradation, and who is incapable of performing miracles, and indeed freely submits to hideous treatment. Yet beneath His distress lies victory. At its very heart there lies the revolutionary secret that will affect the whole

---

[27] On the central place of worship cf. Koch, *Auferstehung*, pp. 331-337.

[28] In Scandinavia Grundtvig's theology is a unique example of a theology of worship and sacraments which does not detract from the first article of the Creed. See in this connexion Aronson, *Mänskligt og kristet*, e.g., pp. 125-166. It is of course true that modern Barthian theology is necessarily critical of Grundtvig's views. Cf. Søe, *Kristelig etik*, pp. 356-358, 417-418, and his *Religionsfilosofi*, p. 136.

world. The Tempter has proved powerless to resist the one who is to die and by dying become the source and sustenance of life to all who are tempted and burdened with guilt. But this is not merely something remembered from the past, it is something acted out here and now. The communicant receives the bread and wine, taking them into his mouth. His old nature stands judged in the light of what he sees. It is to cease to exist and to be swallowed up in death. The whole action is pervaded by judgment on the attitude of acquisitiveness, but it is joyful and triumphant judgment.[29] The new life, which is righteousness in Christ, alone remains when all else has been put to death at a stroke. This righteousness is so specific and concrete that it can be graphically represented to each communicant as consisting in the self-forgetful actions of Jesus as a man, and its specific and concrete character set forth in the picture of the Servant which we have in the Words of Institution. And yet it is not a righteousness which is a moral duty to be done but is something given and offered: "Take, eat . . . drink, all of you." The blood which here flows from the Church's heart to all its members is the blood of the new covenant "for the forgiveness of sins." In the confession of sins the old is held aloft so that it may be branded for what it is: it is *old* and fit only to be rejected. When the new man is set forth specifically and concretely in the Words of the Institution, the old is also seen specifically and concretely.[30] We see before our eyes the profile of the fallen Adam and his lineaments can be traced on our own. We catch glimpses of our daily life in our thoughts, words, and deeds at the sacrament. But here all is bound together in the confession of sin and then covered in the forgiveness of sins. *Since this act is confession, it is Eucharist.*[31] There is only the one total whole of death and resurrection.

The two elements of *prayer* and *praise*, with which we have dealt in the present section, can be recognised quite easily

[29] Cf. Moule in *Background*, pp. 468-476.

[30] On the liturgical function of the Words of Institution as the proclamation of the Gospel according to the view of the Reformers see Jacob Jacobson, *Mässans budskap*, 1958, pp. 40-43.

[31] Cf. Brilioth, *Eucharistic Faith*, pp. 277-278. Confession needs to be delivered from a mechanical interpretation, but to remove it altogether would be to empty the Eucharist of significance. See too Aulén, *Eucharist and Sacrifice*, pp. 105-112.

in the two related parts of confession on the one hand, with its acknowledgment of sin, and Eucharist on the other, with its connexion with Easter Sunday and its reference forward to the heavenly banquet. It is also easy to see how these two component parts came to reflect the two foci in early Christian preaching of the cross and the resurrection. We recollect too that the basic anthropological concept is this duality of "old" man and "new." The death of the old man and the resurrection of the new are both inseparably connected with the Eucharist, the liturgical structure of which involves both the repudiation of the old and the giving of the new.

Here, however, as elsewhere we are to note particularly the connexion with *baptism*. In its classical form the baptismal liturgy contained a renunciation of the devil, that is to say a repudiation of a previous loyalty to the Tempter and a bondage to evil and an affirmation of a new loyalty to Christ.[32] Such a renunciation may seem primitive to us, but it is grounded on the inner reality of baptism. The wording of the renunciation in certain extant liturgies points us back to the prehistory of Genesis, and the implication in them is that in this act one of the vast number of those who are in solidarity with Adam is now incorporated into the new humanity, which is the Church of Christ. The descent into the water of baptism and the rising out of the water also once expressed the same profound reality and made clear in addition the extent of baptism—the whole life of the Christian up to death and eternal life was comprehended within it.[33] Also included within baptism itself were all liturgical acts subsequent to baptism. These brought out the significance of the sacrament and helped to give it the form which it took in daily life. Chief among these is the Eucharist. Its unity of prayer and praise, of confession of sin and thanksgiving, is in its repeated form a new expression of the fundamental denial of the old which we have in the baptismal renunciation and the fundamental

---

[32] In Grundtvig the renunciation at baptism has a place of primary importance. See Aronson, *Mänskligt og kristet*, pp. 29-35, 125.

[33] In an equally clear way even today a child may be lowered and raised up in one of these old, deep baptismal fonts, without the necessity of being plunged in the water, a very small amount of which can be poured on to the bottom of the font.

affirmation of the new in the baptismal confession.[34] Even after baptism fallen Adam still reappears in the temptations which each Christian experiences as an individual. The Christian man lives a life of conflict and he has continually to ask to be forgiven. The natural centre of power for a life that is grounded on baptism, the unrepeated sacrament, is the Eucharist, which, because it has the nature of a meal, is to be repeated frequently.[35]

If, however, this meal is not to become sectarian, it must retain its connexion with daily life. The second use of the law, by which man is accused and judged *coram deo*, derives its content from the first use of the law, which forces a man to do good works. The daily round of home or work is not excluded from the sanctuary, but is caught up into the very heart of worship. The involvements of life in the world outside are part of the burden of guilt which is lifted from the worshipper in his confession of sin. The new man, who is offered in the Eucharist and the word of forgiveness, will live in the midst of the same involvements as "master of all laws" when he lays his prerogatives aside and does the work of a servant. This relationship between worship and daily life is maintained most effectively when each individual has regard to his own special sphere and thus gives individual expression to his Christian service according to the demands of his work or his particular time or place in history.[36] This does not give rise to any individualism or concentration on the individual. The attitude in which I labour in my limited sphere of influence and the faithful pursuit of my vocation is possible only in the context of a recognisable fellowship. Only in the context of the "body" can I conceive of myself as an individual part of it.[37] Only those who are willing to accept that other people are different from them can willingly accept a task of limited dimensions. A similar diversity of function is always communicated in the Eucharist: the body and its members unite in this earthly

[34] The baptismal Creed, the Apostles' Creed, was originally regarded as a hymn of praise like the Nicene.

[35] Cf. Moule, *Sacrifice*, pp. 30, 42.

[36] On the connexion between commandment, Gospel, worship, and daily life, see also Prenter, *Skabelse*, pp. 104-117.

[37] Cf. Odeberg in *En bok om kyrkan*, pp. 70-76.

act in which eternal life is offered to men for whom death is still a reality to be experienced in their lives outside, but who are clothed with power to accept it with the "counter response" at every point (see again the main passage in which this is discussed, II Cor. VI.4-10). The old national Church in Europe, with its heterogeneous assemblage of different callings held together by the unifying worship of the parish church, gave clear expression in its day to the unity which holds together the three articles of the Creed and to the connexion between the sacraments and daily life.[38]

Today, however, the pattern of man's common life is governed by the city. The particular forms of community life in a big city, suburban "dormitories" and places of work which are far removed from the places where men live, are reproduced even in smaller areas where they are not as pressing or necessary as in the teeming centres of population. Wherever we may put the Church in this disintegrated social pattern, an essential element is missing. When night comes, a city church which is set among offices and factories loses the multitudes who have done their work by day, often under difficulties, as it chimed the passing hours. At the same time of day the suburban church begins to be surrounded by thousands of tired returning workers, who have left behind them in the city their trials and duties, which await them when they return next day. The suburb is merely the place to eat and sleep. At the week-end and on Sunday when the regular service of worship and the Eucharist are celebrated, the family is neither in the city nor in the suburb. The family car has brought them to yet a third environment, and little country churches flash past them as they travel. Should they park and enter the church gate, it seems as if they are in a museum, even when they take part in the service from first to last, and even if they take part in communion. When Monday comes and the adults are back again at their jobs in the city, their home remains more or less unoccupied and deserted in the suburbs. This is a completely new situation in society, but it is the daily life of countless thousands, particularly of young parents and their children. It means also that the

[38] Cf. Billing's *Herdabref* in particular, pp. 81-104.

Christian Church is in a wholly new situation.[39] It is pointless to speak of "parishes" in this new setting.

The old territorial church was based on an identity between home, place of work, and place of worship. This identity is now completely and utterly destroyed. But of those who live and dwell in the midst of this disintegrated social pattern the great majority have been baptised. They are already in the Church. The only difficulty is the outworking of the "after effects" of baptism in their lives.

The division of a city into many different local congregations, each of which is thereafter to operate quite independently, might possibly at times represent the modern application of the parish system to a situation where this pattern is no longer applicable. Despite the fact that it sprawls into surrounding districts the city is still a *unity*.[40] This unity is intersected by so many lines of communication that any division into local districts within it will be irrelevant. In any case we must look for other ways of coming to the natural social groupings, and these may differ from place to place. Fellowship at work, often bound up with particular industries, is one such social grouping.[41] We may occasionally wonder if neighbourhood fellowship, especially in suburban dormitories, would also be worth recovering as a complement to other social groupings. There is little doubt that a need for fellowship, which is not being met by radio or television, lies concealed in these depersonalised conglomerations of dwelling-houses. Here is a whole new area which calls for constructive thinking on the part of the Christian Church, and far too little attention has been given to it. The vital thing is the aim and the goal—*we must not lose sight of the connexion between daily life and worship.* From the earliest times Christian worship has been bound up with daily labour, as can also be seen in the constant request

[39] An informative analysis of the effects of a large city on worship is given in Bo Giertz, *Brytningstider*, 1957, pp. 43-45.

[40] The natural unity of the city has had too little effect on modern Church administration. This is true of most denominations. This is all the more strange when we realise that it was the city, overflowing into the surrounding countryside, which once gave Christendom the monarchical episcopate. The unity of the city was then a productive factor, for the "pagans" (*pagani*) lived in the country.

[41] Cf. Berggrav, *Staten*, pp. 161-179.

for prayers to be made for those who exercised "earthly government." Even when these were Gentiles, prayer was still requested for them in early Christian worship.[42] The frequent concern in prayers of the Church for fruitful fields, for the work of all, whatever their office or condition, and for rulers, government, or parliament, is a very early element in our worship and as such a reminder of the place which is to be given to the first article of the Creed and the first use of the law. But such a prayer becomes devoid of meaning if each individual worshipper who comes into the sanctuary allows his presence at worship to become a flight from the many problems which press upon him in daily life. The individual worshipper attests through the prayer and praise which he offers that in his own particular sphere he has held worship and daily life together. This relating of the two is done by those individuals who have the responsibility for doing it—"laymen," as we generally call them, i.e. the baptised who live by their baptism and who therefore also have part in "the events which follow" the sacrament. The connexion between worship and daily life is not an abstract thing, and unless it is made by each individual in his own sphere, the connexion is not made.[43]

Once we have lost this connexion between work and worship, religion becomes escapist in character, and the sanctuary affords a retreat in which we can escape from the multitude of daily problems which we no longer master from the basis of faith. The form of piety which is then best understood is that of the cloister and monasticism. When this is the case, even Churches outside Rome come to be drawn irresistibly into liturgical patterns in which the upward movement of man away from the world is the constructive principle. In the

[42] This is true not only of the demand in 1 Tim. ii.1-2. In a situation of martyrdom in which the state did persecute, the exhortation to pray "for those who persecute you" would acquire a peculiarly vivid meaning (Mt. v.44, Rom. xii.14, cf. 1 Cor. iv.12, 1 Pet. iii.9). See Stauffer, *Theology*, p. 193.

[43] Heinrich Ott, *Denken und Sein*, 1959, pp. 220-225, has a number of interesting references to Heidegger's idea of the annihilation of things by technology, and establishes points of contact between existentialism and theology other than those we should expect to find in Bultmann's demythologising. The broken relationship between man and his material world cannot, however, be restored by fleeing from the world of technology but by working in it. Here, too, theology and the Christian Church have a particular place and task.

area of Eucharistic practice this implies a preference for the doctrine of the sacrifice of the Mass.[44] In these circumstances it does not help to bombard those who have embraced such theories with theocentric arguments about God as the sole agent in worship and Christ's presence in the elements, etc. When the movement "from down below" is lost sight of and "human nature" robbed of its role by a monophysitic Christocentricity in theology, men in desperation usurp the part of God and demonstrate their proficiency in priestly performances directed to God.[45] The Church of Rome, it has been said, having lost the humanity of Christ, has had to find some other human nature, notably Mary, so that there may be at least some place for humanity in the God whom it adores. But once this upward movement, in which the divine continually absorbs the human, has begun its course, nothing can stop it.[46] The more heavenly Mary becomes, the less she is bound to earth. The structure of this whole Roman Catholic concept, as Anders Nygren has pointed out repeatedly is reminiscent of non-Christian *eros*-religion.[47]

Human nature can never remain wholly human if we do not see that divine nature is at its heart outgiving love. God is not the Lord "throned afar" to whom man ascends in worship. He is disclosed in the Gospel and has revealed His nature in the suffering humanity of Christ. This being so, our movement "from below" can have free play in worship as prayer and as praise. The prayer which He uttered in His humanity is a witness to the existence of God—God is the One who condescends to dwell with the needy. Praise is no less human than

[44] On the criticism of the sacrifice of the Mass made during the Lutheran Reformation see Vajta, *Theologie des Gottesdienstes*, pp. 105-112, and also Wisløff, *Nattverd og messe*, pp. 161-172. Cf. Moule, *Sacrifice*, pp. 52-53, on Heb. vi.6.

[45] See the extreme statement in the French quotation in Per Erik Persson's "Vad är romerskt?", in *S.t.k.*, 1958, p. 19. The priest commands and God obeys.

[46] Cf. Gerhard Ebeling, "Zur Frage nach dem Sinn des mariologischen Dogmas," in *Z.T.K.*, 1950, pp. 389-391. See also Persson, *Romerskt och evangeliskt*, pp. 63-66 and the reference there made to an important line of though in Congar. In this context the emphasis on human nature also implies an advocacy of free will. The Lutheran doctrine of the *communicatio idiomatum* is quite different. There the emphasis on human nature implies an emphasis also on the *Gospel* and salvation by grace alone. Cf. Bring, *Dualismen*, pp. 150-152.

[47] Anders Nygren, *Urkristendomen och reformation*, 1932, pp. 28, 122, etc. On the hierarchy and eros-forces cf. the same writer's *Agape and Eros*, pp. 584-588.

prayer and also witnesses to what manner of God God is—
He is near to those who praise Him on earth.

If, then, the free activity of man has its place both in daily
life and in worship, we should not fear the use of psychological
terms in theology, as we do. It would be a stimulating task
to try to define the experience and faith of the Christian
believer.[48]

[48] There is no question here, of course, of deducing the content of the Gospel
from the experience of the individual. But we can begin with daily work and
worship. This brings the preaching of the Gospel into our starting-point. Within
this framework it makes sense to deal systematically with men's experience and
faith. Cf. here also the useful essay by Wilhelm Hahn, "Säkularisation und
Religionszerfall." in *Kerygma und Dogma*, pp. 83-98.

INDEX OF NAMES

INDEX OF SUBJECTS

(n = footnote)

Preaching :
of the gospel : 19-28, 41-3, 59, 72-8,
85, 87-93, 97-101, 105-14, 135 f.,
150 f., 154-60, 162, 169, 177 f., 193 f.,
215 f., 227 f., 257.
of Christ as example: 29-35, 56, 78 f.,
148 f., 177, 182, 189.
See also DISTRIBUTION.
Prehistory : 4, 35, 38 f., 45, 50, 55,
61-6, 78, 85, 98-101, 116, 143, 148 f.,
155 f., 167, 198 f., 207 f., 252.
Privilege : 133, 148 n., 151.

Recapitulatio : 4-6, 9 f., 21, 24 f., 49 f.,
61, 66, 78, 91 f., 120, 156, 166-70, 173,
195, 208, 241-3.
Recognition of sacraments of other
churches : 11-14, 129, 151 f.
Reformation : 16, 36, 117 f., 156-63,
165-7, 170, 188, 236 f.
Renunciation of the devil : 252.
Restoration : *see Recapitulatio.*
Resurrection :
of Christ : 17 f., 23, 40-2, 55-7,
61 f., 65 f., 72-4, 76-101, 109, 145 f.,
169, 215, 235.
of man : 10, 44, 71-3, 78 f., 109,
147-9, 156, 167, 198, 204.

Sacraments, *see* BAPTISM, EUCHARIST,
Cf. ABSOLUTION.
Sanctification : 9 f., 28 f., 143, 238 f.
Satisfaction, doctrine of : 49, 56.
Cf. ATONEMENT.
Sequence of God's acts : 84, 100 f.,
167-71, 175 f., 228 f.
Sharpening of the commandments, 67,
79 f., 179-181, 189 f., 215-19, 228,
234.
Sifting of demands : 117-20, 186-8,
215-17, 229-39.

Sin : 57 f., 78-80, 88 f., 110, 116 f.,
145-7, 155 f., 172, 178, 241 f., 251-3
See also OLD MAN.
Spirit, Holy :
and the gospel : 36, 56 n., 92,
105-12, 121 f., 128-30, 146, 149, 151,
154, 173, 221, 229.
and law : 47, 109-16, 146.
Cf. LAW, SECOND USE OF
Succession : 107 f., 109 n., 128-34,
148 n., 151, 168.
Cf. MINISTRY.
Suffering :
Christ's : 48 f., 57 f., 64, 87, 98 f.,
199, 235, 247.
Ours : 43, 45, 74, 115 f., 143, 218 f.,
246 f.

Temptation :
Adam's (=ours) : 25 f., 46-48, 55 f.,
61, 67 f., 74 f., 94 f., 145, 233 f.,
248-51.
Christ's : 25 f., 46-51, 56, 57-65, 80,
87 f., 94-6, 146, 199, 233 f., 251.
Territorial church : 125-9, 144-53,
160 f., 202, 222, 238, 254-6.
Things of creation purer than man : 5,
79, 242.
Tradition : 12 f., 125-128, 151.

Use of creation : 6, 172 f., 242.

Victory of Christ : 41-8, 59-61,
87 f., 145, 190, 198 f., 234 f., 250.

Worship : 53, 89, 95, 128 f., 135,
141-53, 200-2, 204 f., 219-27,
230-4, 240 f., 243-58.
Wrath of God : 49, 51, 65 f., 87, 97 f.,
108, 110.

INDEX OF BIBLICAL PASSAGES

(n = footnote)

PRINTED IN GREAT BRITAIN BY
OLIVER AND BOYD LTD.
EDINBURGH